THE WORLD OF MAN

THE WORLD OF MAN

PROSE PASSAGES
CHIEFLY FROM THE WORKS OF THE
GREAT HISTORIANS, CLASSICAL
AND ENGLISH

Chosen and arranged
by
L. J. CHENEY, M.A.
Formerly Scholar of Jesus College
Cambridge

"What is man, and whereto serveth he? what is his
good, and what is his evil?"   Ecclesiasticus, xviii

CAMBRIDGE
AT THE UNIVERSITY PRESS
1933

CAMBRIDGE
UNIVERSITY PRESS

University Printing House, Cambridge CB2 8BS, United Kingdom

Published in the United States of America by Cambridge University Press, New York

Cambridge University Press is part of the University of Cambridge.

It furthers the University's mission by disseminating knowledge in the pursuit of
education, learning and research at the highest international levels of excellence.

www.cambridge.org
Information on this title: www.cambridge.org/9781107418394

© Cambridge University Press 1933

First published 1933
First paperback edition 2014

A catalogue record for this publication is available from the British Library

ISBN 978-1-107-41839-4 Paperback

INTRODUCTION

THE study of history is chiefly a matter of thought. The true historian does not reassemble the past from its broken fragments; he re-creates it. If, to-day, owing to the negligence of our ancestors, we are overburdened with the collecting of facts, we would do well to remind ourselves that creation is an act of thought, not a synthesis from a card-index system. Accumulations of historical facts, like accumulations of other sorts of facts, are necessary; but even when arranged and sorted they do not make a history: and students of history should not wish to make too much display, among other men, of their learned compilations—one does not entertain one's guests in the kitchen, however full and well-ordered the shelves may be. Moreover, facts must be recorded in words: and words are not static symbols of a universally common significance, passionless and colourless, but the stuff of thought itself, charged with the emotion and hue of the minds they serve; and so, the facts themselves are apprehended differently by diverse minds. A historian—but the simple name is debased; we should say a *great* historian—is as much a creative artist as is a good scientist: his work is as much an act of thought. He does not subscribe to the fantastic theory of an objective past, ascertainable and recordable by mere drudgery, the toil of ants. He does know that the past can only be re-created by the thoughtful co-operation of writer and reader; that decades can be lived in chapters and centuries in volumes; that he and his reader between them, by the miracle of language, can recapture an image—if not a likeness—of that which time has utterly consumed.

History is best written at length. It is best enjoyed in the works of the masters. It is best realized from the works of the masters. There is little leisure in a democracy, and perhaps the old genus of historians has passed—not to reappear, maybe, until, after pressing the daily and requisite buttons of a standardized world, we sit down to digest each other's masterpieces. That event is preserved for a happier posterity. At present, the precision of the annalist, and the distraction of his daily routine, prevent the scholar from the enterprise of a Hume, a Gibbon, a Macaulay. He puts his work forward with less gusto in short studies and essays. He restricts himself to the intensive exposition of brief periods or limited themes. The quality is still, in many instances, as high as ever, the detail, indeed, more accurately determined; but the technique has altered. Much of the finest history written nowadays is contained in small volumes and single works. Sir James Frazer—I am speaking of Englishmen only—still writes monumentally as well as finely, and Mr F. A. Simpson has begun what one hopes will be a lengthy row of volumes on modern France. Professor G. M. Trevelyan, after celebrating worthily the epic birth of modern Italy, is now heroically continuing Lord Macaulay's narrative. But the bulk of the best histories are of shorter compass, and, owing to the widespread study of the past, much of the most effective commentary on past events is to be found in books whose character is not primarily historical, but philosophical or theological. Such considerations, however, do not affect the main issue here: ancient or modern, at length or in brief, the great historians are worth reading.

This book is not simply a collection of passages from the writings of the great historians. Such collections exist already, and, by themselves, are of small value. It is naturally difficult to regard them as anything more than scrapbooks, compiled arbitrarily, without any continuum of interest. It would be naturally as difficult to compile a collection of passages in illustration of one definite theme from the works of the great historians alone: no educational system has ever yet attempted to train historians: the masters are lucky accidents and what the reader of history requires is not always to be found in them. And it would be a sad charge to bring against students of history that they not only repeat each other but only read each other; since all the world should be their province. Apart from this, restriction to one definite theme, were it possible, would much impair the serviceability of a book such as this. Consequently, I have made two compromises: first, in arranging the passages under convenient headings that indicate some of the chief preoccupations of life; secondly, in widening my net to include a few writers of prose who are not historians.

We are likely to be confused in these days by books showered upon us in streams, copious but not always refreshing; and particularly of those two recent products, the novel and the scientific publication. Neither of these is essentially of interest to the Muse: yet occasionally and incidentally each of them shares some characteristics with purely historical work. So also with books of travel and philosophy. (We would not claim that history embraced philosophy—the two studies are manifestations of the same instinct in man and are complementary.) The great historians are, by this argument, reinforced by a host of men: those who possess the gift of re-creating life by the power of their own thought, and those who—deplorably few—can describe the work and ideas of mankind clearly and easily.

Heroical poetry—the "feigned histories" of Lord Bacon— I have purposely neglected. I am not convinced of the superiority of prose over poetry in the sense of preferring the intellectual to the emotional appeal: if anything, I value most the "emotionalized thought" which is the strongest force in literature, and which finds its purest outlet in poetry. Indeed, I have chosen deliberately some passages of prose that appeal most to the imagination. The omission of poetry is due to the limitations of space: and in some degree to this consideration: that while all educated men should aspire to write good prose, it is a decision outside his power whether a man write good poetry. The "world of man" is here depicted from a restricted palette.

The chief embarrassment in carrying out this project has been the lack of space and the abundance of materials. Every one of the sections into which the book is divided could easily have been expanded to four or five times its size. But the book will have done its work if it sends the reader to a library —or to a bookshop—to expand them for himself. I have rigorously excluded quoting historians in translation— Froissart and the Classics excepted—in spite of the lure of Villani, of Machiavelli, of Guicciardini, and of the flourishing modern French and German schools.

It remains to justify my action. Time is short and the historians are long. In the following of my daily routine I am constrained to read more of them than are most men. That constraint has long since become a willing pursuit, and I here attempt to display a few of its pleasures. I have chosen passages for their matter rather than for their manner; happily, the two are more often than not of equal attraction; since good prose is the garment of a good mind. I have arranged them according to their matter, and, as far as a single volume can do it, I have sketched roughly the world of man. I have but opened the door to a room whose treasure is inexhaustible: he who cares to enter can soon make good my omissions.

There is one more observation to make. The present state of general education gives little time or opportunity for wide reading. I do not think highly of "potted culture", and I do not intend this book as a substitute for study. But I do intend it as a starting-place, an introduction, a series of contacts available in convenient form for the student: a collection of points of view that will stimulate his thought; a collection which, I hope, will lead him on to the wider reading without which education is stunted.

For permission to include extracts from works in copyright, I am indebted to the following:

Messrs Geo. Allen and Unwin, Ltd (*Appearances*, by G. Lowes Dickinson); Edward Arnold and Co. (*In the Desert*, by L. March Phillipps); Edward Arnold and Co., and Mr W. F. Reddaway (*Modern European History*); G. Bell and Sons, Ltd (*Xenophon's Anabasis*, translated by J. S. Watson); G. Bell and Sons, Ltd, and Professor J. Holland Rose (*Life of Napoleon I*); Wm Blackwood and Sons, Ltd (*Invasion of the Crimea*, by A. W. Kinglake); Jonathan Cape, Ltd (*Babbitt*, by Sinclair Lewis); Cassell and Co. Ltd, and the Very Rev. Dean Inge (*Assessments and Anticipations*); Constable and Co. Ltd, and Mr Hilaire Belloc (*The Servile State*); Constable and Co. Ltd, and the Hibbert Trustees (*The Reformation*, by C. Beard); Lady Corbett (*Sir Francis Drake*, by Sir J. Corbett); Gerald Duckworth and Co. Ltd (*The Works of Man*, by L. March Phillipps); Gerald Duckworth and Co. Ltd, and Mr Hilaire Belloc (*Esto Perpetua*); Little, Brown and Co. (*The Influence of Sea Power upon History*, by A. T. Mahan);

Longmans, Green and Co. Ltd (*The Verney Memoirs*; *Medieval and Modern Ideals*, by J. N. Figgis; *History of England*, by J. A. Froude; *The Church and the Age*, by W. R. Inge; *History of England*, by W. E. H. Lecky; *British History in the XIXth Century*, by G. M. Trevelyan; *History of England*, by G. M. Trevelyan); Longmans, Green and Co. Ltd, and Lady Corbett (*England in the Seven Years' War*, by Sir J. Corbett); Sampson Low, Marston and Co. Ltd (*The Influence of Sea Power upon History*); Macmillan and Co. Ltd (*Lectures in Modern History* and *Inaugural Lecture*, by Lord Acton; *History of Greece*, by J. B. Bury; *History of the British Army*, by Sir J. Fortescue; *Historical Essays*, by E. A. Freeman; *Froissart's Chronicles*; *Short History of the English People*, by J. R. Green; *Greek Studies*, by W. H. Pater; *History of European Colonies*, by E. J. Payne; *Histories of Polybius*, translated by E. S. Shuckburgh); Mr John Masefield (*Gallipoli*); Methuen and Co. Ltd (*Regnum Dei*, by A. Robertson); Mr John Murray (*Popular Government*, by Sir H. Maine; *History of Latin Christianity*, by H. H. Milman; *Lives of the Engineers*, by S. Smiles; *The Renaissance in Italy*, by J. A. Symonds); The Delegates of the Oxford University Press (*Monasteries of the Levant*, by the Hon. R. Curzon); George Routledge and Sons, Ltd (*The Service of Man*, by J. C. Morison; *Martyrdom of Man*, by W. Winwood Reade); Seeley, Service and Co. Ltd (*Napoleon the First*, by Sir J. Seeley).

L. J. C.

January 1933

CONTENTS

WAR AND PEACE

ADMIRALTY

THE WORKS OF MAN

HISTORY

So certainly, if a man meditate much upon the universal frame of nature, the earth with men upon it (the divineness of souls except) will not seem much other than an ant-hill, whereas some ants carry corn, and some carry their young, and some go empty, and all to and fro a little heap of dust.

Francis Bacon, 1605

PRAISE OF HISTORY

LORD BERNERS, Preface (1523) to his *Translation of
Sir John Froissart's Chronicles* (1326–1400)

WHAT condign graces and thanks ought men to give to the
writers of histories, who with their great labours have done so
much profit to the human life. They shew, open, manifest
and declare to the reader by example of old antiquity, what
we should enquire, desire and follow, and also what we should
eschew, avoid and utterly fly; for when we (being unexpert of
chances) see, behold and read the ancient acts, gests and deeds,
how and with what labours, dangers and perils they were
gested and done, they right greatly admonish, ensign and
teach us how we may lead forth our lives: and farther, he that
hath the perfect knowledge of others' joy, wealth and high
prosperity, and also trouble, sorrow and great adversity, hath
the expert doctrine of all perils. And albeit that mortal folk
are marvellously separated both by land and water, and right
wondrously situate, yet are they and their acts (done per-
adventure by the space of a thousand year) compact together
by the histographier, as it were the deeds of one self city and
in one man's life: wherefore I say that history may well be
called a divine providence; for as the celestial bodies above
complect all and at every time the universal world, the
creatures therein contained and all their deeds, semblably so
doth history. Is it not a right noble thing for us, by the faults
and errors of other to amend and erect our life into better?
We should not seek and acquire that other did; but what thing
was most best, most laudable and worthily done, we should
put before our eyes to follow. Be not the sage counsels of two
or three old fathers in a city, town or country, whom long age
hath made wise, discreet and prudent, far more praised,
lauded and dearly loved than of the young men? How much
more then ought histories to be commended, praised and loved,
in whom is included so many sage counsels, great reasons and
high wisdoms of so innumerable persons of sundry nations

and of every age, and that in so long space as four or five hundred year. The most profitable thing in this world for the institution of the human life is history. Once the continual reading thereof maketh young men equal in prudence to old men, and to old fathers stricken in age it ministereth experience of things. More, it yieldeth private persons worthy of dignity, rule and governance: it compelleth the emperors, high rulers and governours to do noble deeds, to the end they may obtain immortal glory: it exciteth, moveth and stirreth the strong, hardy warriors, for the great laud that they have after they ben dead, promptly to go in hand with great and hard perils in defence of their country: and it prohibiteth reprovable persons to do mischievous deeds, for fear of infamy and shame. So thus through the monuments of writing, which is the testimony unto virtue many men have been moved, some to build cities, some to devise and establish laws right profitable, necessary and behoveful for the human life, some other to find new arts, crafts and sciences, very requisite to the use of mankind. But above all things, whereby man's wealth riseth, special laud and cause ought to be given to history: it is the keeper of such things as have been virtuously done, and the witness of evil deeds, and by the benefit of history all noble, high and virtuous acts be immortal.

BREVITY OF HUMAN HISTORY

JOHN PEARSON, Bishop of Chester, *An Exposition of the Creed.* Art. i. 1659

IF we look into the historians which give account of ancient times, nay, if we peruse the fictions of the poets, we shall find the first to have no footsteps, the last to feign no actions of so great antiquity. If the race of men had been eternal, or as old as the Egyptians and Chaldees fancy it, how should it come to pass that the poetical inventions should find no actions worthy their heroic verse before the Trojan or the Theban war, or that great adventure of the Argonauts? For whatsoever all the Muses, the daughters of Memory, could rehearse before those times, is nothing but the creation of the World, and the nativity of their gods....

If we search into the nations themselves, we shall see none without some original: and were those authors extant who have written of the first plantations and migrations of people, the foundations and inhabiting of cities and countries, the first rudiments would appear as evident as their later growth and present condition. We know what ways within two thousand years people have made through vast and thick woods for their habitations, now as fertile, as populous, as any. The Hercynian trees, in the time of the Caesars, occupying so great a space as to take up a journey of sixty days, were thought even then coeval with the World. We read without any show of contradiction, how this western part of the World hath been peopled from the east: and all the pretence of the Babylonian antiquity is nothing else, but that we all came from thence. Those eight persons saved in the Ark, descending from the Gordiaean mountains and multiplying to a large collection in the plain of Sinaar, made their first division at that place; and that dispersion, or rather dissemination, hath peopled all other parts of the World, either never before inhabited, or dispeopled by the flood....

Now by the experience of our families, which for their honour and greatness have been preserved, by the genealogies delivered in the Sacred Scriptures, and thought necessary to be presented to us by the blessed evangelists, by the observation and concurrent judgment of former ages, three generations usually take up a hundred years. If then it be not yet three thousand seven hundred years since the birth of Abraham, as certainly it is not; if all men who are or have been since have descended from Noah, as undoubtedly they have; if Abraham were but the tenth from Noah, as Noah from Adam, which Moses hath assured us: then it is not probable that any person now alive is above one hundred and thirty generations removed from Adam. And indeed thus admitting but the Greek account of less than five thousand years since the flood, we may easily bring all sober or probable accounts of the Egyptians, Babylonians, and Chinese, to begin since the dispersion at Babel.

NATURAL SELECTION

Charles Robert Darwin, *Origin of Species by Means of Natural Selection.* 1859

Authors of the highest eminence seem to be fully satisfied with the view that each species has been independently created. To my mind it accords better with what we know of the laws impressed on matter by the Creator, that the production and extinction of the past and present inhabitants of the world should have been due to secondary causes, like those determining the birth and death of the individual. When I view all things not as special creations, but as the lineal descendants of some few beings which lived long before the first bed of the Cambrian system was deposited, they seem to me to become ennobled. Judging from the past, we may safely infer that not one living species will transmit its unaltered likeness to a distant futurity. And of the species now living very few will transmit progeny of any kind to a far distant futurity; for the manner in which all organic beings are grouped, shows that the greater number of species in each genus, and all the species in many genera, have left no descendants, but have become utterly extinct. We can so far take a prophetic glance into futurity as to foretell that it will be the common and widely spread species, belonging to the larger and dominant groups within each class, which will ultimately prevail and procreate new and dominant species. As all the living forms of life are the lineal descendants of those which lived long before the Cambrian Epoch, we may feel certain that the ordinary succession by generation has never once been broken, and that no cataclysm has desolated the whole world. Hence we may look with some confidence to a secure future of great length. And as natural selection works solely by and for the good of each being, all corporeal and mental endowments will tend to progress towards perfection.

It is interesting to contemplate a tangled bank clothed with many plants of many kinds, with birds singing on the bushes, with various insects flitting about, and with worms crawling through the damp earth, and to reflect that these elaborately constructed forms, so different from each other, and dependent upon each other in so complex a manner, have all been produced by laws acting round us. These laws, taken in the largest sense, being Growth and Reproduction; Inheritance which is almost implied by reproduction; Variability from the indirect and direct action of the conditions of life, and from use and disuse: a Ratio of Increase so high as to lead to a Struggle for Life, and as a consequence to Natural Selection, entailing Divergence of Character and the Extinction of less-improved forms. Thus, from the war of nature, from famine and death, the most exalted object which we are capable of conceiving, namely, the production of the higher animals, directly follows. There is grandeur in this view of life with its several powers, having been originally breathed by the Creator into a few forms or into one; and that, whilst this planet has gone cycling on according to the fixed law of gravity, from so simple a beginning endless forms most beautiful and most wonderful have been, and are being evolved.

REALITY A SYSTEM OF ENDS

WILLIAM RALPH INGE, *The Church and the Age.* 1912

I ASK you to consider how our belief that reality is a system of ends, a concatenation of finite purposes willed by the Creator and appointed by Him to be actualised in time, must necessarily affect our judgment of all particular events. We may conveniently draw a distinction between phenomena and facts. A *phenomenon* is a particular occurrence, viewed in isolation, as if it were not part of a system. A *fact* is the working out of some unitary idea. If our view is correct, phenomena are only abstractions: we do not get at the truth of things by regarding them in isolation, or in any other way except as links in a chain by which some particular thought in the mind of God, some particular design in the will of God, is being expressed and actualised. A *fact* has always a beginning, middle, and end, and until we know the end as well as the beginning, we are not in a position to estimate the fact correctly. Now all facts that are really interesting are still unfinished. The world is still in the making, and mankind is in the making too. If it is the characteristic of a teleological series that its rationality is not intelligible until the last term is available for observation, it is no wonder that many things in our experience perplex and baffle us. It is also just what we should expect, that the largest and most far-reaching and exalted of God's purposes, those which have in view the re-presentation and realisation of the grandest ideas and the most divine designs, are precisely those which cause us most difficulty. "What I do thou knowest not now, but thou shalt know hereafter." Even the past is not over and done with when it forms part of a living, growing organic scheme. This is the philosophical proof of the doctrine of repentance and forgiveness. In an organic whole losses may be repaired, waste products utilised. God may even "restore to us the years that the locust hath eaten".

A REASONABLE CREATION

ANICIUS MANLIUS SEVERINUS BOETHIUS, *De consolatione philosophiae*, c. 523. Book IV, Prose VI. Translated by Geoffrey Chaucer. 1377–81

THE engendringe of alle thinges and alle the progressiouns of muable nature, and al that moeveth in any manere, taketh his causes, his ordre, and his formes, of the stablenesse of the divyne thoght; and thilke divyne thought, that is y-set and put in the tour, *that is to seyn, in the heighte*, of the simplicitee of god, stablissheth many maner gyses to thinges that ben to done; the whiche maner, whan that men loken it in thilke pure clennesse of the divyne intelligence, it is y-cleped pur-viaunce; but whan thilke maner is referred by men to thinges that it moeveth and disponeth, thanne of olde men it was cleped destinee....And thus ben the thinges ful wel y-governed, yif that the simplicitee dwellinge in the divyne thoght sheweth forth the ordre of causes, unable to ben y-bowed; and this ordre constreineth by his propre stabletee the moevable thinges, or elles they sholden fleten folily. For which it is, that alle thinges semen to ben confus and trouble to us men, for we ne mowen nat considere thilke ordinaunce; natheles, the propre maner of every thinge, dressinge hem to goode, disponeth hem alle.

ACCIDENT IN HISTORY

WILLIAM EDWARD HARTPOLE LECKY, *A History of England in the Eighteenth Century.* Vol. i, chap. i. 1878

Whoever will study the history of the downfall of the Roman Republic; of the triumph of Christianity in the Roman Empire; of the dissolution of that empire; of the mediæval transition from slavery to serfdom; of the Reformation, or of the French Revolution, may easily convince himself that each of these great changes was the result of a long series of religious, social, political, economical, and intellectual causes, extending over many generations. So eminently is this the case, that some distinguished writers have maintained that the action of special circumstances and of individual genius, efforts, and peculiarities, counts for nothing in the great march of human affairs, and that every successful revolution must be attributed solely to the long train of intellectual influences that prepared and necessitated its triumph.

It is not difficult, however, to show that this, like most very absolute historical generalisations, is an exaggeration, and several instances might be cited in which a slight change in the disposition of circumstances, or in the action of individuals, would have altered the whole course of history. There are, indeed, few streams of tendency, however powerful, that might not, at some early period of their career, have been arrested or deflected. Thus the whole religious and moral sentiment of the most advanced nations of the world has been mainly determined by the influence of that small nation which inhabited Palestine; but there have been periods when it was more than probable that the Jewish race would have been as completely absorbed or extirpated as were the ten tribes, and every trace of the Jewish writings blotted from the world. Not less distinctive, not less unique in its kind, has been the place which the Greek, and especially the Athenian, intellect has occupied in history. It has been the great dynamic agency in European civilisation. Directly or indirectly it has contributed more than any other single influence, to stimulate its energies, to shape its intellectual type, to determine its political ideals and canons of taste, to impart to it the qualities that distinguish it most widely from the Eastern world. But how much of this influence would have arisen or have survived if, as might easily have happened, the invasion of Xerxes had succeeded, and an Asiatic despotism been planted in Greece? It is a mere question of strategy whether Hannibal, after Cannaë, might not have marched upon Rome and burnt it to the ground, and had he done so, the long train of momentous consequences that flowed from the Roman Empire would never have taken place, and a nation widely different in its position, its character, and its pursuits, would have presided over the developments of civilisation. It is, no doubt, true that the degradation or disintegration of Oriental Christianity assisted the triumph of Mohammedanism; but if Mahomet had been killed in one of the first skirmishes of his career, there is no reason to believe that a great monotheistic and military religion would have been organised in Arabia, destined to sweep with resistless fanaticism over an immense part both of the Pagan and of the Christian world, and to establish itself for many centuries and in three continents as a serious rival to Christianity. As Gibbon truly says, had Charles Martel been defeated at the battle of Poitiers, Mohammedanism would have almost certainly overspread the whole of Gallic and Teutonic Europe, and the victory of the Christians was only gained after several days of doubtful and indecisive struggle. The obscure blunder of some forgotten captain, who perhaps moved his troops to the right when he should have moved them to the left, may have turned the scale, and determined the future of Europe. Even the changes of the

French Revolution, prepared as they undoubtedly were by a long train of irresistible causes, might have worn a wholly different complexion had the Duke of Burgundy succeeded Lewis XIV and directed, with the intelligence, and the liberality that were generally expected from the pupil of Fénelon, the government of his country. Profound and searching changes in the institutions of France were inevitable, but had they been effected peacefully, legally, and gradually, had the shameless scenes of the Regency and Lewis XV been avoided, that frenzy of democratic enthusiasm which has been the most distinctive product of the Revolution, and which has passed, almost like a new religion, into European life, might never have arisen, and the whole Napoleonic episode, with its innumerable consequences, would never have occurred.

UNIVERSAL HISTORY

THOMAS CARLYLE, "On History Again", *Frazer's Magazine*. 1833

To use a ready-made similitude, we might liken Universal History to a magic web; and consider with astonishment how, by philosophic insight and indolent neglect, the ever-growing fabric wove itself forward, out of that ravelled immeasurable mass of threads and thrums, which we name *Memoirs*; nay, at each new lengthening, at each new *epoch*, changed its whole proportions, its hue and structure to the very origin. Thus, do not the records of a Tacitus acquire new meaning, after seventeen hundred years, in the hands of a Montesquieu? Niebuhr has to reinterpret for us, at a still greater distance, the writings of a Titus Livius: nay, the religious archaic chronicles of a Hebrew Prophet and Lawgiver escape not the like fortune; and many a ponderous Eichhorn scans, with new-ground philosophic spectacles, the revelation of a Moses, and strives to reproduce for this century what, thirty centuries ago, was of plainly infinite significance to all. Consider History with the beginnings of it stretching dimly into the remote Time; emerging darkly out of the mysterious Eternity: the ends of it enveloping *us* at this hour, whereof we at this hour, both as actors and relators, form part! In shape we might mathematically name it *Hyperbolic-Asymptotic*; ever of *infinite* breadth around us; soon shrinking within narrow limits: ever narrowing more and more into the infinite depth behind us. In essence and significance it has been called "the true Epic Poem, and universal Divine Scripture, *whose* 'plenary inspiration' no man, out of Bedlam or in it, shall bring in question".

THE PERFECT HISTORIAN

THOMAS BABINGTON, LORD MACAULAY,
Edinburgh Review. May 1828

A HISTORY in which every particular incident may be true may on the whole be false. The circumstances which have most influence on the happiness of mankind, the changes of manners and morals, the transition of communities from poverty to wealth, from knowledge to ignorance, from ferocity to humanity—these are, for the most part, noiseless revolutions. Their progress is rarely indicated by what historians are pleased to call important events. They are not achieved by armies, or enacted by senates. They are sanctioned by no treaties, and recorded in no archives. They are carried on in every school, in every church, behind ten thousand counters, at ten thousand firesides. The upper current of society presents no certain criterion by which we can judge of the direction in which the under current flows. We read of defeats and victories. But we know that nations may be miserable amidst victories and prosperous amidst defeats. We read of the fall of wise ministers and of the rise of profligate favourites. But we must remember how small a proportion the good or evil effected by a single statesman can bear to the good or evil of a great social system.

Bishop Watson compares a geologist to a gnat mounted on

an elephant, and laying down theories as to the whole internal structure of the vast animal, from the phenomena of the hide. The comparison is unjust to the geologists; but it is very applicable to those historians who write as if the body politic were homogeneous, who look only on the surface of affairs, and never think of the mighty and various organisation which lies deep below.

In the works of such writers as these, England, at the close of the Seven Years' War, is in the highest state of prosperity: at the close of the American war she is in a miserable and degraded condition; as if people were not on the whole as rich, as well governed, and as well educated at the latter period as at the former. We have read books called Histories of England, under the reign of George the Second, in which the rise of Methodism is not even mentioned. A hundred years hence this breed of authors will, we hope, be extinct. If it should still exist, the late ministerial interregnum will be described in terms which will seem to imply that all government was at an end; that the social contract was annulled; and that the hand of every man was against his neighbour, until the wisdom and virtue of the new cabinet educed order out of the chaos of anarchy. We are quite certain that misconceptions as gross prevail at this moment respecting many important parts of our annals.

The effect of historical reading is analogous, in many respects, to that produced by foreign travel. The student, like the tourist, is transported into a new state of society. He sees new fashions. He hears new modes of expression. His mind is enlarged by contemplating the wide diversities of laws, of morals, and of manners. But men may travel far, and return with minds as contracted as if they had never stirred from their own market-town. In the same manner, men may know the dates of many battles and the genealogies of many royal houses, and yet be no wiser. Most people look at past times as princes look at foreign countries. More than one illustrious stranger has landed on our island amidst the shouts of a mob, has dined with the king, has hunted with the master of the stag-hounds, has seen the guards reviewed, and a knight of the garter installed, has cantered along Regent Street, has visited St Paul's, and noted down its dimensions; and has then departed, thinking that he has seen England. He has, in fact, seen a few public buildings, public men, and public ceremonies. But of the vast and complex system of society, of the fine shades of national character, of the practical operation of government and laws, he knows nothing. He who would understand these things rightly must not confine his observations to palaces and solemn days. He must see ordinary men as they appear in their ordinary business and in their ordinary pleasures. He must mingle in the crowds of the exchange and the coffee-house. He must obtain admittance to the convivial table and the domestic hearth. He must bear with vulgar expressions. He must not shrink from exploring even the retreats of misery. He who wishes to understand the condition of mankind in former ages must proceed on the same principle. If he attends only to public transactions, to wars, congresses, and debates, his studies will be as unprofitable as the travels of those imperial, royal, and serene sovereigns who form their judgment of our island from having gone in state to a few fine sights, and from having held formal conferences with a few great officers.

The perfect historian is he in whose work the character and spirit of an age is exhibited in miniature. He relates no fact, he attributes no expression to his characters, which is not authenticated by sufficient testimony. But, by judicious selection, rejection, and arrangement, he gives to truth those attractions which have been usurped by fiction. In his narrative a due subordination is observed: some transactions are prominent; others retire. But the scale on which he represents them is increased or diminished, not according to the dignity of the persons concerned in them, but according to the degree in which they elucidate the condition of society and the nature of man. He shows us the court, the camp, and the senate. But he shows us also the nation. He considers no anecdote, no peculiarity of manner, no familiar saying, as too insignificant for his notice which is not too insignificant to illustrate the operation of laws, of religion, and of education, and to mark the progress of the human mind. Men will not merely be described, but will be made intimately known to us. The changes of manners will be indicated, not merely by a few general phrases or a few extracts from statistical documents, but by appropriate images presented in every line.

If a man, such as we are supposing, should write the history of England, he would assuredly not omit the battles, the sieges, the negotiations, the seditions, the ministerial changes. But with these he would intersperse the details which are the charm of historical romances. At Lincoln Cathedral there is a beautiful painted window, which was made by an apprentice out of the pieces of glass which had been rejected by his master. It is so far superior to every other in the church, that, according to the tradition, the vanquished artist killed himself from mortification. Sir Walter Scott, in the same manner, has used those fragments of truth which historians have scornfully thrown behind them in a manner which may well excite their envy. He has constructed out of their gleanings works which, even considered as histories, are scarcely less valuable than their's. But a truly great historian would reclaim those materials which the novelist has appropriated. The history of the government, and the history of the people, would be exhibited in that mode in which alone they can be exhibited justly, in inseparable conjunction and intermixture. We should not then have to look for the wars and votes of the Puritans in Clarendon, and for their phraseology in Old Mortality; for one half of King James in Hume, and for the other half in the Fortunes of Nigel.

The early part of our imaginary history would be rich with colouring from romance, ballad, and chronicle. We should find ourselves in the company of knights such as those of Froissart, and of pilgrims such as those who rode with Chaucer from the Tabard. Society would be shown from the highest to the lowest,—from the royal cloth of state to the den of the outlaw; from the throne of the legate, to the chimney-corner where the begging friar regaled himself. Palmers, minstrels, crusaders,—the stately monastery, with the good cheer in its refectory and the high-mass in its chapel,—the manor-house, with its hunting and hawking,—the tournament, with the heralds and ladies, the trumpets and the cloth of gold,—would give truth and life to the representation. We should perceive, in a thousand slight touches, the importance of the privileged burgher, and the fierce and haughty spirit which swelled under the collar of the degraded villain. The revival of letters would not merely be described in a few magnificent periods. We should discern, in innumerable particulars, the fermentation of mind, the eager appetite for knowledge, which distinguished the sixteenth from the fifteenth century. In the Reformation we should see, not merely a schism which changed the ecclesiastical constitution of England and the mutual relations of the European powers, but a moral war which raged in every family, which set the father against the son, and the son against the father, the mother against the daughter, and the daughter against the mother. Henry would be painted with the skill of Tacitus. We should have the change of his character from his profuse and joyous youth to his savage and imperious old age. We should perceive the gradual progress of selfish and tyrannical passions in a mind not naturally insensible or ungenerous; and to the last we should detect some remains of that open and noble temper which endeared him to a people whom he oppressed, struggling with the hardness of despotism and the irritability of disease. We should see Elizabeth in all her weakness and in all her strength, surrounded by the handsome favourites whom she never trusted, and the wise old statesmen whom she never dismissed, uniting in herself the most contradictory qualities of both her parents, —the coquetry, the caprice, the petty malice of Anne,—the haughty and resolute spirit of Henry. We have no hesitation in saying that a great artist might produce a portrait of this remarkable woman at least as striking as that in the novel of Kenilworth, without employing a single trait not authenticated by ample testimony. In the meantime, we should see arts cultivated, wealth accumulated, the conveniences of life improved. We should see the keeps, where nobles, insecure themselves, spread insecurity around them, gradually giving place to the halls of peaceful opulence, to the oriels of Longleat, and the stately pinnacles of Burleigh. We should see towns extended, deserts cultivated, the hamlets of fishermen turned into wealthy havens, the meal of the peasant improved, and his hut more commodiously furnished. We should see those opinions and feelings which produced the great struggle against the house of Stuart slowly growing up in the bosom of private families, before they manifested themselves in parliamentary debates. Then would come the civil war. Those skirmishes on which Clarendon dwells so minutely would be told, as Thucydides would have told them, with perspicuous conciseness. They are merely connecting links. But the great characteristics of the age, the loyal enthusiasm of the brave English gentry, the fierce licentiousness of the swearing, dicing, drunken reprobates, whose excesses disgraced the royal cause,—the austerity of the Presbyterian Sabbaths in the city, the extravagance of the independent preachers in the camp, the precise garb, the severe countenance, the petty scruples, the affected accent, the absurd names and phrases which marked the Puritans,—the valour, the policy, the public spirit, which lurked beneath these ungraceful disguises,—the dreams of the raving Fifth-monarchy-man, the dreams, scarcely less wild, of the philosophic republican,—all these would enter into the representation, and render it at once more exact and more striking.

The instruction derived from history thus written would be of a vivid and practical character. It would be received by the imagination as well as by the reason. It would be not merely traced on the mind, but branded into it. Many truths, too, would be learned, which can be learned in no other manner. As the history of states is generally written, the greatest and most momentous revolutions seem to come upon them like supernatural inflictions, without warning or cause. But the fact is, that such revolutions are almost always the consequences of moral changes, which have gradually passed on the mass of the community, and which ordinarily proceed far before their progress is indicated by any public measure. An intimate knowledge of the domestic history of nations is therefore absolutely necessary to the prognosis of political events....

A historian, such as we have been attempting to describe, would indeed be an intellectual prodigy. In his mind, powers scarcely compatible with each other must be tempered into an exquisite harmony. We shall sooner see another Shakspeare or another Homer. The highest excellence to which any single faculty can be brought would be less surprising than such a happy and delicate combination of qualities. Yet the contemplation of imaginary models is not an unpleasant or useless employment of the mind. It cannot indeed produce perfection; but it produces improvement, and nourishes that generous and liberal fastidiousness which is not inconsistent with the strongest sensibility to merit, and which, while it exalts our conceptions of the art, does not render us unjust to the artist.

OBLIVION

Sir Thomas Browne, *Hydriotaphia: Urne Burial.* 1658

But the iniquity of oblivion blindly scattereth her poppy, and deals with the memory of men without distinction to merit of perpetuity. Who can but pity the founder of the Pyramids? *Herostratus* lives that burnt the Temple of *Diana*, he is almost lost that built it; Time hath spared the Epitaph of Adrians horse, confounded that of himself. In vain we compute our felicities by the advantage of our good names, since bad have equal durations; and *Thersites* is like to live as long as *Agamemnon*. Who knows whether the best of men be known? or whether there be not more remarkable persons forgot, then any that stand remembred in the known account of time? Without the favour of the everlasting Register the first man had been as unknown as the last, and Methuselahs long life had been his only Chronicle.

Oblivion is not to be hired: The greater part must be content to be as though they had not been, to be found in the register of God, not in the record of man. Twenty seven names make up the first story, and the recorded names ever since contain not one living Century. The number of the dead long exceedeth all that shall live. The night of time far surpasseth the day, and who knows when was the Æquinox? Every houre addes unto that current Arithmetique, which scarce stands one moment. And since death must be the *Lucina* of life, and even Pagans could doubt whether thus to live, were to die; Since our longest Sun sets at right descensions, and makes but winter arches, and therefore it cannot be long before we lie down in darknesse, and have our light in ashes; Since the brother of death daily haunts us with dying *memento's*, and time that grows old itself, bids us hope no long duration: Diuturnity is a dream and folly of expectation.

PRINCIPALITIES AND POWERS

*Public life is a situation of power and energy; he
trespasses against his duty who sleeps upon his watch,
as well as he that goes over to the enemy.*

EDMUND BURKE, 1770

ORDINARY PEOPLE

Francis, Lord Jeffrey, *Edinburgh Review.* March 1817

Nothing is more delusive, or at least more woefully imperfect, than the suggestions of authentic history, as it is
generally—or rather universally—written, and nothing more
exaggerated than the impressions it conveys of the actual
state and condition of those who live in its most agitated
periods. The great public events of which alone it takes
cognisance, have but little direct influence upon the body of
the people, and do not, in general, form the principal business,
or happiness or misery even of those who are in some measure
concerned in them. Even in the worst and most disastrous
times—in periods of civil war and revolution and public
discord and oppression, a great part of the time of a great
part of the people is spent in making love and money—in
social amusement or professional industry—in schemes for
worldly advancement or personal distinction, just as in periods
of general peace and prosperity. Men court and marry very
nearly as much in the one season as in the other; and are as
merry at weddings and christenings—as gallant at balls and
races—as busy in their studies and counting-houses—eat as
heartily, in short, and sleep as soundly—prattle with their
children as pleasantly—and thin their plantations and scold
their servants as zealously, as if their contemporaries were
not furnishing materials thus abundantly for the tragic muse
of history. The quiet undercurrent of life, in short, keeps its
deep and steady course in its eternal channels, unaffected, or
but slightly disturbed, by the storms that agitate its surface;
and while long tracts of time, in the history of every country,
seem, to the distant student of its annals to be darkened over
with one thick and oppressive cloud of unbroken misery, the
greater part of those who have lived through the whole acts
of the tragedy, will be found to have enjoyed a fair average
share of felicity, and to have been much less affected by the
shocking events of their day, than those who know nothing
else of it than that such events took place in its course.

SOCIAL STRATA

WALTER BAGEHOT, *The English Constitution.*
Chap. i. 1867

WE have in a great community like England crowds of
people scarcely more civilized than the majority of two thousand years ago; we have others, even more numerous, such
as the best people were a thousand years since. The lower
orders, the middle orders, are still, when tried by what is the
standard of the educated "ten thousand", narrow-minded,
unintelligent, incurious. It is useless to pile up abstract
words. Those who doubt should go out into their kitchens.
Let an accomplished man try what seems to him most obvious, most certain, most palpable in intellectual matters,
upon the housemaid and the footman, and he will find that
what he says seems unintelligible, confused, and erroneous—
that his audience think him mad and wild when he is speaking
what is in his own sphere of thought the dullest platitude of
cautious soberness. Great communities are like great mountains—they have in them the primary, secondary, and tertiary
strata of human progress; the characteristics of the lower
regions resemble the life of old times rather than the present
life of the higher regions. And a philosophy which does not
ceaselessly remember, which does not continually obtrude,
the palpable differences of the various parts, will be a theory
radically false, because it has omitted a capital reality—will
be a theory essentially misleading, because it will lead men
to expect what does not exist, and not to anticipate that which
they will find.

A MIGRATION

GILBERT MURRAY, *The Rise of the Greek Epic.*
3rd ed. 1924

THE centre of Greece is really not Athens nor Sparta nor any state of the mainland. The real centre is the Aegean; and the migrations by sea are both more characteristic and for after-history, I venture to suggest, more important. When a tribe moved by land it took most of its belongings with it. When it had to cross the sea a possession must needs be very precious indeed before it could be allowed room in those small boats. Of course there are cases where a deliberate invasion is planned, as the Saxons, for instance, planned their invasion of Britain. The fighting men go first and secure a foothold; the rest of the nation can follow when things are safe. In historical times, when the Athenians left Attica before the advance of the Persian army, they took their wives and even their herds across the narrow waters to Salamis and Aegina. When the Phocaeans deserted their city and fled to the west, they seem to have begun by taking their womankind at least as far as Chios, where they might hope to find a breathing-place. But these were more organised or at least less helpless peoples; the movement was well thought out beforehand, and there was friendly land near. In the earlier migrations of the Dark Age a tribe, or mass of people, seldom took to the sea till driven by the fear of death. That was no time to think of taking women or herds. You might desire greatly to take your young wife—or your old wife, for that matter; but you would scarcely dare to make such a proposal to the hungry fighters about you. You might wish to take your little boy. But would the rest of us, think you, choose to be encumbered with another consumer of bread who could never help in a fight, who might delay us in charging or flying, might cry from the pain of hunger or fatigue and betray us all? No, leave him on the beach and come! Put some mark on him. Probably some one will make him a slave, and then, with good luck, you may some day knock up against him and pay his ransom.

When we are off on the sea, what is the prospect before us? We have some provisions, though no water. Instead, we take guides who know where there are springs near the sea-shore in divers islands and unfrequented promontories. We can move by night and hide in caves during the day. The guide probably knows places where cattle may, with some risk, be raided. Better still, he knows of some villages that have been lately attacked by other pirates, where the men are still weak with their wounds. Not all their flocks have been killed. We might well take the rest. If we stay at sea, we die of thirst. If we are seen landing, we are for certain massacred by any human beings who find us. Piracy on the high seas will not keep us alive. In the good old days, when the Northmen first came, pirates could live like fighting-cocks and be buried like princes. But the business has been spoiled. There are too many men like ourselves, and too few ships with anything on them to steal. If we go back to our old home, the invaders have by this time got our women as slaves, and will either kill us or sell us in foreign countries. Is there any where an island to seize? There are many little desert rocks all studded over the Aegean, where doubtless we have rested often enough when the constrained position of sitting everlastingly at the oars has been too much for us; rested and starved, and some of us gone mad with thirst under that hot sun. A water-less rock will be no use. Can we seize some inhabited island? Alone we are too weak; but what if we combined with some other outlaws? There are some outcast Carians in like plight with ourselves in one of the desert caves near. In our normal life we would not touch a Carian. Their weapons are no gentle-man's weapons. Their voices make one sick. And their hair...! But what does it matter now?...And with them are some Leleges, who worship birds; some unknown savages from the eastern side, dark-bearded hook-nosed creatures answering to babyish names like "Atta" and "Babba" and "Duda"; and—good omen!—some of our old enemies from near home, the tribe that we were always fighting with and had learned to hate in our cradles. A pleasure to meet them again! One can understand their speech. We swear an oath that makes us brothers. We cut one another's arms, pour the blood in a bowl and drink some all round. We swear by our gods: to make things pleasanter, we swear by one another's gods, so far as we can make out their outlandish names. And then forth to attack our island.

After due fighting it is ours. The men who held it yesterday are slain. Some few have got away in boats, and may someday come back to worry us, but not just yet, not for a good long time. There is water to drink; there is bread and curded milk and onions. There is flesh of sheep or goats. There is wine, or, at the worst, some coarser liquor of honey or grain, which will at least intoxicate. One needs that, after such a day....No more thirst, no more hunger, no more of the cramped galley benches, no more terror of the changes of wind and sea. The dead men are lying all about us. We will fling them into the sea tomorrow. The women are suitably tied up and guarded. The old one who kept shrieking curses has been spiked with a lance and tossed over the cliff. The wailing and sobbing of the rest will stop in a day or two: if it torments you, you can easily move a few paces away out of the sound. If it still rings in your ears, drink two more cups and you will not mind it. The stars are above us, and the protecting sea round us, we have got water and food and roofs over our heads. And we wrought it all by our own wisdom and courage and the manifest help of Zeus and Apollo. What good men we are, and valiant and pious; and our gods—what short work they make of other men's gods!

THE LEVIATHAN

Thomas Hobbes, *Leviathan.* Part i, chap. xiii; part ii, chap. xvii. 1651

Hereby it is manifest, that during the time men live without a common Power to keep them all in awe, they are in that condition which is called Warre; and such a warre, as is of every man, against every man. For warre, consisteth not in Battell onely, or the act of fighting; but in a tract of time, wherein the Will to contend by Battell is sufficiently known:

and therefore the notion of *Time*, is to be considered in the nature of Warre; as it is in the nature of Weather. For as the nature of Foule weather, lyeth not in a showre or two of rain; but in an inclination thereto of many dayes together; So the nature of War, consisteth not in actuall fighting; but in the known disposition thereto, during all the time there is no assurance to the contrary. All other time is PEACE.

Whatsoever therefore is consequent to a time of Warre, where every man is Enemy to every man; the same is consequent to the time, wherein men live without other security, than what their own strength, and their own invention shall furnish them withall. In such condition, there is no place for Industry; because the fruit thereof is uncertain: and consequently no Culture of the Earth, no Navigation, nor use of the commodities that may be imported by Sea; no commodious Building; no Instruments of moving, and removing such things as require much force; no Knowledge of the face of the Earth; no account of Time; no Arts; no Letters; no Society; and which is worst of all, continuall feare, and danger of violent death; And the life of man, solitary, poore, nasty, brutish, and short....

The only way to erect such a Common Power, as may be able to defend them from the invasion of Forraigners, and the injuries of one another, and thereby to secure them in such sort, as that by their owne industrie, and by the fruites of the Earth, they may nourish themselves and live contentedly; is, to conferre all their power and strength upon one Man, or upon one Assembly of men, that may reduce all their Wills, by plurality of voices, unto one Will: which is as much as to say, to appoint one Man, or Assembly of men, to beare their Person; and every one to owne, and acknowledge himselfe to be Author of whatsoever he that so beareth their Person, shall Act, or cause to be Acted, in those things which concerne the Common Peace and Safetie; and therein to submit their Wills, every one to his Will, and their Judgements, to his Judgment. This is more than Consent, or Concord; it is a reall Unitie of them all, in one and the same Person, made by Covenant of every man with every man, in such manner, as if every man should say to every man, *I Authorise and give up my Right of*

Governing my selfe, to this Man, or to this Assembly of men, on this condition, that thou give up thy Right to him, and Authorise all his Actions in like manner. This done, the Multitude so united in one Person, is called a COMMON-WEALTH, in latine CIVITAS. This is the Generation of that great LEVIATHAN, or rather (to speake more reverently) of that *Mortall God,* to which wee owe under the *Immortall God,* our peace and defence. For by this Authoritie, given him by every particular man in the Common-Wealth, he hath the use of so much Power and Strength conferred on him, that by terror thereof, he is inabled to forme the wills of them all, to Peace at home, and mutuall ayd against their enemies abroad.

FORMS OF GOVERNMENT

ARISTOTLE's *Politics,* c. 330 B.C. Book III, sect. 7.
Translated by Benjamin Jowett. 1885

THE true forms of government, therefore, are those in which the one, or the few, or the many, govern with a view to the common interest; but governments which rule with a view to the private interest, whether of the one, or of the few, or of the many, are perversions. For citizens, if they are truly citizens, ought to participate in the advantages of a state. Of forms of government in which one rules, we call that which regards the common interests, kingship or royalty; that in which more than one, but not many, rule, aristocracy; and it is so called, either because the rulers are the best men, or because they have at heart the best interests of the state and of the citizens. But when the citizens at large administer the state for the common interest, the government is called by the generic name—a constitution. And there is a reason for this use of language. One man or a few may excel in virtue; but of virtue there are many kinds: and as the number increases it becomes more difficult for them to attain perfection in every kind, though they may in military virtue, for this is found in the masses. Hence, in a constitutional government the fighting-men have the supreme power, and those who possess arms are the citizens.

Of the above-mentioned forms, the perversions are as follows:—of royalty, tyranny; of aristocracy, oligarchy; of constitutional government, democracy. For tyranny is a kind of monarchy which has in view the interest of the monarch only; oligarchy has in view the interest of the wealthy; democracy, of the needy: none of them the common good of all.

MAN AND OFFICE

WILLIAM EDWARD HARTPOLE LECKY, *A History of England in the Eighteenth Century.* Vol. I, chap. iii. 1878

THERE have been legislative bodies, constructed on the largest, freest, and most symmetrical plan, which have been the passive instruments of despotism; and there have been others which, though saturated with corruption and disfigured by every description of anomaly, have never wholly lost their popular character. The parliamentary system at the time we are considering was a government by the upper classes of the nation; those classes possessed in an eminent degree political capacity, and although public spirit had sunk very low among them, it was by no means extinguished. Men who on ordinary occasions voted through party or personal motives rose on great emergencies to real patriotism. The enthusiasm and the genius of the country aspired in a great degree to political life; and large boroughowners, who disposed of some seats for money and of others for the aggrandisement of their families, were accustomed also, through mingled motives of patriotism and vanity, to bring forward young men of character and promise. Even if they restricted their patronage to their sons they at least provided that many young men should be in the House, and they thus secured the materials of efficient legislators. Statesmanship is not like poetry, or some of the other forms of higher literature, which can only be brought to perfection by men endowed with extraordinary natural genius. The art of management, whether applied to public business or to assemblies, lies strictly within the limits of education, and what is required is much less transcendent abilities than early practice, tact, courage, good temper, courtesy, and industry. In the immense majority of cases the function of statesmen is not creative, and its excellence lies much more in execution than in conception. In politics possible combinations are usually few, and the course that should be pursued is sufficiently obvious. It is in the management of details, the necessity of surmounting difficulties, that chiefly taxes the abilities of statesmen, and these things can to a very large degree be acquired by practice. The natural capacities, even of a Walpole, a Palmerston, or a Peel, were far short of prodigy or genius. Imperfect and vicious as was the system of parliamentary government, it at least secured a school of statesmen quite competent for the management of affairs, and the reign of corruption among them, though very threatening, was by no means absolute.

THE PHILOSOPHER IN POWER

PLATO's *Republic*, c. 390 B.C. Book VII. Translated by
Benjamin Jowett. 1871

You have again forgotten, my friend, I said, the intention of the legislator, who did not aim at making any one class in the State happy above the rest; the happiness was to be in the whole State, and he held the citizens together by persuasion and necessity, making them benefactors of the State, and therefore benefactors of one another; to this end he created them, not to please themselves, but to be his instruments in binding up the State.

True, he said, I had forgotten.

Observe, Glaucon, that there will be no injustice in compelling our philosophers to have a care and providence of others; we shall explain to them that in other States, men of their class are not obliged to share in the toils of politics: and this is reasonable, for they grow up at their own sweet will, and the government would rather not have them. Being self-taught, they cannot be expected to show any gratitude for a culture which they have never received. But we have brought you into the world to be rulers of the hive, kings of yourselves and of the other citizens, and have educated you far better and more perfectly than they have been educated, and you are better able to share in the double duty. Wherefore each of you, when his turn comes, must go down to the general underground abode, and get the habit of seeing in the dark. When you have acquired the habit, you will see ten thousand times better than the inhabitants of the den, and you will know what the several images are, and what they represent, because you have seen the beautiful and just and good in their truth. And thus our State, which is also yours, will be a reality, and not a dream only, and will be administered in a spirit unlike that of other States, in which men fight with one another about shadows only and are distracted in the struggle for power, which in their eyes is a great good. Whereas the truth is that the State in which the rulers are most reluctant to govern is always the best and most quietly governed, and the State in which they are most eager, the worst.

Quite true, he replied.

And will our pupils, when they hear this, refuse to take their turn at the toils of State, when they are allowed to spend the greater part of their time with one another in the heavenly light?

Impossible, he answered; for they are just men, and the commands which we impose upon them are just; there can be no doubt that every one of them will take office as a stern necessity, and not after the fashion of our present rulers of State.

REPUBLIC OF ATHENS

EDMUND BURKE, *A Vindication of Natural Society.* 1756

THE whole history of this celebrated republic is but one tissue of rashness, folly, ingratitude, injustice, tumult, violence, and tyranny, and indeed of every species of wickedness that can well be imagined. This was a city of wise men, in which a minister could not exercise his functions; a warlike people, amongst whom a general did not dare either to gain or lose a battle; a learned nation in which a philosopher could not venture on a free enquiry. This was the city which banished Themistocles, starved Aristides, forced into exile Miltiades, drove out Anaxagoras, and poisoned Socrates. This was a city which changed the form of its government with the moon; eternal conspiracies, revolutions daily, nothing fixed and established. A republic, as an ancient philosopher has observed, is no one species of government, but a magazine of every species; here you find every sort of it, and that in the worst form. As there is a perpetual change, one rising and the other falling, you have all the violence and wicked policy, by which a beginning power must always acquire its strength, and all the weakness by which falling states are brought to a complete destruction.

CARTHAGINIAN CONSTITUTION

ARISTOTLE'S *Politics*, c. 330 B.C. Book II, sect. 11. Translated by Benjamin Jowett. 1885

THE Carthaginians are also considered to have an excellent form of government, which differs from that of any other state in several respects, though it is in some very like the Lacedaemonian. Indeed, all three states—the Lacedaemonian, the Cretan and the Carthaginian—nearly resemble one another, and are very different from any others. Many of the Carthaginian institutions are excellent. The superiority of their constitution is proved by the fact that, although containing an element of democracy, it has been lasting; the Carthaginians have never had any rebellion worth speaking of, and have never been under the rule of a tyrant.

Among the points in which the Carthaginian constitution resembles the Lacedaemonian are the following:—The common tables of the clubs answer to the Spartan phiditia, and their magistracy of the 104 to the Ephors; but, whereas the Ephors are any chance persons, the magistrates of the Carthaginians are elected according to merit—this is an improvement. They have also their kings and their gerusia, or council of elders, who correspond to the kings and elders of Sparta. Their kings, unlike the Spartan, are not always of the same family, and this an ordinary one, but if there is some distinguished family they are selected out of it and not appointed by seniority—this is far better. Such officers have great power, and therefore, if they are persons of little worth, do a great deal of harm, and they have already done harm at Lacedaemon.

Most of the defects or deviations from the perfect state, for which the Carthaginian constitution would be censured, apply equally to all the forms of government which we have mentioned. But of the deflections from aristocracy and constitutional government, some incline more to democracy and some to oligarchy. The kings and elders, if unanimous, may determine whether they will or will not bring a matter before the people, but when they are not unanimous, the people may decide whether or not the matter shall be brought forward. And whatever the kings and elders bring before the people is not only heard but also determined by them, and any one who likes may oppose it; now this is not permitted in Sparta or Crete. That the magistracies of five who have under them many important matters should be co-opted, that they should choose the supreme council of 100, and should hold office longer than other magistrates (for they are virtually rulers both before and after they hold office)—these are oligarchical features; their being without salary and not elected by lot, and any similar points, such as the practice of having all suits tried by the magistrates, and not some by one class of judges or jurors and some by another, as at Lacedaemon, are characteristic of aristocracy. The Carthaginian constitution deviates from aristocracy and inclines to oligarchy, chiefly on a point where popular opinion is on their side. For men in general think that magistrates should be chosen not only for their merit, but for their wealth: a man, they say, who is poor cannot rule well—he has not the leisure. If, then, election of magistrates for their wealth be characteristic of oligarchy, and election for merit of aristocracy, there will be a third form under which the constitution of Carthage is comprehended; for the Carthaginians choose their magistrates, and particularly the highest of them—their kings and generals—with an eye both to merit and to wealth.

But we must acknowledge that, in thus deviating from aristocracy, the legislator has committed an error. Nothing is more absolutely necessary than to provide that the highest class, not only when in office, but when out of office, should have leisure and not demean themselves in any way; and to this his attention should be first directed. Even if you must have regard to wealth, in order to secure leisure, yet it is surely a bad thing that the greatest offices, such as those of kings and generals, should be bought. The law which allows this abuse makes wealth of more account than virtue, and the whole state becomes avaricious. For, whenever the chiefs of the state deem anything honourable, the other citizens are sure to follow their example; and, where virtue has not the first place, there aristocracy cannot be firmly established. Those who have been at the expense of purchasing their places will be in the habit of repaying themselves; and it is absurd to suppose that a poor and honest man will be wanting to make gains, and that a lower stamp of man who has incurred a great expense will not. Wherefore they should rule who are able to rule best. And even if the legislator does not care to protect the good from poverty, he should at any rate secure leisure for those in office.

It would seem also to be a bad principle that the same person should hold many offices, which is a favourite practice among the Carthaginians, for one business is better done by one man. The legislator should see to this and should not appoint the same person to be a flute-player and a shoe-maker. Hence, where the state is large, it is more in accordance both with constitutional and with democratic principles that the offices of state should be distributed among many persons. For, as I was saying, this arrangement is more popular, and any action familiarized by repetition is better and sooner performed. We have a proof in military and naval matters; the duties of command and of obedience in both these services extend to all.

The government of the Carthaginians is oligarchical, but they successfully escape the evils of oligarchy by their wealth, which enables them from time to time to send out some portion of the people to their colonies. This is their panacea and the means by which they give stability to the state. Accident favours them, but the legislator should be able to provide against revolution without trusting to accidents. As things are, if any misfortune occurred, and the people revolted from their rulers, there would be no way of restoring peace by legal methods.

THE LORD OF ASIA

JOHN BAGNELL BURY, *A History of Greece to the Death of Alexander the Great.* Chap. xvii. 1900

THE Macedonian king, the commander-in-chief of the Greek confederates, had set forth as a champion of Greeks against mere barbarians, as a leader of Europeans against effeminate Asiatics, as the representative of a higher folk against beings lower in the human scale. All the Greeks and Macedonians who followed him regarded the east as a world to be plundered and rifled by their higher intelligence and courage, and considered the orientals as inferiors meant by nature to be their own slaves. "Slaves by nature" they seemed to the political wisdom of Aristotle himself, Alexander's teacher; and the victories of Issus and Gaugamela were calculated to confirm the Europeans in their sense of unmeasured superiority. But, as Alexander advanced, his view expanded, and he rose to a loftier conception of his own position and his relation to Asia. He began to transcend the familiar distinction of Greek and barbarian, and to see that, for all the truth it contained, it was not the last word that could be said. He formed the notion of an empire, both European and Asiatic, in which the Asiatics should not be dominated by the European invaders, but Europeans and Asiatics alike should be ruled on an equality by a monarch, indifferent to the distinction of Greek and barbarian, and looked upon as their own king by Persians as well as by Macedonians. The idea begins to show itself after the battle of Gaugamela. The Persian lords and satraps who submit are received with favour and confidence; Alexander learns to know and appreciate the fine qualities of the Iranian noblemen. Some of the eastern provinces are entrusted to Persian satraps, for example Babylonia to Mazaeus, and the court of Alexander ceases to be purely European. With oriental courtiers, the forms of an oriental court are also gradually introduced; the Asiatics prostrate themselves before the lord of Asia; and presently Alexander adopts the dress of a Persian king at court ceremonies, in order to appear less a foreigner in the eyes of his eastern subjects. The idea which prompted this policy was new and bold, and it harmonised with the great work of Alexander,—the breaking down of the barriers between west and east; but it was accompanied by a certain imperious self-exaltation, which we do not find in the earlier part of Alexander's career, and it involved him in troubles with his own folk. The Macedonians strongly disapproved of their king's new paths; they disliked the rival influence of the Asiatic nobles, and their prejudices were shocked at seeing Alexander occasionally assume oriental robes. The Macedonian royalty was indeed inadequate for Alexander's imperial position; but it is unfortunate that he had no other model than the royalty of Persia, hedged round by forms which were so distasteful to the free spirit of Greece. The life of Alexander was spent in solving difficult problems, political and military; and none was harder than this, to create a kingship which should conciliate the prejudices of the east without offending the prejudices of the west.

THE DOMINION OF ROME

(i) POLYBIUS OF MEGALOPOLIS, *Histories*. Book I, chaps. i, ii.
C. 150 B.C. Translated by Evelyn Shirley Shuckburgh.
1889
(ii) GAIUS CORNELIUS TACITUS, *Life of Agricola*. Chap. XXX.
A.D. 97. Translated by Arthur Murphy. 1793

(i)

CAN any one be so indifferent or idle as not to care to know by what means, and under what kind of polity, almost the whole inhabited world was conquered and brought under the dominion of the single city of Rome, and that too within a period of not quite fifty-three years?* Or who again can be so completely absorbed in other subjects of contemplation or study, as to think any of them superior in importance to the accurate understanding of an event for which the past affords no precedent?

We shall best show how marvellous and vast our subject is by comparing the most famous Empires which preceded, and which have been the favourite themes of historians, and measuring them with the superior greatness of Rome. There are but three that deserve even to be so compared and measured: and they are these. The Persians for a certain length of time were possessed of a great empire and dominion. But every time they ventured beyond the limits of Asia, they found not only their empire, but their own existence also in danger. The Lacedaemonians, after contending for supremacy in Greece for many generations, when they did get it, held it without dispute for barely twelve years. The Macedonians obtained dominion in Europe from the lands bordering on the Adriatic to the Danube,—which after all is but a small fraction of this continent,—and, by the destruction of the Persian Empire, they afterwards added to that the dominion of Asia. And yet, though they had the credit of having made themselves masters of a larger number of countries and states than any people had ever done, they still left the greater half of the

* 219 B.C. to 167 B.C.

inhabited world in the hands of others. They never so much as thought of attempting Sicily, Sardinia, or Libya: and as to Europe, to speak the plain truth, they never even knew of the most warlike tribes of the West. The Roman conquest, on the other hand, was not partial. Nearly the whole inhabited world was reduced by them to obedience: and they left behind them an empire not to be paralleled in the past or rivalled in the future.

(ii)

From the speech of Galgacus, the Caledonian chief

THIS is the end of the habitable world, and rocks and brawling waves fill all the space behind. The Romans are in the heart of our country; no submission can satisfy their pride; no concessions can appease their fury. While the land has anything left, it is the theatre of war; when it can yield no more, they explore the sea for hidden treasure. Are the nations rich, Roman avarice is their enemy. Are they poor, Roman ambition lords it over them. The east and the west have been rifled, and the spoiler is still insatiate. The Romans, by a strange singularity of nature, are the only people who invade, with equal ardour, the wealth and the poverty of nations. To rob, to ravage, and to murder, in their imposing language, are the arts of civil policy. When they have made the world a solitude, they call it peace.

SUBJECTION TO AUTHORITY

Epistle to the Romans. Chap. xiii. C. A.D. 58.
Revised Version. 1881

LET every soul be in subjection to the higher powers: for there is no power but of God; and the powers that be are ordained of God. Therefore he that resisteth the power, withstandeth the ordinance of God: and they that withstand shall receive to themselves judgement. For rulers are not a terror to the good work, but to the evil. And wouldest thou have no fear of the power? do that which is good, and thou shalt have praise from the same: for he is a minister of God to thee for good. But if thou do that which is evil, be afraid; for he beareth not the sword in vain: for he is a minister of God, an avenger for wrath to him that doeth evil. Wherefore ye must needs be in subjection, not only because of the wrath, but also for conscience sake. For for this cause ye pay tribute also; for they are ministers of God's service, attending continually upon this very thing. Render to all their dues: tribute to whom tribute is due; custom to whom custom; fear to whom fear; honour to whom honour.

AN APPEAL TO CAESAR

Acts of the Apostles. Chaps. xxii–xxv. C. A.D. 70.
Authorized Version. 1611

AND as they bound him with thongs, Paul said unto the centurion that stood by, "Is it lawful for you to scourge a man that is a Roman, and uncondemned?" When the centurion heard that, he went and told the chief captain, saying, "Take heed what thou doest: for this man is a Roman". Then the chief captain came, and said unto him, "Tell me, art thou a Roman?" He said, "Yea". And the chief captain answered, "With a great sum obtained I this freedom". And Paul said, "But I was free born". Then straightway they departed from him which should have examined him: and the chief captain also was afraid, after he knew that he was a Roman, and because he had bound him.

On the morrow, because he would have known the certainty wherefore he was accused of the Jews, he loosed him from his bands, and commanded the chief priests and all their council to appear, and brought Paul down, and set him before them.... And when there arose a great dissension, the chief captain, fearing lest Paul should have been pulled in pieces of them, commanded the soldiers to go down, and to take him by force from among them, and to bring him into the castle.... And he called unto him two centurions, saying, "Make ready two hundred soldiers to go to Caesarea, and horsemen three score and ten, and spearmen two hundred, at the third hour of the night; and provide them beasts, that they may set Paul on, and bring him safe unto Felix the governor". And he wrote a letter after this manner:

Claudius Lysias unto the most excellent governor Felix, sendeth greeting. This man was taken of the Jews, and should have been killed of them: then came I with an army, and rescued him, having understood that he was a Roman. And when I would have known the cause wherefore they accused him, I brought him forth into their council: whom I perceived to be accused of questions of their law, but to have nothing laid to his charge worthy of death or of bonds. And when it was told me how that the Jews laid wait for the man, I sent straightway to thee, and gave commandment to his accusers also to say before thee what they had against him. Farewell.

Then the soldiers, as it was commanded them, took Paul, and brought him by night to Antipatris. On the morrow they left the horsemen to go with him, and returned to the castle: who, when they came to Caesarea, and delivered the epistle to the governor, presented Paul also before him. And when the governor had read the letter, he asked of what province he was. And when he understood that he was of Cilicia; "I will hear thee", said he, "when thine accusers are also come". And he commanded him to be kept in Herod's judgment hall.

And after five days Ananias the high priest descended with the elders, and with a certain orator named Tertullus, who informed the governor against Paul....

And when Felix heard these things, having more perfect knowledge of that way, he deferred them, and said, "When Lysias the chief captain shall come down, I will know the uttermost of your matter". And he commanded a centurion to keep Paul, and to let him have liberty, and that he should forbid none of his acquaintance to minister or come unto him....

But after two years Porcius Festus came into Felix' room: and Felix, willing to shew the Jews a pleasure, left Paul bound. Now when Festus was come into the province, after three days he ascended from Caesarea to Jerusalem. Then the high priest and the chief of the Jews informed him against

Paul, and besought him, and desired favour against him, that
he would send for him to Jerusalem, laying wait in the way
to kill him. But Festus answered, that Paul should be kept
at Caesarea, and that he himself would depart shortly thither.
"Let them therefore," said he, "which among you are able,
go down with me, and accuse this man, if there be any
wickedness in him."

And when he had tarried among them more than ten days,
he went down unto Caesarea; and the next day sitting on the
judgment seat commanded Paul to be brought. And when he
was come, the Jews which came down from Jerusalem stood
round about, and laid many and grievous complaints against
Paul, which they could not prove. While he answered for
himself, "Neither against the law of the Jews, neither against
the temple, nor yet against Caesar, have I offended anything
at all". But Festus, willing to do the Jews a pleasure,
answered Paul, and said, "Wilt thou go up to Jerusalem, and
there be judged of these things before me?" Then said Paul,
"I stand at Caesar's judgment seat, where I ought to be judged:
to the Jews have I done no wrong, as thou very well knowest.
For if I be an offender, or have committed anything worthy
of death, I refuse not to die: but if there be none of these
things whereof these accuse me, no man may deliver me unto
them. I appeal unto Caesar". Then Festus, when he had
conferred with the council, answered, "Hast thou appealed
unto Caesar? Unto Caesar shalt thou go".

EGYPTIAN HERMITS

WILLIAM EDWARD HARTPOLE LECKY, *History of European
Morals from Augustus to Charlemagne*. Vol. II, chap. iv. 1869

THE progress of the monastic movement, as has been truly
said, "was not less rapid or universal than that of Christianity itself". Of the actual number of the anchorites, those
who are acquainted with the extreme unveracity of the first
historians of the movement will hesitate to speak with con-

fidence. It is said that St Pachomius, who, early in the fourth century, founded the cœnobitic mode of life, enlisted under his jurisdiction 7,000 monks; that in the days of St Jerome nearly 50,000 monks were sometimes assembled at the Easter festivals; that in the desert of Nitria alone there were, in the fourth century, 5,000 monks under a single abbot; that an Egyptian city named Oxyrynchus devoted itself almost exclusively to the ascetic life, and included 20,000 virgins and 10,000 monks; that St Serapion presided over 10,000 monks; and that, towards the close of the fourth century, the monastic population in a great part of Egypt was nearly equal to the population of the cities. Egypt was the parent of monachism, and it was there that it attained both its extreme development and its most austere severity; but there was very soon scarcely any Christian country in which a similar movement was not ardently propagated. St Athanasius and St Zeno are said to have introduced it into Italy, where it soon afterwards received a great stimulus from St Jerome. St Hilarion instituted the first monks in Palestine, and he lived to see many thousands subject to his rule, and towards the close of his life to plant monachism in Cyprus. Eustathius, Bishop of Sebastia, spread it through Armenia, Paphlagonia, and Pontus. St Basil laboured along the wild shores of the Euxine. St Martin of Tours founded the first monastery in Gaul, and 2,000 monks attended his funeral. Unrecorded missionaries planted the new institution in the heart of Æthiopia, amid the little islands that stud the Mediterranean, in the secluded valleys of Wales and Ireland. But even more wonderful than the many thousands who thus abandoned the world is the reverence with which they were regarded by those who, by their attainments or their character, would seem most opposed to the monastic ideal. No one had more reason than Augustine to know the dangers of enforced celibacy, but St Augustine exerted all his energies to spread monasticism through his diocese. St Ambrose, who was by nature an acute statesman; St Jerome and St Basil, who were ambitious scholars; St Chrysostom, who was pre-eminently formed to sway the refined throngs of a metropolis—all exerted their powers in favour of the life of solitude, and the last three practised it themselves. St Arsenius, who was surpassed by no one in the extravagance of his penances, had held a high office at the court of the Emperor Arcadius. Pilgrims wandered among the deserts, collecting accounts of the miracles and the austerities of the saints, which filled Christendom with admiration; and the strange biographies which were thus formed, wild and grotesque as they are, enable us to realise very vividly the general features of the anchorite life which became the new ideal of the Christian world.

There is, perhaps, no phase in the moral history of mankind of a deeper or more painful interest than this ascetic epidemic. A hideous, sordid, and emaciated maniac, without knowledge, without patriotism, without natural affection, passing his life in a long routine of useless and atrocious self-torture, and quailing before the ghastly phantoms of his delirious brain, had become the ideal of the nations which had known the writings of Plato and Cicero and the lives of Socrates and Cato. For about two centuries, the hideous maceration of the body was regarded as the highest proof of excellence. St Jerome declares, with a thrill of admiration, how he had seen a monk, who for thirty years had lived exclusively on a small portion of barley bread and of muddy water; another, who lived in a hole and never ate more than five figs for his daily repast; a third who cut his hair only on Easter Sunday, who never washed his clothes, who never changed his tunic till it fell to pieces, who starved himself till his eyes grew dim, and his skin "like a pumice stone", and whose merits, shown by these austerities, Homer himself would be unable to recount. For six months, it is said, St Macarius of Alexandria slept in a marsh, and exposed his body naked to the stings of venomous flies. He was accustomed to carry about with him eighty pounds of iron. His disciple, St Eusebius, carried one hundred and fifty pounds of iron, and lived for three years in a dried-up well. St Sabinus would only eat corn that had become rotten by remaining for a month in water. St Besarion spent forty days and nights in the middle of thorn-bushes, and for forty years never lay down when he slept, which last penance was also during fifteen years practised by St Pachomius. Some saints, like St Marcian, restricted themselves to one meal a day, so small that they continually suffered the pangs of hunger. Of one of them it is related that his daily food was six ounces of bread and a few herbs; that he was never seen to recline on a mat or bed, or even to place his limbs easily for sleep; but that some-times, from excess of weariness, his eyes would close at his meals, and the food would drop from his mouth. Other saints, however, ate only every second day; while many, if we could believe the monkish historian, abstained for whole weeks from all nourishment. St Macarius of Alexandria is said during an entire week to have never lain down, or eaten anything but a few uncooked herbs on Sunday. Of another famous saint, named John, it is asserted that for three whole years he stood in prayer, leaning upon a rock; that during all that time he never sat or lay down, and that his only nourishment was the Sacrament, which was brought him on Sundays. Some of the hermits lived in deserted dens of wild beasts, others in dried-up wells, while others found a congenial resting-place among the tombs. Some disdained all clothes, and crawled abroad like the wild beasts, covered only by their matted hair. In Mesopotamia, and part of Syria, there existed a sect known by the name of "Grazers", who never lived under a roof, who ate neither flesh nor bread, but who spent their time for ever on the mountain side, and ate grass like cattle. The cleanliness of the body was regarded as a pollution of the soul, and the saints who were most admired had become one hideous mass of clotted filth. St Athanasius relates with enthusiasm how St Anthony, the patriarch of monachism, had never, to ex-treme old age, been guilty of washing his feet. The less con-stant St Pœmen fell into this habit for the first time when a very old man, and, with a glimmering of common sense, de-fended himself against the astonished monks by saying that he had "learnt to kill not his body, but his passions". St Abraham the hermit, however, who lived for fifty years after his conversion, rigidly refused from that date to wash either his face or his feet. He was, it is said, a person of singular beauty, and his biographer somewhat strangely remarks that "his face reflected the purity of his soul".

St Ammon had never seen himself naked. A famous virgin named Silvia, though she was sixty years old and though bodily sickness was a consequence of her habits, resolutely refused, on religious principles, to wash any part of her body except her fingers. St Euphraxia joined a convent of one hundred and thirty nuns, who never washed their feet, and who shuddered at the mention of a bath. An anchorite once imagined that he was mocked by an illusion of the devil, as he saw gliding before him through the desert a naked creature black with filth and years of exposure, and with white hair floating to the wind. It was a once beautiful woman, St Mary of Egypt, who had thus, during forty-seven years, been expiating her sins.

THE EMPIRE OF CONSTANTINE

EDWARD GIBBON, *Decline and Fall of the Roman Empire.*
Vol. II, chap. xvii. 1781

As long as the Roman consuls were the first magistrates of a free state, they derived their right to power from the choice of the people. As long as the emperors condescended to disguise the servitude which they imposed, the consuls were still elected by the real or apparent suffrage of the senate. From the reign of Diocletian even these vestiges of liberty were abolished, and the successful candidates, who were invested with the annual honours of the consulship, affected to deplore the humiliating condition of their predecessors. The Scipios and the Catos had been reduced to solicit the votes of plebeians, to pass through the tedious and expensive forms of a popular election, and to expose their dignity to the shame of a public refusal; while their own happier fate had reserved them for an age and government in which the rewards of virtue were assigned by the unerring wisdom of a gracious sovereign. In the epistles which the emperor addressed to the two consuls elect, it was declared that they were created by his sole authority. Their names and portraits, engraved on gilt tablets of ivory, were dispersed over the empire as presents to the provinces, the cities, the magistrates, the senate, and the people. Their solemn inauguration was performed at the place of the Imperial residence; and during a period of one hundred and twenty years Rome was constantly deprived of the presence of her ancient magistrates. On the morning of the first of January the consuls assumed the ensigns of their dignity. Their dress was a robe of purple, embroidered in silk and gold, and sometimes ornamented with costly gems. On this solemn occasion they were attended by the most eminent officers of the state and army in the habit of senators; and the useless fasces, armed with the once formidable axes, were borne before them by the lictors. The procession moved from the palace to the Forum or principal square of the city; where the consuls ascended their tribunal, and seated themselves in the curule chairs, which were framed after the fashion of ancient times. They immediately exercised an act of juris-diction, by the manumission of a slave who was brought before them for that purpose; and the ceremony was intended to represent the celebrated action of the elder Brutus, the author of liberty and of the consulship, when he admitted among his fellow-citizens the faithful Vindex, who had revealed the conspiracy of the Tarquins. The public festival was continued during several days in all the principal cities; in Rome, from custom; in Constantinople, from imitation; in Carthage, Antioch, and Alexandria, from the love of pleasure and the superfluity of wealth. In the two capitals of the empire the annual games of the theatre, the circus, and the amphitheatre cost four thousand pounds of gold, (about) one hundred and sixty thousand pounds sterling; and if so heavy an expense surpassed the faculties or the inclination of the magistrates themselves, the sum was supplied from the Imperial treasury. As soon as the consuls had discharged these customary duties, they were at liberty to retire into the shade of private life, and to enjoy during the remainder of the year the undis-turbed contemplation of their own greatness. They no longer presided in the national councils; they no longer executed the resolutions of peace or war. Their abilities (unless they were employed in more effective offices) were of little moment; and their names served only as the legal date of the year in which they had filled the chair of Marius and of Cicero. Yet it was still felt and acknowledged, in the last period of Roman servitude, that this empty name might be compared, and even preferred, to the possession of substantial power. The title of consul was still the most splendid object of ambition, the noblest reward of virtue and loyalty. The emperors themselves, who disdained the faint shadow of the republic, were conscious that they acquired an additional splendour and majesty as often as they assumed the annual honours of the consular dignity.

The proudest and most perfect separation which can be found in any age or country between the nobles and the people is perhaps that of the Patricians and the Plebeians, as it was established in the first age of the Roman republic. Wealth and honours, the offices of the state, and the ceremonies of religion, were almost exclusively possessed by the former; who, preserving the purity of their blood with the most insulting jealousy, held their clients in a condition of specious vassalage. But these distinctions, so incompatible with the spirit of a free people, were removed, after a long struggle, by the persevering efforts of the Tribunes. The most active and successful of the Plebeians accumulated wealth, aspired to honours, deserved triumphs, contracted alliances, and, after some generations, assumed the pride of ancient nobility. The Patrician families, on the other hand, whose original number was never recruited till the end of the commonwealth, either failed in the ordinary course of nature, or were extinguished in so many foreign and domestic wars, or, through a want of merit or fortune, insensibly mingled with the mass of the people. Very few remained who could derive their pure and genuine origin from the infancy of the city, or even from that of the republic, when Cæsar and Augustus, Claudius and Vespasian, created from the body of the senate a competent number of new Patrician families, in the hope of perpetuating an order which was still considered as honourable and sacred. But these artificial supplies (in which the reigning house was always included) were rapidly swept away by the rage of tyrants, by frequent revolutions, by the change of manners, and by the intermixture of nations. Little more was left when Constantine ascended the throne than a vague and imperfect tradition that the Patricians had once been the first of the Romans. To form a body of nobles, whose influence may restrain while it secures the authority of the monarch, would have been very inconsistent with the character and policy of Constantine; but, had he seriously entertained such a design, it might have exceeded the measure of his power to ratify by an arbitrary edict an institution which must expect the sanction of time and of opinion. He revived, indeed, the title of PATRICIANS, but he revived it as a personal, not as a hereditary distinction. They yielded only to the transient superiority of the annual consuls; but they enjoyed the pre-eminence over all the great officers of state, with the most familiar access to the person of the prince. This honourable rank was bestowed on them for life; and, as they were usually favourites and ministers who had grown old in the Imperial court, the true etymology of the word was perverted by ignorance and flattery; and the Patricians of Constantine were reverenced as the adopted *Fathers* of the emperor and the republic.

The fortunes of the Prætorian præfects were essentially different from those of the consuls and Patricians. The latter saw their ancient greatness evaporate in a vain title. The former, rising by degrees from the most humble condition, were invested with the civil and military administration of the Roman world. From the reign of Severus to that of Diocletian, the guards and the palace, the laws and the finances, the armies and the provinces, were intrusted to their superintending care; and, like the vizirs of the East, they held with one hand the seal, and with the other the standard, of the empire. The ambition of the præfects, always formidable, and sometimes fatal to the masters whom they served, was supported by the strength of the Prætorian bands; but, after those haughty troops had been weakened by Diocletian and finally suppressed by Constantine, the præfects, who survived their fall, were reduced without difficulty to the station of useful and obedient ministers. When they were no longer responsible for the safety of the emperor's person, they resigned the jurisdiction which they had hitherto claimed and exercised over all the departments of the palace. They were deprived by Constantine of all military command as soon as they had ceased to lead in the field, under their immediate orders, the flower of the Roman troops; and, at length, by a singular revolution, the captains of the guards were transformed into the civil magistrates of the provinces. According to the plan of government instituted by Diocletian, the four princes had each their Prætorian præfect; and after the monarchy was once more united in the person of Constantine, he still continued to create the same number of FOUR PRÆ-FECTS, and intrusted to their care the same provinces which they had already administered. The præfect of the East stretched his ample jurisdiction into the three parts of the globe which were subject to the Romans, from the cataracts of the Nile to the banks of the Phasis, and from the mountains of Thrace to the frontiers of Persia. The important provinces of Pannonia, Dacia, Macedonia, and Greece once acknow-ledged the authority of the præfect of Illyricum. The power of the præfect of Italy was not confined to the country from whence he derived his title; it extended over the additional territory of Rhætia as far as the banks of the Danube, over the dependent islands of the Mediterranean, and over that part of the continent of Africa which lies between the confines of Cyrene and those of Tingitania. The præfect of the Gauls comprehended under that plural denomination the kindred provinces of Britain and Spain, and his authority was obeyed from the walls of Antoninus to the foot of Mount Atlas.

After the Prætorian præfects had been dismissed from all military command, the civil functions which they were or-dained to exercise over so many subject nations were adequate to the ambition and abilities of the most consummate ministers. To their wisdom was committed the supreme ad-ministration of justice and of the finances, the two objects which, in a state of peace, comprehend almost all the respec-tive duties of the sovereign and of the people; of the former, to protect the citizens who are obedient to the laws; of the latter, to contribute the share of their property which is required for the expenses of the state. The coin, the highways, the posts, the granaries, the manufactures, whatever could interest the public prosperity, was moderated by the authority of the Prætorian præfects. As the immediate representatives of the Imperial majesty, they were empowered to explain, to enforce, and on some occasions to modify, the general edicts by their discretionary proclamations. They watched over the conduct of the provincial governors, removed the negligent, and inflicted punishments on the guilty. From all the inferior jurisdictions an appeal in every matter of importance, either civil or criminal, might be brought before the tribunal of the præfect: but *his* sentence was final and absolute; and the emperors themselves refused to admit any complaints against the judgment or the integrity of a magistrate whom they honoured with such unbounded confidence. His appointments were suitable to his dignity; and, if avarice was his ruling passion, he enjoyed frequent opportunities of collecting a rich harvest of fees, of presents, and of perquisites. Though the emperors no longer dreaded the ambition of their præfects, they were attentive to counterbalance the power of this great office by the uncertainty and shortness of its duration.

From their superior importance and dignity, Rome and Constantinople were alone excepted from the jurisdiction of the Prætorian præfects. The immense size of the city, and the experience of the tardy, ineffectual operation of the laws, had furnished the policy of Augustus with a specious pretence for introducing a new magistrate, who alone could restrain a servile and turbulent populace by the strong arm of arbitrary power. Valerius Messalla was appointed the first præfect of Rome, that his reputation might countenance so invidious a measure; but at the end of a few days that accomplished citizen resigned his office, declaring, with a spirit worthy of the friend of Brutus, that he found himself incapable of exercising a power incompatible with public freedom. As the sense of liberty became less exquisite, the advantages of order were more clearly understood; and the præfect, who seemed to have been designed as a terror only to slaves and vagrants, was permitted to extend his civil and criminal jurisdiction over the equestrian and noble families of Rome.... After the office of Roman consuls had been changed into a vain pageant, which was rarely displayed in the capital, the præfects assumed their vacant place in the senate, and were soon acknowledged as the ordinary presidents of that venerable assembly....About thirty years after the foundation of Constantinople a similar magistrate was created in that rising metropolis, for the same uses and with the same powers. A perfect equality was established between the dignity of the *two* municipal and that of the *four* Prætorian præfects.

   Those who in the Imperial hierarchy were distinguished by the title of *Respectable* formed an intermediate class between the *illustrious* præfects and the *honourable* magistrates of the provinces. In this class the proconsuls of Asia, Achaia, and Africa claimed a pre-eminence, which was yielded to the remembrance of their ancient dignity; and the appeal from their tribunal to that of the præfects was almost the only mark of their dependence. But the civil government of the empire was distributed into thirteen great DIOCESES, each of which equalled the just measure of a powerful kingdom. The first of these dioceses was subject to the jurisdiction of the *count* of the East; and we may convey some idea of the importance and variety of his functions by observing that six hundred apparitors, who would be styled at present either secretaries, or clerks, or ushers, or messengers, were employed in his immediate office. The place of *Augustal præfect* of Egypt was no longer filled by a Roman knight, but the name was retained; and the extraordinary powers which the situation of the country and the temper of the inhabitants had once made indispensable were still continued to the governor. The eleven remaining dioceses—of Asiana, Pontica, and Thrace; of Macedonia, Dacia, Pannonia, or Western Illyricum; of Italy and Africa; of Gaul, Spain, and Britain—were governed by twelve *vicars* or *vice-præfects*, whose name sufficiently explains the nature and dependence of their office. It may be added that the lieutenant-generals of the Roman armies, the military counts and dukes, who will be hereafter mentioned, were allowed the rank and title of *Respectable*.

   As the spirit of jealousy and ostentation prevailed in the councils of the emperors, they proceeded with anxious diligence to divide the substance and to multiply the titles of power. The vast countries which the Roman conquerors had united under the same simple form of administration were imperceptibly crumbled into minute fragments, till at length the whole empire was distributed into one hundred and sixteen provinces, each of which supported an expensive and splendid establishment. Of these, three were governed by *proconsuls*, thirty-seven by *consulars*, five by *correctors*, and seventy-one by *presidents*. The appellations of these magistrates were different; they ranked in successive order, the ensigns of their dignity were curiously varied, and their situation, from accidental circumstances, might be more or less agreeable or advantageous. But they were all (excepting only the proconsuls) alike included in the class of *honourable* persons; and they were alike intrusted, during the pleasure of the prince, and under the authority of the præfects or their deputies, with the administration of justice and the finances in their respective districts. The ponderous volumes of the Codes and Pandects would furnish ample materials for a minute inquiry into the system of provincial government, as in the space of six centuries it was improved by the wisdom of the Roman statesmen and lawyers. It may be sufficient for the historian to select two singular and salutary provisions, intended to restrain the abuse of authority. For the preservation of peace and order, the governors of the provinces were armed with the sword of justice. They inflicted corporal punishments, and they exercised, in capital offences, the power of life and death. But they were not authorised to indulge the condemned criminal with the choice of his own execution or to pronounce a sentence of the mildest and most honourable kind of exile. These prerogatives were reserved to the præfects, who alone could impose the heavy fine of fifty pounds of gold: their vicegerents were confined to the trifling weight of a few ounces. This distinction, which seems to grant the larger while it denies the smaller degree of authority, was founded on a very rational motive. The smaller degree was infinitely more liable to abuse. The passions of a provincial magistrate might frequently provoke him into acts of oppression, which affected only the freedom or the fortunes of the subject; though, from a principle of prudence, perhaps of humanity, he might still be terrified by the guilt of innocent blood. It may likewise be considered that exile, considerable fines, or the choice of an easy death, relate more particularly to the rich and the noble; and the persons the most exposed to the avarice or resentment of a provincial magistrate were thus removed from his obscure persecution to the more august and impartial tribunal of the Prætorian præfect. As it was reasonably apprehended that the integrity of the judge might be biassed, if his interest was concerned or his affections were engaged, the strictest regulations were established to exclude any person, without the special dispensation of the emperor, from the government of the province where he was born; and to prohibit the governor or his son from contracting marriage with a native or an inhabitant, or from purchasing slaves, lands, or houses within the extent of his jurisdiction.. . .

In the system of policy introduced by Augustus, the governors, those at least of the Imperial provinces, were invested with the full powers of the sovereign himself. Ministers of peace and war, the distribution of rewards and punishments depended on them alone, and they successively appeared on their tribunal in the robes of civil magistracy, and in complete armour at the head of the Roman legions. The influence of the revenue, the authority of law, and the command of a military force, concurred to render their power supreme and absolute; and whenever they were tempted to violate their allegiance, the loyal province which they involved in their rebellion was scarcely sensible of any change in its political state. From the time of Commodus to the reign of Constantine near one hundred governors might be enumerated, who, with various success, erected the standard of revolt; and though the innocent were too often sacrificed, the guilty might be sometimes prevented, by the suspicious cruelty of their master. To secure his throne and the public tranquillity from these formidable servants, Constantine resolved to divide the military from the civil administration, and to establish, as a permanent and professional distinction, a practice which had been adopted only as an occasional expedient. The supreme jurisdiction exercised by the Prætorian præfects over the armies of the empire was transferred to the two *masters general* whom he instituted, the one for the *cavalry*, the other for the *infantry*; and though each of these *illustrious* officers was more peculiarly responsible for the discipline of those troops which were under his immediate inspection, they both indifferently commanded in the field the several bodies, whether of horse or foot, which were united in the same army. Their number was soon doubled by the division of the East and West; and as separate generals of the same rank and title were appointed on the four important frontiers of the Rhine, the Upper and the Lower Danube, and of the Euphrates, the defence of the Roman empire was at length committed to eight masters general of the cavalry and infantry. Under their orders, thirty-five military commanders were stationed in the provinces: three in Britain, six in Gaul, one in Spain, one in Italy, five on the Upper, and four on the Lower Danube, in Asia eight, three in Egypt, and four in Africa. The titles of *counts* and *dukes*, by which they were properly distinguished, have obtained in modern languages so very different a sense that the use of them may occasion some surprise. But it should be recollected that the second of these appellations is only a corruption of the Latin word which was indiscriminately applied to any military chief. All these provincial generals were therefore *dukes*; but no more than ten among them were dignified with the rank of *counts* or companions, a title of honour, or rather of favour, which had been recently invented in the court of Constantine. A gold belt was the ensign which distinguished the office of the counts and dukes; and, besides their pay, they received a liberal allowance sufficient to maintain one hundred and ninety servants and one hundred and fifty-eight horses. They were strictly prohibited from interfering in any matter which related to the administration of justice or of the revenue; but the command which they exercised over the troops of their department was independent of the authority of the magistrates. About the same time that Constantine gave a legal sanction to the ecclesiastical order, he instituted in the Roman empire the nice balance of the civil and the military powers. The emulation, and sometimes the discord, which reigned between two professions of opposite interests and incompatible manners, was productive of beneficial and of pernicious consequences. It was seldom to be expected that the general and the civil governor of a province should either conspire for the disturbance, or should unite for the service, of their country. While the one delayed to offer the assistance which the other disdained to solicit, the troops very frequently remained without orders or without supplies, the public safety was betrayed, and the defenceless subjects were left exposed to the fury of the barbarians. The divided administration, which had been formed by Constantine, relaxed the vigour of the state, while it secured the tranquillity of the monarch.

GREENS AND BLUES

EDWARD GIBBON, *Decline and Fall of the Roman Empire.*
Vol. IV, chap. xl. 1788

A MATERIAL difference may be observed in the games of antiquity: the most eminent of the Greeks were actors, the Romans were merely spectators. The Olympic stadium was open to wealth, merit, and ambition; and, if the candidates could depend on their personal skill and activity, they might pursue the footsteps of Diomede and Menelaus, and conduct their own horses in the rapid career. Ten, twenty, forty, chariots, were allowed to start at the same instant; a crown of leaves was the reward of the victor; and his fame, with that of his family and country, was chanted in lyric strains more durable than monuments of brass and marble. But a senator, or even a citizen, conscious of his dignity, would have blushed to expose his person or his horses in the circus of Rome. The games were exhibited at the expense of the republic, the magistrates, or the emperors; but the reins were abandoned to servile hands; and, if the profits of a favourite charioteer sometimes exceeded those of an advocate, they must be considered as the effects of popular extravagance, and the high wages of a disgraceful profession. The race, in its first in-

stitution, was a simple contest of two chariots, whose drivers
were distinguished by *white* and *red* liveries; two additional
colours, a light *green* and a cærulean *blue*, were afterwards
introduced; and, as the races were repeated twenty-five times,
one hundred chariots contributed in the same day to the
pomp of the circus. The four *factions* soon acquired a legal
establishment, and a mysterious origin; and their fanciful
colours were derived from the various appearances of nature
in the four seasons of the year: the red dog-star of summer,
the snows of winter, the deep shades of autumn, and the cheerful verdure of the spring. Another interpretation preferred
the elements to the seasons, and the struggle of the green and
blue was supposed to represent the conflict of the earth and
sea. Their respective victories announced either a plentiful
harvest or a prosperous navigation, and the hostility of the
husbandmen and mariners was somewhat less absurd than
the blind ardour of the Roman people, who devoted their
lives and fortunes to the colour which they had espoused.
Such folly was disdained and indulged by the wisest princes;
but the names of Caligula, Nero, Vitellius, Verus, Commodus,
Caracalla, and Elagabalus, were enrolled in the blue or green
factions of the circus; they frequented their stables, applauded
their favourites, chastised their antagonists, and deserved the
esteem of the populace by the natural or affected imitation
of their manners. The bloody and tumultuous contest continued to disturb the public festivity till the last age of the
spectacles of Rome; and Theodoric, from a motive of justice
or affection, interposed his authority to protect the greens
against the violence of a consul and a patrician who were
passionately addicted to the blue faction of the circus.

Constantinople adopted the follies, though not the virtues,
of ancient Rome; and the same factions which had agitated
the circus raged with redoubled fury in the hippodrome.
Under the reign of Anastasius, this popular frenzy was in-
flamed by religious zeal; and the greens, who had treacher-
ously concealed stones and daggers under baskets of fruit,
massacred at a solemn festival three thousand of their blue
adversaries. From the capital, this pestilence was diffused
into the provinces and cities of the East, and the sportive

distinction of two colours produced two strong and irrecon-
cilable factions, which shook the foundations of a feeble
government. The popular dissensions, founded on the most
serious interest or holy pretence, have scarcely equalled the
obstinacy of this wanton discord, which invaded the peace of
families, divided friends and brothers, and tempted the female
sex, though seldom seen in the circus, to espouse the inclina-
tions of their lovers or to contradict the wishes of their
husbands. Every law, either human or divine, was trampled
underfoot, and as long as the party was successful, its deluded
followers appeared careless of private distress or public
calamity. The licence, without the freedom, of democracy,
was revived at Antioch and Constantinople, and the support
of a faction became necessary to every candidate for civil or
ecclesiastical honours. A secret attachment to the family or
sect of Anastasius was imputed to the greens; the blues were
zealously devoted to the cause of orthodoxy and Justinian,
and their grateful patron protected, above five years, the disorders of a faction whose seasonable tumults overawed the
palace, the senate, and the capitals of the East. Insolent with
royal favour, the blues affected to strike terror by a peculiar
and Barbaric dress—the long hair of the Huns, their close
sleeves and ample garments, a lofty step, and a sonorous
voice. In the day they concealed their two-edged poniards,
but in the night they boldly assembled in arms and in
numerous bands, prepared for every act of violence and rapine.
Their adversaries of the green faction, or even inoffensive
citizens, were stripped and often murdered by these nocturnal
robbers, and it became dangerous to wear any gold buttons
or girdles, or to appear at a late hour in the streets of a peaceful
capital. A daring spirit, rising with impunity, proceeded to
violate the safeguard of private houses; and fire was employed
to facilitate the attack, or to conceal the crimes, of these
factious rioters. No place was safe or sacred from their
depredations; to gratify either avarice or revenge they profusely spilt the blood of the innocent; churches and altars
were polluted by atrocious murders, and it was the boast of
the assassins that their dexterity could always inflict a mortal
wound with a single stroke of their dagger.

LEGACY OF ROME

SIR FRANCIS PALGRAVE, *History of Normandy and of England*. Vol. I, chap. i. 1851

ROME's cruelties, baffling conception by their infinity, her vices, so detestable that no tongue can risk the pollution of holding them up to infamy, her absolute hatred against God, received their chastisement; but her dominion was not extinguished. Races the most adverse, who divided her provinces amongst them as a spoil, who executed vengeance against her temples, who led her children into captivity, who insulted and loathed her imbecility and baseness, nevertheless humbly knelt before their Captive as the dispenser of their temporal power. Not of the blood of Rome, they claimed to be her heirs, engrafting their heroic ancestors upon the stem of the Caesars.

This devolution of authority from Rome, this absorption of Roman authority by the Barbarians, this political, and more than political, this moral unity, this confirmation of a dominion which they seemed to subvert, this acknowledgment of the authority they defied, is the great truth upon which the whole history of European society, and more than European society, European civilization, depends....

We, therefore, all live in the Roman world: the departed generations are not distinguishable in these reasonings from ourselves; the "dark ages" and the "middle ages" are merely bights and bends in the great stream of Time, which we contemplate from the bridge by which the river is arched over. Rome conferred upon the Sovereigns of Modern Europe their principles of prerogative, their attributes of majesty. The powers of the State were concentrated in the Monarch by the *Lex Regia*, he the sole Legislator, though acting by advice; he the supreme Magistrate, delegating his powers. The Comites, the companions of Augustus, installed their successors in the palace of Clovis. European aristocracy is plumed by the stately nomenclature of the declining Empire. The Romans bestowed upon us that Institution so directly antagonistic to Teutonic ethos, nobility created by the

Sovereign's grant. Every Duke and Dukedom, every Count and County, testifies to the Roman influence, and confesses the Barbarian's exulting appropriation of Roman spoils. No King of the Cherusci or of the old Saxons, no Marcomannic or Alemannic Sovereign, was ever the fountain of honour....

Rome presented to Europe the platform of her great Councils: but for the Imperial administration of the Empire combining with the Synods and Councils of the Church, never would the European Commonwealth have known her Diets, her States-General, her Cortes, her Parliaments, her representative Assemblies....

Roman taste gave the fashion to the garment; Roman skill the models for the instruments of war. We have been told to seek in the Forests of Germany the origin of the feudal system and the conception of the Gothic aisle. We shall discover neither there. Architecture is the costume of society, and throughout European Christendom that costume was patterned from Rome. Unapt and unskilful pupils, she taught the Ostrogothic workman to plan the palace of Theodoric; the Frank, to decorate the Hall of Charlemagne; the Lombard, to vault the Duomo; the Norman, to design the Cathedral.

Above all, Rome imparted to our European civilization her luxury, her grandeur, her richness, her splendour, her exaltation of human reason, her spirit of free enquiry, her ready mutability, her unwearied activity, her expansive and devouring energy, her hardness of heart, her intellectual pride, her fierceness, her insatiate cruelty, that unrelenting cruelty which expels all other races out of the very pale of humanity: whilst our direction of thought, our literature, our languages, concur in uniting the Dominions, Kingdoms, States, Principalities and Powers, composing our Civilized Commonwealth in the Old Continent and the New, with the terrible People through whom that Civilized Commonwealth wields the thunderbolts of the dreadful Monarchy, diverse from all others which preceded amongst mankind.

MOHAMMEDANISM

LISLE MARCH PHILLIPPS, *In the Desert.* Chap. xv. 1909

MOHAMMEDANISM gave the Arabs two great things. It gave them for the first time a kind of national unity, and it gave them a tremendous incentive to action and conquest. By temperament and precept the Arab is a propagandist. Every movement to-day of any consequence that agitates the desert has the spread of Islam at the root of it; the features of the first great mission are reproduced in miniature in every rising and under every Mahdi in turn. Only whereas these later ebullitions are sporadic, and agitate only scattered and weakened tribes, the original outburst was a solid national effort, towards which the Arab race had been concentrating its strength for centuries. In that effort the desert delivered its shock and scattered its seed. Its religion was carried east and west through the world, but the exertion drained the desert itself of its store of energy. Apparently Arab nationality was forged and cast for the delivery of one tremendous blow, and having delivered that blow it collapsed.

THE PAPACY

EDWARD GIBBON, *Decline and Fall of the Roman Empire.* Vol. ii, chap. xvi. 1781

THOSE who survey with a curious eye the revolutions of mankind may observe that the gardens and circus of Nero on the Vatican, which were polluted with the blood of the first Christians, have been rendered still more famous by the triumph and by the abuse of the persecuted religion. On the same spot a temple, which far surpasses the ancient glories of the Capitol, has been since erected by the Christian Pontiffs, who, deriving their claim of universal dominion from an humble fisherman of Galilee, have succeeded to the throne of the Cæsars, given laws to the barbarian conquerors of Rome, and extended their spiritual jurisdiction from the coast of the Baltic to the shores of the Pacific Ocean.

A THEOCRACY

WILLIAM RALPH INGE, *Assessments and Anticipations.*
Pp. 104–5. 1929

IF Jesus Christ had never existed, it is practically certain that the mantle of the Roman Caesars would have descended upon some great ecclesiastical corporation, very like the Catholic Church. Plato, with wonderful foresight, laid down the conditions for such a form of Government; he did not even forget the Inquisition. Plato also, in another part of his works, drew a picture of the perfectly just man, who would end by being crucified; but he never thought of bringing the two pictures together. Some kind of theocratic political corporation, deriving its religious ideas from the east, where religions grow wild, its theology from Greece, and its organisation from Rome, would have appeared anyhow, quite independently of what happened in Galilee and Judaea. The Olympian gods would not have stood in the way; they died a natural death when their worshippers became extinct. The history of the Catholic Church, as a political institution, has not much more than an accidental connexion with the life of the Founder.

IDEAL OF GREGORY VII

ARCHIBALD ROBERTSON, *Regnum Dei.* Bampton Lectures.
Lecture VI. 1901

GREGORY was indeed no narrow ascetic; he lived and worked as a man among men, a man of affairs. But he was inspired through and through by the dualism which forms so marked an element in medieval religion, a dualism first applied to political theory as we have seen in Augustine's *de Civitate Dei*. Only whereas to Augustine the Church is the one divine *Society*, to Gregory it is the one divine *Government*. To Gregory as to Augustine the civil government is founded on mere force, is in its essence profane. Augustine ascribed the bond of justice, by which civil society holds together, to the inscrutable commingling of the two *civitates* in the complex web of human history. His conception of the *civitas Dei* as consisting of the elect tempered his tendency to identify the antithesis between the two *civitates* as that between Church and Realm. But Gregory, whose interest was wholly that of the ecclesiastical statesman, conceived of the State as wholly secular, the Church as wholly sacred. The *iustitia* necessary to the well-being and coherence of the state must be imposed upon it by the legislative, judicial, and administrative action of the Church. But the Church at large, *i.e.* the episcopate, was, as a matter of fact, honeycombed with secularity, dependent upon emperors and kings. This must be remedied by a clear separation between the Kingdom of GOD and the kingdoms of the world. To the former belong all persons, all offices, all possessions of the Church, which must accordingly be at the disposal of the Church's supreme head. And not only so. Every Christian man, peasant, prince, or emperor, is a citizen or subject of this kingdom. All questions of rule and possession are moral questions, to be decided by the supreme arbiter of Christian duty. It is for the Church, by her supreme ruler, to award to each his rights, to undo and punish wrong. And so the pope holds the disposal, not only of ecclesiastical but of royal and imperial dignities. He alone can confirm the emperor in his throne, and for just cause he can also depose him.

So vast a power must be infallible in its exercise. Gregory lays it down that a papal decision can never be revised (*retractari*) save by a pope himself, and that the Roman Church never has erred, nor, as Scripture witnesses, ever can err. This is no doubt a vague declaration as compared with later definitions of infallibility, but it marks a very distinct advance upon previous papal claims to doctrinal authority.

Gregory defined once for all the attitude of the papacy

toward the civil power. Neither Alexander III nor Innocent III nor Boniface VIII added or could add anything in
principle to the Gregorian system. In Gregory we have the
famous appeals to the two great lights that GOD placed in the
firmament, to the two swords in the hand of Peter, the spiritual
sword to be wielded by his successors, the secular at their
command.

KINGDOM OF DARKNESS

THOMAS HOBBES, *Leviathan.* Part IV, chap. xlvii. 1651

FROM the time that the Bishop of Rome had gotten to be
acknowledged for Bishop Universall by pretence of Succession
to St Peter, their whole Hierarchy, or Kingdome of Darknesse, may be compared not unfitly to the *Kingdome of Fairies*;
that is, to the old wives *Fables* in England, concerning *Ghosts*
and *Spirits*, and the feats they play in the night. And if a
man consider the originall of this great Ecclesiasticall Dominion, he will easily perceive, that the *Papacy*, is no other,
than the *Ghost* of the deceased *Romane Empire*, sitting
crowned upon the grave thereof: For so did the Papacy start
up on a Sudden out of the Ruines of that Heathen Power.

THE ROMAN CATHOLIC CHURCH

THOMAS BABINGTON, LORD MACAULAY, "Essay on Von
Ranke's *History of the Popes*", *Edinburgh Review*. 1840

THERE is not, and there never was on this earth, a work of
human policy so well deserving of examination as the Roman
Catholic Church. The history of that Church joins together
the two great ages of human civilization. No other institution
is left standing which carries the mind back to the times when
the smoke of sacrifice rose from the Pantheon, and when
camelopards and tigers bounded in the Flavian amphitheatre.

The proudest royal houses are but of yesterday, when compared with the line of the Supreme Pontiffs. That line we trace back in an unbroken series, from the Pope who crowned Napoleon in the nineteenth century to the Pope who crowned Pepin in the eighth; and far beyond the time of Pepin the august dynasty extends, till it is lost in the twilight of fable. The republic of Venice came next in antiquity. But the republic of Venice was modern when compared with the Papacy; and the republic of Venice is gone, and the Papacy remains. The Papacy remains, not in decay, not a mere antique, but full of life and youthful vigour. The Catholic Church is still sending forth to the farthest ends of the world, missionaries as zealous as those who landed in Kent with Augustin, and still confronting hostile kings with the same spirit with which she confronted Attila. The number of her children is greater than in any former age. Her acquisitions in the New World have more than compensated her for what she has lost in the Old. Her spiritual ascendancy extends over the vast countries which lie between the plains of the Missouri and Cape Horn, countries which, a century hence, may not improbably contain a population as large as that which now inhabits Europe. The members of her communion are certainly not fewer than a hundred and fifty millions; and it will be difficult to show that all the other Christian sects united amount to a hundred and twenty millions. Nor do we see any sign which indicates that the term of her long dominion is approaching. She saw the commencement of all the governments and of all the ecclesiastical establishments that now exist in the world; and we feel no assurance that she is not destined to see the end of them all. She was great and respected before the Saxon had set foot on Britain, before the Frank had passed the Rhine, when Grecian eloquence still flourished in Antioch, when idols were still worshipped in the temple of Mecca. And she may still exist in undiminished vigour when some traveller from New Zealand shall, in the midst of a vast solitude, take his stand on a broken arch of London Bridge to sketch the ruins of St Paul's.

MONKS

George Gordon Coulton, *Five Centuries of Religion*.
Vol. i, chaps. i and xx. 1923

The heroism of the great Religious becomes more comprehensible in proportion as we visualize the ordinary monk or
friar or nun. Though Newman was not a monk in the strictest
technical sense (for the Oratorians are a secular congregation),
yet his life illustrates monastic vocation and conversion more
vividly, perhaps, than any other modern book. He was an
accomplished musician and violinist; his palate was so delicate that he was made official wine-taster for the cellars of his
Oxford college; his letters from abroad show a wonderful
sense of form and colour; he apprehends and describes with
an effortless accuracy which puts him absolutely in the first
rank. All these things he seems to have subordinated, early
and completely, to what he felt an incomparably higher
vocation. He broke a stubborn and masterful will to obedience,
and often to the pettiest obedience, though here the struggle
was life-long and never, perhaps, completely victorious.
St Bernard, again, was born and bred for human society; he
had every personal and intellectual charm. Though he chose
to make himself unobservant of natural beauty for what
seemed Christ's sake, yet his very sermons show a keenness of
observation and (where necessary) of satire which tell their
own tale of struggle and renunciation. Nor did the choice
seem as simple to those men, perhaps, as it seems to their
modern panegyrists who pitch the note of admiration upwards
and upwards till it reaches a falsetto. We can see the final
triumph of the dead saint's ideal; but we are apt to forget his
own inevitable doubts and misgivings; St Bernard himself,
though his mind was one of the serenest, was vividly conscious of the temptation to welcome as divine truth that
which was really devilish falsehood. Even in the Middle Ages,
Religious must sometimes have doubted not only of final
perseverance (as they constantly confess) but also, to some
extent, even of wisdom in their choice. They must have asked
not only: "Need I give up so much?" but even: "Is it right

to look upon the abandonment of some of these things as a sacrifice to God?" With all their worship of celibacy, the best of them generally recognized the value of married life; they were not blind to parental love; they saw the natural innocence and beauty of many "worldly" relations and enjoyments; and they knew how truly a man may give praise to God as he tastes them. They do not often put these things into plain words; they would perhaps not even have frankly confessed so much to themselves; yet something of the bitterness which we often find in the very sweetest of these ascetic natures —the 22nd chapter, for instance, of the 1st book of the *Imitatio* —suggests that the writer is crying aloud in order to deaden his own pangs; that he does not always float in a serene sense of victory over evil, but needs to work himself up into artificial indignation against that which he is now professionally pledged to hate, yet which God in the beginning may have formed him to love. The Religious sometimes gives the World the go-by not in the lofty indifference of impenetrable armour, but seamed with soul-scars that are still tender to the lightest touch of memory, and with a conscience not altogether free from suggestions of treachery towards things which the Almighty had created and found very good:

respiciens udis prodita luminibus.

Behind the dullest of these monastic records there lurks tragedy, in the fullest dramatic sense of the word—the inspiration of human endeavour and endurance,—and pity for all that human flesh and nerves must suffer in the struggle— and sympathy with those far more pitiable figures who despaired sooner or later as we ourselves might well have despaired, and who sank into self-confessed failure. Thousands were sincerely converted in the spirit, yet not in the flesh; they remained unrefinedly and almost unrepentantly fond of all merriment and good cheer and good fellowship; but such men, even through their lapses, bear true witness to the immensity of their ordinary sacrifice, as the death of the common soldier is often more significant than the officer's.

* * * *

"Time, the devourer of all things, deadeneth even monastic

religion, since mankind is more prone to imitate vice than virtue." So wrote the chronicler of the *Exordium Magnum* in about 1200 A.D.; but we, while admitting his facts, shall hardly accept his explanation. One of the most decisive social gains since the Middle Ages is the gradual decline of that pessimism which saw little hope but in the speedy coming of Antichrist, and Armageddon, and the end of all created things. We believe in the gradual perfectibility of human nature; and, though our temptation may be to take this belief too easily, that is at least a nobler error than to make it a point of faith that man is more prone to vice than to virtue. If monachism in general failed to satisfy the best minds even in 1200, and has since lost ground steadily with the large majority of thinking people, we must seek the causes of failure not in human nature, but in the nature of this institution which fails to satisfy the legitimate demands of humanity.

That is the key to the revival which we connect with the names of Francis and Dominic. If, a century after St Bernard, it needed a greater than he to institute reforms which rather superseded than recalled true Benedictinism, then the fault was not in Bernard but in the system. Not but that the earlier monastic leaders, and the best of their followers, had shown as fine qualities as any that we can trace in history; but there was something in the ideal itself which the later Middle Ages were outgrowing. The inmost core of St Benedict's Rule is suited to every age; we can scarcely conceive a society in which a few groups, here and there, might not find profit in his type of celibate common life, devoted to a high ideal and controlled in details by sound common-sense. But as a world-institution, richly endowed in lands and rents, and even richer in the prestige of its spiritual past, built upon the conservative instincts of an uneducated population which regarded monachism as an apostolic ordinance, coeval with and inseparable from the Christian church—as an institution of that kind, monachism was beginning to outlive its day; and not even those eight great revivals of 1020–1120 could save it from decadence. What was mainly wrong with it was that tinge of "holy boorishness" which it had partly inherited from the anchorites of the desert, and partly been forced into by the corruption and turbulence of Western society in those centuries from which the monks took their character. Incidentally, the monk did a great deal of good in the world, even directly; but his primary object was, confessedly, to save his own soul by retiring from the world; we have seen this already, and shall see it again. Therefore men like St Bernard, overflowing with the milk of human kindness, had to force themselves to be less generally sociable than society would have desired of them. Bernard did, indeed, constantly mix with the outer world, but most reluctantly, and only because the world could not do without him. And to a little extent even in him—far more clearly, therefore, in inferior saints—we may trace this tendency to puritanical aloofness which was very strong indeed in certain quarters of the medieval church, and especially among cloisterers of all Orders—for even the friars often fell back into it. One of the few really remarkable utterances of the late Cardinal Vaughan was delivered in reply to Cardinal Manning. The latter, who by nature was somewhat cold-blooded, remarked once with just a tinge of religious superiority: "The natural man in me has no love of the world". To which the full-blooded cardinal instantly retorted: "So God loved the world, that He gave His only-begotten Son—". We must not thus array Bernard and Francis personally against each other; but we may fairly put the average monk here in Manning's place, and the average friar in Vaughan's.

GHIBELLINE AND GUELF

John Addington Symonds, *Renaissance in Italy.*
Vol. I. 1875

The Ghibelline heard Italy calling upon him to build a citadel that should be guarded by the lance and shield of chivalry, where the hierarchies of feudalism, ranged beneath the daïs of the Empire, might dispense culture and civil order in due measure to the people. The Guelf believed that she was bidding him to multiply arts and guilds within the burgh, beneath the mantle of the Pope, who stood for Christ, the preacher of equality and peace for all mankind, in order that the beehive of industry should in course of time evolve a civil order and a culture representative of its own freely acting forces....

The Divine Comedy, written after the culmination of the Guelf and Ghibelline dissensions, yields the measure of their animosity. Dante finds no place in Hell, Heaven, or Purgatory for the souls who stood aloof from strife, the angels who were neither Guelf nor Ghibelline in Paradise. His Vigliacchi, "wretches who never lived", because they never felt the pangs or ecstasies of partisanship, wander homeless on the skirts of Limbo, among the abortions and offscourings of creation. Even so there was no standing-ground in Italy outside one or the other hostile camp. Society was riven down to its foundation. Rancours dating from the thirteenth century endured long after the great parties ceased to have a meaning. They were perpetuated in customs, and expressed themselves in the most trivial details. Banners, ensigns, and heraldic colours followed the divisions of the factions. Ghibellines wore the feathers in their caps upon one side, Guelfs upon the other. Ghibellines cut fruit at table crosswise, Guelfs straight down. In Bergamo some Calabrians were murdered by their host, who discovered from their way of slicing garlic that they sided with the hostile party. Ghibellines drank out of smooth, and Guelfs out of chased, goblets. Ghibellines wore white, and Guelfs red, roses. Yawning, passing in the street, throwing dice, gestures in speaking or swearing, were used as pretexts for distinguishing the one half of Italy from the other. So late as the middle of the fifteenth century, the Ghibellines of Milan tore Christ from the high-altar of the Cathedral at Crema and burned him because he turned his face to the Guelf shoulder. Every great city has a tale of love and death that carries the contention of its adverse families into the region of romance and legend. Florence dated her calamities from the insult offered by Buondelmonte dei Buondelmonti to the Amidei in a broken marriage. Bologna never forgot the pathos of Imelda Lambertazzi stretched in death upon her lover Bonifazio

Gieremei's corpse. The story of Romeo and Juliet at Verona is a myth which brings both factions into play, the well-meaning intervention of peace-making monks, and the ineffectual efforts of the Podestà to curb the violence of party warfare.

HELL, PURGATORY, HEAVEN

HENRY HART MILMAN, *History of Latin Christianity.*
Vol. IX. 1855

THROUGHOUT the middle ages the world after death continued to reveal more and more fully its awful secrets. Hell, Purgatory, Heaven became more distinct, if it may be so said, more visible. Their site, their topography, their torments, their trials, their enjoyments, became more conceivable, almost more palpable to sense: till Dante summed up the whole of this traditional lore, or at least, with a Poet's intuitive sagacity, seized on all which was most imposing, effective, real, and condensed it in his three co-ordinate poems. That Hell had a local situation, that immaterial spirits suffered bodily and material torments, none, or scarcely one hardy speculative mind, presumed to doubt. Hell had admitted, according to legend, more than one visitant from this upper world, who returned to relate his fearful journey to wondering man: St Fiercy, St Vettin, a layman, Bernilo. But all these early descents interest us only as they may be supposed to have been faint types of the great Italian Poet. Dante is the one authorised topographer of the mediæval Hell. His originality is no more called in question by these mere signs and manifestations of the popular belief than by the existence and reality of those objects or scenes in external nature which he describes with such unrivalled truth. In Dante meet unreconciled (who thought of or cared for their reconciliation?) those strange contradictions, immaterial souls subject to material torments: spirits which had put off the mortal body, cognisable by the corporeal sense. The mediaeval Hell had gathered from all ages, all lands, all races, its imagery, its denizens, its site, its access, its commingling horrors; from the old Jewish traditions, perhaps from regions beyond the sphere of the Old Testament; from the Pagan poets, with their black rivers, their Cerberus, their boatman and his crazy vessel; perhaps from the Teutonic Hela, through some of the earlier visions. Then came the great Poet, and reduced all this wild chaos to a kind of order, moulded it up with the cosmical notions of the times, and made it, as it were, one with the prevalent mundane system. Above all, he brought it to the very borders of our world; he made the life beyond the grave one with our present life; he mingled in close and intimate relation the present and the future. Hell, Purgatory, Heaven, were but an immediate expansion and extension of the present world. And this is among the wonderful causes of Dante's power, the realising the unreal by the admixture of the real: even as in his imagery the actual, homely, everyday language or similitude mingles with and heightens the fantastic, the vague, the transmundane. What effect had Hell produced, if peopled by ancient, almost immemorial objects of human detestation, Nimrod or Iscariot, or Julian or Mohammed? It was when Popes all but living, Kings but now on their thrones, Guelfs who had hardly ceased to walk the streets of Florence, Ghibellines almost yet in exile, revealed their awful doom— this it was which, as it expressed the passions and the fears of mankind of an instant, immediate, actual, bodily, comprehensible place of torment: so, wherever it was read, it deepened that notion, and made it more distinct and natural. This was the Hell, conterminous to the earth, but separate, as it were, by a gulph passed by almost instantaneous transition, of which the Priesthood held the keys. These keys the audacious Poet had wrenched from their hands, and dared to turn on many of themselves, speaking even against Popes the sentence of condemnation. Of that which Hell, Purgatory, Heaven, were in popular opinion during the Middle Ages, Dante was but the full, deep, concentered expression; what he embodied in verse all men believed, feared, hoped.

Purgatory had now its intermediate place between Heaven and Hell, as unquestioned, as undisturbed by doubt; its existence was as much an article of uncontested popular belief as Heaven or Hell. It were as unjust and unphilosophical to attribute all the legendary lore which realised Purgatory, to the sordid invention of the Churchman or the Monk, as it would be unhistorical to deny the use which was made of this superstition to exact tribute from the fears or the fondness of mankind. But the abuse grew out of the belief; the belief was not slowly, subtly, deliberately instilled into the mind for the sake of the abuse. Purgatory, possible with St Augustine, probable with Gregory the Great, grew up, I am persuaded (its growth is singularly indistinct and untraceable), out of the mercy and modesty of the Priesthood. To the eternity of Hell torments there is and ever must be—notwithstanding the peremptory decrees of dogmatic theology, and the reverential dread in so many religious minds of tampering with what seems the language of the New Testament—a tacit repugnance. But when the doom of every man rested on the lips of the Priest, on his absolution or refusal of absolution, that Priest might well tremble with some natural awe—awe not confessed to himself—at dismissing the soul to an irrevocable, unrepealable, unchangeable destiny. He would not be averse to pronounce a more mitigated, a reversible sentence. The keys of Heaven and of Hell were a fearful trust, a terrible responsibility; the key of Purgatory might be used with far less presumption, with less trembling confidence. Then came naturally, as it might seem, the strengthening and exaltation of the efficacy of prayer, of the efficacy of the religious ceremonials, of the efficacy of the sacrifice of the altar, and the efficacy of the intercession of the Saints: and these all within the province, within the power of the Sacerdotal Order. Their authority, their influence, their intervention, closed not with the grave. The departed soul was still to a certain degree dependent upon the Priest. They had yet a mission, it might be of mercy; they had still some power of saving the soul after it had departed from the body. Their faithful love, their inexhaustible interest might yet rescue the sinner; for he had not reached those gates—over which alone was written, "There is no Hope"—the gates of Hell. That which was a mercy, a consolation, became a trade, an inexhaustible source of wealth. Praying souls out of Purgatory by Masses said on their behalf, became an ordinary office, an office which deserved, which could demand, which did demand, the most prodigal remuneration. It was later that the Indulgence, originally the remission of so much penance, of so many days, weeks, months, years; or of that which was the commutation for penance, so much almsgiving or munificence to churches or Churchmen, in sound at least extended (and mankind, the high and low vulgar of mankind, are governed by sound) its significance: it was literally understood, as the remission of so many years, sometimes centuries, of Purgatory.

If there were living men to whom it had been vouchsafed to visit and to return and to reveal the secrets of remote and terrible Hell, there were those too who were admitted in vision, or in actual life to more accessible Purgatory, and brought back intelligence of its real local existence, and of the state of souls within its penitential circles. There is a legend of St Paul himself; of the French monk St Farcy; of Drithelm, related by Bede; of the Emperor Charles the Fat, by William of Malmesbury. Matthew Paris relates two or three journeys of the Monk of Evesham, of Thurkill, an Essex peasant, very wild and fantastic. The Purgatory of St Patrick, the Purgatory of Owen Miles, the vision of Alberic of Monte Casino, were among the most popular and wide-spread legends of the ages preceding Dante; and as in Hell, so in Purgatory, Dante sums up in his noble verses the whole theory, the whole popular belief as to this intermediate sphere.

If Hell and Purgatory thus dimly divulged their gloomy mysteries, if they had been visited by those who returned to actual life, Heaven was unapproached, unapproachable. To be rapt to the higher Heaven remained the privilege of the Apostle; the popular conception was content to rest in modest ignorance. Though the Saints might descend on beneficent missions to the world of man; of the site of their beatitude, of the state of the Blest, of the joys of the supernal world, they brought but vague and indefinite tidings. In truth, the notion of Heaven was inextricably mingled up with the astronomical and cosmogonical as well as with the theological notions of the age. Dante's Paradise blends the Ptolemaic system with the nine angelic circles of the Pseudo Dionysius; the material heavens in their nine circles; above and beyond them, in the invisible heavens, the nine Hierarchies; and yet higher than the highest heavens the dwelling of the Ineffable Trinity. The Beatific Vision, whether immediate or to await the Last Day, had been eluded rather than determined, till the rash and presumptuous theology of Pope John XXII compelled a declaration from the Church. But yet this ascent to the Heaven of Heavens would seem from Dante, the best interpreter of the dominant conceptions, to have been an especial privilege, if it may be so said, of the most Blessed of the Blessed, the Saint of Saints. There is a manifest gradation in Beatitude and Sanctity. According to the universal cosmical theory, the Earth, the round and level earth, was the centre of the whole system. It was usually supposed to be encircled by the vast, circumambient, endless ocean; but beyond that ocean (with a dim reminiscence, it should seem, of the Elysian Fields of the poets) was placed a Paradise, where the souls of men hereafter to be blest, awaited the final resurrection. Dante takes the other theory: he peoples the nine material heavens—that is, the cycle of the Moon, Venus, Mercury, the Sun, Mars, Jupiter, Saturn, the fixed stars, and the firmament above, or the Primum Mobile—with those who are admitted to a progressively advancing state of glory and blessedness. All this, it should seem, is below the ascending circles of the Celestial Hierarchies, that immediate vestibule or fore-court of the Holy of Holies, the Heaven of Heavens, into which the most perfect of the Saints are admitted. They are commingled with, yet unabsorbed by, the Redeemer, in mystic union; yet the mysticism still reverently endeavours to maintain some distinction in regard to this Light, which, as it has descended upon earth, is drawn up again to the highest Heavens, and has a kind of communion with the yet Incommunicable Deity. That in all the Paradise of Dante there should be a dazzling sameness, a mystic indistinctness, an inseparable blending of the real and the unreal, is not wonderful, if we consider the nature of the subject, and the still more incoherent and incongruous popular conceptions which he had to represent and to harmonise. It is more wonderful that, with these few elements, Light, Music, and Mysticism, he should, by his singular talent of embodying the purely abstract and metaphysical thought in the liveliest imagery, represent such things with the most objective truth, yet without disturbing their fine spiritualism. The subtlest scholasticism is not more subtle than Dante. It is perhaps a bold assertion, but what is there on these transcendent subjects, in the vast theology of Aquinas, of which the essence and sum is not in the Paradise of Dante? Dante, perhaps, though expressing to a great extent the popular conception of Heaven, is as much by his innate sublimity above it, as St Thomas himself.

THE MIDDLE AGES

DAVID HUME, *History of England.* Chap. xxiii. 1762

THOSE who cast their eye on the general revolutions of society, will find, that, as all the improvements of the human mind had reached nearly to their state of perfection about the age of Augustus, there was a sensible decline from that point or period; and men thenceforth relapsed gradually into ignorance and barbarism. The unlimited extent of the Roman empire, and the consequent despotism of the monarchs, extinguished all emulation, debased the generous spirits of men, and depressed that noble flame, by which all the refined arts must be cherished and enlivened. The military government, which soon succeeded, rendered even the lives and properties of men insecure and precarious; and proved destructive to those vulgar and more necessary arts of agriculture, manufactures, and commerce; and in the end, to the military art and genius itself, by which alone the immense fabric of the empire could be supported. The irruption of the barbarous nations, which soon followed, overwhelmed all human knowledge, which was already far in its decline; and men sunk every age deeper into ignorance, stupidity, and superstition; till the light of antient science and history, had very nearly suffered a total extinction in all the European nations.

But there is an ultimate point of depression, as well as of exaltation, from which human affairs naturally return in a contrary progress, and beyond which they seldom pass either in their advancement or decline. The period, in which the people of Christendom were the lowest sunk in ignorance, and consequently in disorders of every kind, may justly be fixed at the eleventh century, about the age of William the Conqueror; and from that æra, the sun of science, beginning to re-ascend, threw out many gleams of light, which preceded the full morning, when letters were revived in the fifteenth century. The Danes and other northern people, who had so long infested all the coasts, and even the inland parts of Europe, by their depredations, having now learned the arts of tillage and agriculture, found a settled subsistence at home, and were no longer tempted to desert their industry, in order to seek a precarious livelihood by rapine and by the plunder of their neighbours. The feudal governments also, among the more southern nations, were reduced to a kind of system; and tho' that strange species of civil polity was ill fitted to ensure either liberty or tranquillity, it was preferable to the universal license and disorder which had everywhere preceded it.

MEDIEVAL AND MODERN IDEALS

JOHN NEVILLE FIGGIS, *Civilisation at the Cross Roads*.
Lecture I. 1912

CIVILISATION works hand in hand with religion, in so far as it treats men as ends not means, and by its ordered variety of life gives freer place to development. It is just these things, however, that are in question today; there we are at the Cross Roads. They are right who speak of the "Gifts of Civilisation" as they see the Church and culture marching hand in hand in the warfare with barbarism and unordered passion. Only, while civilisation begins by ministering to man as a spiritual being, by making freedom and all personal values a reality and preserving space for that leisure of spirit in which the peace of God may reign, it by no means ends at that point. Apart from a Godward outlook it may tend to destroy these personal values by permitting men to rest in the "much goods laid up in store" and allow the fortunate in a purely material-ist ambition, while from its true benefits the masses of man-kind may become more and more shut out. This has been its great vice in past history. It looks a little as though it were being repeated in the present. Do we not see before us a world intoxicated with material prosperity, reckless of the life of the spirit, and callous to the misery of vast masses of its fellow-men?

We may look back to the age when these spiritual ends of civilised life were partially attained and all its treasures en-joyed as the gift of God, but can the modern world claim as its own the glories of the ages which, so far from being dark, are still the refuge of souls wearied with the squalid fever of our time? It cannot. We must admit the profound difference between the thoughts and feelings of our own day and those of the age which produced the *Sainte-Chapelle*, the frescoes of Giotto, and the *Divina Commedia*. Nor would any statistics about railroads and steamships ever persuade me that a world of which these things are the characteristic symbols is inferior to that which flowers in the factory town or the mammoth hotel.

Medieval civilisation was no flawless crystal. Then as now men gave free play "to the lust of the flesh, the lust of the eyes, and the pride of life", but they did not worship these things. In all ages men have been bad. But the achievements of the thirteenth century were owing precisely to the opposite of these elements men admire most today. As a hostile writer puts it, "they had one *idée fixe*, religion". They may not have always served God very well, but they knew that He was "the chief end of man". That world presents neither the oleo-graphic picture dear to sentimentalists, nor yet the mere battle of kites and crows conceived by Puritan and Renais-sance pride. Yet its most notable qualities—the things that made it what it was—the cathedral, the minster, the uni-versity (and each of us here owes more to the University of the Middle Ages than he is apt to imagine), the orders of chivalry, the hierarchy of society, the communal life and all its pageantry, that unity which outlasted so much conflict, all these things were what they were because of men's faith in God and man and the love which makes him free. None of them could have been at all in the form they took, had that faith not been present; and hence Walter Pater, summing up the qualities of the differing cultures of the world, speaks in the famous passage on Mona Lisa of "the reverie of the middle age with its spiritual ambitions and imaginative souls" as contrasted with "the animalism of Greece, the lust of Rome, the return of the Pagan world, the sins of the Borgias". Always rather by its ideals than its achievements do we judge a nation or epoch. These ideals can be seen reflected as in a mirror all through the life of the Middle Ages, in the peace as of a strange land which pervades the *Historia Ecclesiastica* of the great Northumbrian monk, the Venerable Bede, in the love and universal reverence felt for S. Francis even in his lifetime, in the mystery plays like *Everyman*, in the almost autocratic influence of a mystic like S. Bernard, even indeed in the strength of the Papacy (for it rested not on material force, but on the faith of men), above all in the most characteristic of all its fruits—books such as *The Imitation of Christ*, similar works like the writings of Walter Hilton, or Richard Rolle, or Dame Julian, the anchoress of Norwich. All these are the natural fruit of the time; they express its spirit. So far as we have anything like them, it is rather as protests, reactions, the work of those who repudiate the prevalent ideals, *unzeitgemässe Betrachtungen*, as Nietzsche would call them. No one can deny the beauty of a work like the *Pathway of the Eternal Wisdom* or Tyrrell's *Oil and Wine*, but their distinction consists in thus expressing a side of life far from popular. The dominant feeling of the age shrieks itself hoarse in the newspapers and expresses itself artistically in the *New Machiavelli* or *L'Ile des Pingouins*, and I cannot feel convinced that we have gained by the exchange.

The world in the Middle Ages was far enough from the practice of holiness, but at least it did not question the ideal. What are men's ideals today? It would be hard to tell. But so far as their main energies are concerned and we can form any judgment as to what animates the man in the street, I cannot doubt that it is truer to say that Christianity runs counter to our civilisation than that it fulfils it.

THE VALLEY OF THE SHADOW

JAMES COTTER MORISON, *The Service of Man.*
Chap. vii. 1887

THE soft autumnal calm, and purple tints as of an Indian summer, which lingered, up to the Antonines, over that wide expanse of empire, from the Persian Gulf to the Pillars of Hercules, and from the Nile to the Clyde, broken as it was by the year of Revolution of A.D. 69 and the black tyranny of Domitian's reign, was only a misleading transition to that bitter winter which filled the half of the second and the whole of the third century, to be soon followed by the abiding dark and cold of the Middle Ages. The Empire was moribund when Christianity arose. Indeed, Rome had practically slain the ancient world before the Empire replaced the effete Republic. The barbarous Roman soldier who killed Archimedes absorbed in a problem, is but an instance and a type of what Rome had done always and everywhere by Greek art, civilization and science. The Empire lived upon and consumed the capital of preceding ages, which it did not replace. Population, production, knowledge, all declined and slowly died. The Christian apologists, headed by St Augustine, were justly indignant at the pagan slander which attributed the fall of the Empire to the spread of Christianity. Their answer to the objection was complete, as we can see far better even than they did themselves. But what they could not be expected to see, and what we can see very well is, that the fall of the Empire, including the loss and ruin of the old philosophy and knowledge, was an indispensable condition of the spread of Christianity. If the blood of the martyrs was truly said to be the seed of the Church, the decay of knowledge was an equally needed prerequisite. It will not be denied that this decay of knowledge was present and startlingly rapid. After the silver age which ended nobly with Tacitus and the younger Pliny, later pagan literature almost ceases to exist; and the falling off in the form is not more striking than in the value and quality of the contents. All superstitions revived and flourished apace in the ever-waning light of knowledge. A shudder of religious awe ran through the Roman world, and grew more sombre and searching with the progressive gloom and calamities of the time. A spirit wholly different from the light-hearted scepticism of the Augustan age and later Republic stirred men's hearts, and the strongest minds did not escape it.... The sun of ancient science, which had risen in such splendour from Thales to Hipparchus, was now sinking rapidly to the horizon; and when it at last disappeared, say, in the fifth century, the long night of the Middle Ages began.

But it was in this period of decaying knowledge and civilization that the Christian religion was elaborated and constituted in the historical form which it practically still wears. The creeds and chief dogmas of the Church were worked out in the period which extends from the Council of Jerusalem to the Councils of Nice, Chalcedon, Alexandria, and Ephesus. No evolutionist would think of speaking in any but respectful terms of the great churchmen who laid down the lines along which European thought was destined to travel for a thousand years. The sneering tone of sceptics in the last age is wholly out of place, and arose from pure ignorance of the laws which govern social and intellectual development. The Nicene Creed in the fourth century after Christ was as natural and legitimate a product of the conditions of the time, as was the Socratic philosophy in the fourth century before Christ. What we have to note is, that the Nicene Creed was the product of an age of decay, of disaster, and approaching death, so far as civilization and science were concerned. In every light, one of the most memorable, and in many respects one of the most noble of human compositions, it yet, as it could not fail to do, bears the marks of its birth-time; and that time was one of extreme calamity, of growing gloom, ignorance and misery. Within two centuries of its promulgation, the Graeco-Roman world had descended into the great hollow which is roughly called the Middle Ages, extending from the fifth to the fifteenth century, a hollow in which many great, beautiful and heroic things were done and created, but in which knowledge, as we understand it, and as Aristotle understood it, had no place. The revival of learning and the Renaissance are memorable as the first sturdy breasting by humanity of the hither slope of the great hollow which lies between us and the ancient world. The modern man, reformed and regenerated by knowledge, looks across it, and recognizes on the opposite ridge, in the far-shining cities and stately porticoes, in the art, politics, and science of antiquity, many more ties of kinship and sympathy than in the mighty concave between, wherein dwell his Christian ancestry, in the dim light of scholasticism and theology.

THE RENAISSANCE

JAMES ANTHONY FROUDE, *History of England*.
Vol. VIII, chap. xlvii. 1863

IN 1497 John Cabot, the Venetian, with his son Sebastian—then a little boy—sailed from Bristol for "the islands of Cathay". He struck the American continent at Nova Scotia, sailed up into the Greenland seas till he was blocked by the ice, then coasted back to Florida, and returned with the news of another continent waiting to be occupied. The English mariners turned away with indifference; their own soil and their own seas had been sufficient for the wants of their fathers; "their fathers had more wit and wisdom than they"; and it was left to Spain, in that grand burst of energy which followed on the expulsion of the Moors and the union of the crowns, to add a hemisphere to the known world and found empires in lands beyond the sunset.

Strange indeed was the contrast between the two races, and stranger still the interchange of character, as we look back over three hundred years. Before the sixteenth century had measured half its course the shadow of Spain already stretched beyond the Andes; from the mines of Peru and the custom-houses of Antwerp, the golden rivers streamed into her Imperial treasury; the crowns of Arragon and Castile, of Burgundy, Milan, Naples, and Sicily, clustered on the brow of her sovereigns; and the Spaniards themselves, before their national liberties were broken, were beyond comparison the noblest, grandest, and most enlightened people in the known world.

The spiritual earthquake shook Europe: the choice of the ways was offered to the nations; on the one side liberty, with the untried possibilities of anarchy and social dissolution; on the other the reinvigoration of the creeds and customs of ten centuries, in which Christendom had grown to its present stature.

Fools and dreamers might follow their ignis fatuus till it led them to perdition: the wise Spaniard took his stand on the old ways. He too would have his reformation, with an inspired Santa Teresa for a prophetess, an army of ascetics to combat with prayer the legions of the evil one, a most holy Inquisition to put away the enemies of God with sword and dungeon, stake and fire. That was the Spaniard's choice, and his intellect shrivelled in his brain, and the sinews shrank in his self-bandaged limbs; and only now at last, with such imperfect deliverance as they have found in French civilization and Voltairian philosophy, is the life-blood stealing again into the veins of the descendants of the conquerors of Granada.

Meanwhile a vast intellectual revolution, of which the religious reformation was rather a sign than a cause, was making its way in the English mind. The discovery of the form of the earth and of its place in the planetary system, was producing an effect on the imagination which long familiarity with the truth renders it hard for us now to realize. The very heaven itself had been rolled up like a scroll, laying bare the illimitable abyss of space; the solid frame of the earth had become a transparent ball, and in a hemisphere below their feet men saw the sunny Palm Isles and the golden glories of the tropic seas. Long impassive, long unable from the very toughness of their natures to apprehend these novel wonders, indifferent to them, even hating them as at first they hated the doctrines of Luther, the English opened their eyes at last. In the convulsions which rent England from the Papacy a thousand superstitions were blown away, a thousand new thoughts rushed in, bringing with them their train of new desires and new emotions; and when the fire was once kindled, the dry wood burnt fiercely in the wind.

RETAINERS

JOHN STOW, *Survey of London.* 1598

NEARER to our time, I read, in the 36th of Henry VI, that the greater estates of the realm being called up to London,

The Earl of Salisbury came with five hundred men on horseback, and was lodged in the Herber. Richard, Duke of York, with four hundred men, lodged at Baynard's castle. The Dukes of Excester and Sommerset, with eight hundred men. The Earl of Northumberland, the Lord Egremont, and the Lord Clifford, with fifteen hundred men. Richard Nevill, Earl of Warwick, with six hundred men, all in red jackets, embroidered with ragged staves before and behind, and was lodged in Warwicke lane; in whose house there was oftentimes six oxen eaten at a breakfast, and every tavern was full of his meat; for he that had any acquaintance in that house, might have there so much of sodden and roast meat as he could prick and carry upon a long dagger.

Richard Redman, Bishop of Ely, 1500, the 17th of Henry VII, besides his great family, housekeeping, alms dish, and relief to the poor, wheresoever he was lodged. In his travelling, when at his coming or going to or from any town, the bells being rung, all the poor would come together, to whom he gave every one six pence at least. . . .

Nicholas West, Bishop of Ely, in the year 1532, kept continually in his house an hundred servants, giving to the one half of them 53s. 4d. the piece yearly; to the other half each

40*s.* the piece; to every one for his winter gown four yards of broad cloth, and for his summer coat three yards and a half: he daily gave at his gates, besides bread and drink, warm meat to two hundred poor people.

The housekeeping of Edward, late Earl of Derby, is not to be forgotten, who had two hundred and twenty men in check roll: his feeding aged persons twice every day, sixty and odd, besides all comers, thrice a week, appointed for his dealing days, and every Good Friday two thousand seven hundred, with meat, drink, and money.

Thomas Audley, lord chancellor, his family of gentlemen, before him, in coats garded with velvet, and chains of gold; his yeomen after him in the same livery, not garded.

William Powlet, lord great master, Marquis of Winchester, kept the like number of gentlemen and yeomen in a livery of Reading tawny, and a great relief at his gate.

Thomas Lord Cromwell, Earl of Essex, kept the like or greater number in a livery of grey marble; the gentlemen garded with velvet, the yeomen with the same cloth, yet their skirts large enough for their friends to sit upon them.

Edward, Duke of Sommerset, was not inferior in keeping a number of tall and comely gentlemen and yeomen, though his house was then in building, and most of his men were lodged abroad.

The late Earl of Oxford, father to him that now liveth, hath been noted within these forty years to have ridden into this city, and so to his house by London stone, with eighty gentlemen in a livery of Reading tawny, and chains of gold about their necks, before him, and one hundred tall yeomen, in the like livery, to follow him without chains, but all having his cognisance of the blue boar embroidered on their left shoulder.

THE ITALIAN DESPOTS

JOHN ADDINGTON SYMONDS, *Renaissance in Italy*.
Vol. I. 1875

I T will be observed in this classification of Italian tyrants
that the tenure of their power was almost uniformly forcible.
They generally acquired it through the people in the first
instance, and maintained it by the exercise of violence. Rank
had nothing to do with their claims. The bastards of Popes,
who like Sixtus IV had no pedigree, merchants like the
Medici, the son of a peasant like Francesco Sforza, a rich
usurer like Pepoli, had almost equal chances with nobles of
the ancient houses of Este, Visconti, or Malatesta. The chief
point in favour of the latter was the familiarity which through
long years of authority had accustomed the people to their
rule. When exiled, they had a better chance of return to
power than parvenus, whose party-cry and ensigns were
comparatively fresh and stirred no sentiment of loyalty—if
indeed the word loyalty can be applied to that preference for
the established and the customary which made the mob, distracted by the wrangling of doctrinaires and intriguers,
welcome back a Bentivoglio or a Malatesta. Despotism in
Italy as in ancient Greece was democratic. It recruited its
ranks from all classes and erected its thrones upon the
sovereignty of the peoples it oppressed. The impulse to the
free play of ambitious individuality which this state of things
communicated was enormous. Capacity might raise the
meanest monk to the chair of S. Peter's, the meanest soldier
to the Duchy of Milan. Audacity, vigour, unscrupulous
crime were the chief requisites for success. It was not till
Cesare Borgia displayed his magnificence at the French Court,
till the Italian adventurer matched himself with royalty in
its legitimate splendour, that the lowness of his origin and
the frivolity of his pretensions appeared in any glaring light.
In Italy itself, where there existed no time-honoured hierarchy of classes and no fountain of nobility in the person of
a sovereign, one man was a match for another, provided he
knew how to assert himself. To the conditions of a society

based on these principles we may ascribe the unrivalled emergence of great personalities among the tyrants, as well as the extraordinary tenacity and vigour of such races as the Visconti. In the contest for power and in the maintenance of an illegal authority, the picked athletes came to the front. The struggle by which they established their tyranny, the efforts by which they defended it against foreign foes and domestic adversaries, trained them to endurance and to daring. They lived habitually in an atmosphere of peril which taxed all their energies. Their activity was extreme, and their passions corresponded to their vehement vitality. About such men there could be nothing on a small or mediocre scale. When a weakling was born in a despotic family, his brothers murdered him, or he was deposed by a watchful rival. Thus only gladiators of tried capacity and iron nerve, superior to religious and moral scruples, dead to natural affection, perfected in perfidy, scientific in the use of cruelty and terror, employing first-rate faculties of brain and will and bodily powers in the service of transcendent egotism, only the *virtuosi* of political craft as theorised by Machiavelli, could survive and hold their own upon this perilous arena.

The life of the Despot was usually one of prolonged terror. Immured in strong places on high rocks, or confined to gloomy fortresses like the Milanese Castello, he surrounded his person with foreign troops, protected his bedchamber with a picked guard, and watched his meat and drink lest they should be poisoned. His chief associates were artists, men of letters, astrologers, buffoons, and exiles. He had no real friends or equals, and against his own family he adopted an attitude of fierce suspicion, justified by the frequent intrigues to which he was exposed. His timidity verged on monomania. Like Alfonso II of Naples, he was tortured with the ghosts of starved or strangled victims; like Ezzelino, he felt the mysterious fascination of astrology; like Filippo Maria Visconti, he trembled at the sound of thunder, and set one band of body-guards to watch another next his person. He dared not hope for a quiet end. No one believed in the natural death of a prince: princes must be poisoned or poignarded. Out of thirteen of the Carrara family, in little more than a century

(1318–1485) three were deposed or murdered by near relatives, one was expelled by a rival from his state, four were executed by the Venetians. Out of five of the La Scala family three were killed by their brothers, and a fourth was poisoned in exile.

HENRY VIII IN THE LORDS

JOHN LINGARD, *History of England.*
Vol. IV, chap. v. 1820

THE parliament, as often as it was opened or closed by the king in person, offered a scene not unworthy of an oriental divan. The form indeed differed but little from our present usage. The king sate on his throne; on the right hand stood the chancellor, on the left the lord treasurer: whilst the peers were placed on their benches, and the commons stood at the bar. But the addresses made on these occasions by the chancellor or the speaker, usually lasted more than an hour; and their constant theme was the character of the king. The orators, in their efforts to surpass each other, fed his vanity with the most hyperbolical praise. Cromwell was unable, he believed all men were unable, to describe the unutterable qualities of the royal mind, the sublime virtues of the royal heart. Rich told him that in wisdom he was equal to Solomon, in strength and courage to Sampson, in beauty and address to Absalom: and Audley declared before his face, that God had anointed him with the oil of wisdom above his fellows, above the other kings of the earth, above all his predecessors; had given him a perfect knowledge of the Scriptures, with which he had prostrated the Roman Goliath; a perfect knowledge of the art of war, by which he had gained the most brilliant victories at the same time in remote places; and a perfect knowledge of the art of government, by which he had for thirty years secured to his own realm the blessings of peace, while all the other nations of Europe suffered the calamities of war.

During these harangues, as often as the words "most sacred majesty" were repeated, or any emphatic expression was pronounced, the lords rose, and the whole assembly, in token of respect and assent, bowed profoundly to the demigod on the throne. Henry himself affected to hear such fulsome adulation with indifference. His answer was invariably the same: that he had no claim to superior excellence; but that, if he did possess it, he gave the glory to God, the Author of all good gifts: it was, however, a pleasure to him to witness the affection of his subjects, and to learn that they were not insensible of the blessings which they enjoyed under his government.

RICH AND POOR

SIR THOMAS MORE, *Utopia*. Book II. 1516. Translated
by Ralph Robinson, 1551

Is not this an unjust and an unkind public weal, which giveth great fees and rewards to gentlemen, as they call them, and to goldsmiths, and to such other, which be either idle persons, or else only flatterers and devisers of vain pleasures: and of the contrary part maketh no gentle provision for poor ploughmen, colliers, labourers, carters, ironsmiths, and carpenters, without whom no commonwealth can continue? But after it hath abused the labours of their lusty and flowering age, at the last when they be oppressed with old age and sickness, being needy, poor, and indigent of all things, then forgetting their so many painful watchings, not remembering their so many and so great benefits, recompenseth them and acquitteth them most unkindly with miserable death. And yet besides this the rich men not only by private fraud, but also by common laws, do every day pluck and snatch away from the poor some part of their daily living. So whereas it seemed before unjust to recompense with unkindness their pains that have been beneficial to the public weal, now they have to this their wrong and unjust dealing (which is yet a much worse point) given the name of justice, yea and that by force of a law. Therefore, when I consider and weigh in my mind all these commonwealths which nowadays anywhere do flourish, so God help me, I can perceive nothing but a certain conspiracy of rich men procuring their own commodities under the name and title of the commonwealth. They invent and devise all means and crafts, first how to keep safely without fear of losing that they have unjustly gathered together, and next how to hire and abuse the work and labour of the poor for as little money as may be. These devices, when the rich men have decreed to be kept and observed under colour of the commonalty, that is to say, also of the poor people, then they be made laws.

THE TUDORS

FRANCIS BACON, *Advancement of Learning.*
Book II. 1605

(Addressed to James I)

THERE is an excellent period of a much smaller compass of time, as to the story of England; that is to say, from the uniting of the Roses to the uniting of the kingdoms; a portion of time wherein, to my understanding, there hath been the rarest varieties that in like number of successions of any hereditary monarchy hath been known. For it beginneth with the mixed adeption of a crown by arms and title; an entry by battle, an establishment by marriage; and therefore times answerable, like waters after a tempest, full of working and swelling, though without extremity of storm; but well passed through by the wisdom of the pilot, being one of the most sufficient kings of all the number. Then followeth the reign of a king, whose actions, howsoever conducted, had much intermixture with the affairs of Europe, balancing them and inclining them variably; in whose time also began that great alteration in the state ecclesiastical, an action which seldom cometh upon the stage. Then the reign of a minor:

then an offer of an usurpation (though it was but as *febris ephemera*). Then the reign of a queen matched with a foreigner: then of a queen that lived solitary and unmarried, and yet her government so masculine, as it had greater impression and operation upon the states abroad than it any ways received from thence. And now last, this most happy and glorious event, that this island of Brittany, divided from all the world, should be united in itself: and that oracle of rest given to Aeneas, "antiquam exquirite matrem", should now be performed, and fulfilled upon the nations of England and Scotland, being now reunited in the ancient mother name of Brittany, as a full period of all instability and peregrinations.

OF THE CIVIL MAGISTRATES

Book of Common Prayer; Articles of Religion.
No. xxxvii. 1571

THE King's Majesty hath the chief power in this Realm of *England*, and other his Dominions, unto whom the chief Government of all Estates of this Realm, whether they be Ecclesiastical or Civil, in all causes doth appertain, and is not, nor ought to be, subject to any foreign Jurisdiction.

Where we attribute to the King's Majesty the chief government, by which Titles we understand the minds of some slanderous folks to be offended; we give not to our Princes the ministering either of God's Word, or of the Sacraments, the which thing the Injunctions also lately set forth by *Elizabeth* our Queen do most plainly testify; but that only prerogative, which we see to have been given always to all godly Princes in holy Scriptures by God himself; that is, that they should rule all estates and degrees committed to their charge by God, whether they be Ecclesiastical or Temporal, and restrain with the civil sword the stubborn and evil-doers.

The Bishop of *Rome* hath no jurisdiction in this Realm of *England*.

The Laws of the Realm may punish Christian men with death, for heinous and grievous offences.

It is lawful for Christian men, at the commandment of the Magistrate, to wear weapons, and serve in the wars.

JESUITS

THOMAS BABINGTON, LORD MACAULAY, "Essay on Von Ranke's *History of the Popes*", *Edinburgh Review*. 1840

Two reformations were pushed on at once with equal energy and effect, a reformation of doctrine in the North, a reformation of manners and discipline in the South. In the course of a single generation, the whole spirit of the Church of Rome underwent a change. From the halls of the Vatican to the most secluded hermitage of the Apennines, the great revival was everywhere felt and seen. All the institutions anciently devised for the propagation and defence of the faith were furbished up and made efficient. Fresh engines of still more formidable power were constructed. Everywhere old religious communities were remodelled and new religious communities called into existence. Within a year after the death of Leo, the order of Camaldoli was purified. The Capuchins restored the old Franciscan discipline, the midnight prayer and the life of silence. The Barnabites and the society of Somasca devoted themselves to the relief and education of the poor. To the Theatine order a still higher interest belongs. Its great object was the same with that of our early Methodists, namely to supply the deficiencies of the parochial clergy. The Church of Rome, wiser than the Church of England, gave every countenance to the good work. The members of the new brotherhood preached to great multitudes in the streets, and in the fields, prayed by the beds of the sick, and administered the last sacraments to the dying. Foremost among them in zeal and devotion was Gian Pietro Caraffa, afterwards Pope Paul the Fourth. In the convent of the Theatines at Venice, under the eye of Caraffa, a Spanish gentleman took

up his abode, tended the poor in the hospitals, went about in
rags, starved himself almost to death, and often sallied into
the streets, mounted on stones, and waving his hat to invite
the passers-by, began to preach in a strange jargon of mingled
Castilian and Tuscan. The Theatines were among the most
zealous and rigid of men; but to this enthusiastic neophyte
their discipline seemed lax, and their movements sluggish;
for his own mind, naturally passionate and imaginative, had
passed through a training which had given to all its peculiarities a morbid intensity and energy. In his early life he had
been the prototype of the hero of Cervantes. The single study
of the young Hidalgo had been chivalrous romance; and his
existence had been one gorgeous day-dream of princesses
rescued and infidels subdued. He had chosen a Dulcinea, "no
countess, no duchess,"—these are his own words,—"but one
of far higher station"; and he flattered himself with the hope
of laying at her feet the keys of Moorish castles and the
jewelled turbans of Asiatic kings. In the midst of these
visions of martial glory and prosperous love, a severe wound
stretched him on a bed of sickness. His constitution was
shattered and he was doomed to be a cripple for life. The
palm of strength, grace, and skill in knightly exercises, was
no longer for him. He could no longer hope to strike down
gigantic soldans, or to find favour in the sight of beautiful
women. A new vision then arose in his mind, and mingled
itself with his old delusions in a manner which to most Englishmen must seem singular, but which those who knew how close
was the union between religion and chivalry in Spain will be
at no loss to understand. He would still be a soldier; he would
still be a knight errant; but the soldier and knight errant of
the spouse of Christ. He would smite the Great Red Dragon.
He would be the champion of the Woman clothed with the
Sun. He would break the charm under which false prophets
held the souls of men in bondage. His restless spirit led him
to the Syrian deserts, and to the chapel of the Holy Sepulchre.
Thence he wandered back to the farthest West, and astonished
the convents of Spain and the schools of France by his penances
and vigils. The same lively imagination which had been employed in picturing the tumult of unreal battles, and the

charms of unreal queens, now peopled his solitude with saints and angels. The Holy Virgin descended to commune with him. He saw the Saviour face to face with the eye of flesh. Even those mysteries of religion which are the hardest trial of faith were in his case palpable to sight. It is difficult to relate without a pitying smile that, in the sacrifice of the mass, he saw transubstantiation take place, and that as he stood praying on the steps of St Dominic, he saw the Trinity in Unity, and wept aloud with joy and wonder. Such was the celebrated Ignatius Loyola, who, in the great Catholic reaction, bore the same part which Luther bore in the great Protestant movement.

Dissatisfied with the system of the Theatines, the enthusiastic Spaniard turned his face towards Rome. Poor, obscure, without a patron, without recommendations, he entered the city where now two princely temples, rich with painting and many-coloured marble, commemorate his great services to the Church; where his form stands sculptured in massive silver; where his bones, enshrined amidst jewels, are placed beneath the altar of God. His activity and zeal bore down all opposition; and under his rule the order of Jesuits began to exist, and grew rapidly to the full measures of his gigantic powers. With what vehemence, with what policy, with what exact discipline, with what dauntless courage, with what self denial, with what forgetfulness of the dearest private ties, with what intense and stubborn devotion to a single end, with what unscrupulous laxity and versatility in the choice of means, the Jesuits fought the battle of their church, is written in every page of the annals of Europe during several generations. In the order of Jesus was concentrated the quintessence of the Catholic spirit; and the history of the order of Jesus is the history of the great Catholic reaction. That order possessed itself at once of all the strongholds which command the public mind, of the pulpit, of the press, of the confessional, of the academies. Wherever the Jesuit preached, the church was too small for the audience. The name of Jesuit on a title-page secured the circulation of a book. It was in the ears of the Jesuit that the powerful, the noble, and the beautiful, breathed the secret history of their lives. It was at the feet of the Jesuit that the youth of the higher and middle classes were brought up from childhood to manhood, from the first rudiments to the courses of rhetoric and philosophy. Literature and science, lately associated with infidelity or with heresy, now became the allies of orthodoxy. Dominant in the South of Europe, the great order soon went forth conquering and to conquer. In spite of oceans and deserts, of hunger and pestilence, of spies and penal laws, of dungeons and racks, of gibbets and quartering-blocks, Jesuits were to be found under every disguise, and in every country; scholars, physicians, merchants, serving-men; in the hostile court of Sweden, in the old manor-houses of Cheshire, among the hovels of Connaught; arguing, instructing, consoling, stealing away the hearts of the young, animating the courage of the timid, holding up the crucifix before the eyes of the dying. Nor was it less their office to plot against the thrones and lives of apostate kings, to spread evil rumours, to raise tumults, to inflame civil wars, to arm the hand of the assassin. Inflexible in nothing but in their fidelity to the Church, they were equally ready to appeal in her cause to the spirit of loyalty and to the spirit of freedom. Extreme doctrines of obedience and extreme doctrines of liberty, the right of rulers to misgovern the people, the right of every one of the people to plunge his knife in the heart of a bad ruler, were inculcated by the same man, according as he addressed himself to the subject of Philip or to the subject of Elizabeth. Some described these divines as the most rigid, others as the most indulgent of spiritual directors. And both descriptions were correct. The truly devout listened with awe to the high and saintly morality of the Jesuit. The gay cavalier who had run his rival through the body, the frail beauty who had forgotten her marriage vow, found in the Jesuit an easy well-bred man of the world, who knew how to make allowance for the little irregularities of people of fashion. The confessor was strict or lax, according to the temper of the penitent. His first object was to drive no person out of the pale of the Church. Since there were bad people, it was better that they should be bad Catholics than bad Protestants. If a person were so unfortunate as to be a bravo, a libertine, or a gambler, that was no reason for making him a heretic too.

The Old World was not wide enough for this strange activity. The Jesuits invaded all the countries which the great maritime discoveries of the preceding age had laid open to European enterprise. They were to be found in the depths of the Peruvian mines, at the marts of the African slave-caravans, on the shores of the Spice Islands, in the observatories of China. They made converts in regions which neither avarice nor curiosity had tempted any of their countrymen to enter; and preached and disputed in tongues of which no other native of the West understood a word.

QUAKER PRACTICES

WILLIAM PENN, *Rise and Progress of the People called Quakers.* 1694

NOT fighting, but suffering, is another testimony peculiar to this people: they affirm that Christianity teacheth people to beat their swords into ploughshares, and their spears into pruning hooks, and to learn war no more, that so the wolf may lie down with the lamb, and the lion with the calf, and nothing that destroys be entertained in the hearts of people: exhorting them to employ their zeal against sin, and turn their anger against Satan, and no longer war one against another; because all wars and fightings come of men's own hearts' lusts, according to the apostle James, and not of the meek spirit of Christ Jesus, who is captain of another warfare, and which is carried on with other weapons. Thus as truth-speaking succeeded swearing, so faith and patience succeeded fighting in the doctrine and practice of this people. Nor ought they for this to be obnoxious to civil government, since if they cannot fight for it neither can they fight against it; which is no mean security to any state. Nor is it reasonable that people should be blamed for not doing more for others than they can do for themselves. And, Christianity set aside, if the costs and fruits of war were well considered, peace with all its inconveniences is generally preferable. But though they were not for fighting, they were for submitting to government; and that not only for fear but for conscience sake; where government doth not interfere with conscience; believing it to be an ordinance of God, and where it is justly administered a great benefit to mankind. Though it has been their lot through blind zeal in some and interest in others to have felt the strokes of it with greater weight and rigour than any other persuasion in this age; whilst they of all others, religion set aside, have given the civil magistrate the least occasion of trouble in the discharge of his office.

Another part of the character of this people was, and is, they refuse to pay tithes or maintenance to a national ministry; and that for two reasons: the one is they believe all compelled maintenance even to gospel ministers to be unlawful, because expressly contrary to Christ's command, who said, freely you have received, freely give: at least, that the maintenance of gospel ministers should be free, and not forced. The other reason of their refusal is because those ministers are not gospel ones, in that the Holy Ghost is not their foundation, but human arts and parts. So that it is not a matter of humour or sullenness, but pure conscience towards God, that they cannot help to support national ministries where they dwell, which are but too much and too visibly become ways of worldly advantage and preferment.

SECULAR MONARCHY

JOHN EMERICH EDWARD DALBERG-ACTON, LORD ACTON,
Lectures on Modern History, XVII. 1906

THOSE who remember with honour men like Hampden and Washington, regard with a corresponding aversion Peter the Great and Frederic William I. But without the first Europe might be French, and without the other it might be Russian. That which arose in Northern Europe about the time of our revolution settlement was a new form of practical absolutism. Theological monarchy had done its time, and was now followed by military monarchy. Church and State had oppressed mankind together; henceforth the State oppressed for its own sake. And this was the genuine idea which came in with the Renaissance, according to which the State alone governs, and all other things obey. Reformation and Counter-Reformation had pushed religion to the front: but after two centuries the original theory, that government must be undivided and un-controlled, began to prevail. It is a new type, not to be con-founded with that of Henry VIII, Philip II, or Lewis XIV, and better adapted to a more rational and economic age. Government so understood is the intellectual guide of the nation, the promoter of wealth, the teacher of knowledge, the guardian of morality, the mainspring of the ascending move-ment of man. That is the tremendous power, supported by millions of bayonets, which grew up in the days of which I have been speaking at Petersburg, and was developed, by much abler minds, chiefly at Berlin; and it is the greatest danger that remains to be encountered by the Anglo-Saxon race.

A NEW EUROPE

EDWARD JOHN PAYNE, *History of European Colonies.*
Chap. i. 1875

THE history we are going to write is that of the New Europe, that is, of Europe beyond seas: of America, Australia, South Africa, and other places where European communities are growing up away from their native soil. These nations are Colonies, or offshoots, of the Old Europe; and they have been planted at different times within the last four hundred years. To the historian this is but a short space of time. This world of nations that we are going to write about is an infant world: and the history we are going to write is something like what a history of the Jews would have been in the time of Joshua, or a history of Greece in the time of Agamemnon, or the history of England in the time of Alfred the Great. But it is on a much bigger scale than any of these; it is in fact on about as big a scale as the history of anything upon this globe can possibly be. On the other hand, the main changes which have directed the course of the present history are few in number and easily remembered: so that if we once understand them well, half the difficulty of the business will be over. Although this history drops at length into the common historical forms, and deals with generals and emperors, ministers and parties, revolutions and constitutions, we shall find that for a long time it is chiefly a history of the ventures of merchants and planters, and that its mainsprings are navigation and trade. After an episode or two of mediæval conquest, it will turn to a history of commercial navigation; of the quest of spices and metals, coffee and sugar, wool and hides. Its leading types, such as the quick-witted Athenian is for the history of Greece, and the Norman baron in the midst of his liege men for the history of England, will be the grave merchant of Amsterdam, or Bristol, or Lisbon, in his counting-house: the bronzed skipper, lading his unwieldy hulk in the Indian roadstead: the Western planter among his canes, and the half-breed miner toiling on the slopes of the South American Cordillera. As we go on we shall see these things exercising a surprising change upon European ideas. We shall see a mediaeval military order turning West Indian planters: religious bodies founding Americ an states: the European world leaving off fighting for religion, and fighting for sugar hogsheads instead: the outcasts of the Batavian marshes suddenly becoming the first nation in Europe, and the Hague the centre of the world's diplomacy: the humble trade-guild grown into the rich and powerful commercial company, and the commercial company speedily transformed into a sovereign power, holding in its hands the welfare of millions. We shall see revolutions in national finance: feel the social balance of old kingdoms displaced by colonial wealth, and listen to dreams of making the fortune of everybody in the old Europe at the expense of the new. We shall see the old Europe finally wax fat and dull with its unnatural prosperity, and the face of affairs change: the decline of the old Europe now becomes the rise of the new. We shall then see colonial empires, built up by generations of acute statesmen, totter to their ruin, and two of the proudest monarchies the world has ever seen humbled in the dust one after the other before their outlawed subjects. We shall see a revolution of races—the despised negro expelling his master from the fairest regions of the earth, which he had been forced thither to cultivate like a beast of labour, and asserting for himself a place among civilised nations: and even the American Indian rising up at last to shake off the tyranny of the priest and the government official. We shall see political movements derived from the old world reflected on a vaster scale in the new; and the beginnings made of a history whose development the wisest cannot forecast. These beginnings are all that we can study; but, if we please, we can study them very thoroughly. For the whole of this history has taken place since the invention of printing. Records have been kept of it in abundance; and the historian of New Europe will be the first historian who goes to work armed completely with facts.

TIES OF EMPIRE

EDMUND BURKE, *Speech on Conciliation with the Colonies.* 1775

My hold of the Colonies is in the close affection which grows from common names, from kindred blood, from similar privileges, and equal protection. These are ties, which, though light as air, are as strong as links of iron. Let the Colonists always keep the idea of their civil rights associated with your Government;—they will cling and grapple to you; and no force under heaven will be of power to tear them from their allegiance. But let it be once understood, that your government may be one thing, and their Privileges another; that these two things may exist without any mutual relation;— the cement is gone; the cohesion is loosened; and everything hastens to decay and dissolution. As long as you have the wisdom to keep the sovereign authority of this country as the sanctuary of liberty, the sacred temple consecrated to our common faith, wherever the chosen race and sons of England worship freedom, they will turn their faces towards you. The more they multiply, the more friends you will have; the more ardently they love liberty, the more perfect will be their obedience. Slavery they can have anywhere. It is a weed that grows in every soil. They may have it from Spain, they may have it from Prussia. But, until you become lost to all feeling of your true interest and your natural dignity, freedom they can have from none but you. This is the commodity of price, of which you have the monopoly. This is the true Act of Navigation, which binds to you the commerce of the Colonies, and through them secures to you the wealth of the world. Deny them this participation of freedom, and you break that sole bond, which originally made, and must still preserve, the unity of the Empire. Do not entertain so weak an imagination, as that your registers and your bonds, your affidavits and your sufferances, your cockets and your clearances, are what form the great securities of your commerce. Do not dream that your letters of office, and your instructions, and your suspending clauses, are the things that hold together the great contexture of the mysterious whole. These things do not make your government. Dead instruments, passive tools as they are, it is the spirit of the English communion that gives all their life and efficacy to them. It is the spirit of the English Constitution, which, infused through the mighty mass, pervades, feeds, unites, invigorates, vivifies every part of the empire, even down to the minutest member.

Is it not the same virtue which does everything for us here in England? Do you imagine then, that it is the Land Tax Act which raises your revenue? that it is the annual vote in the Committee of Supply which gives you your army? or that it is the Mutiny Bill which inspires it with bravery and discipline? No! surely no! It is the love of the people; it is their attachment to their government, from the sense of the deep stake they have in such a glorious institution—which gives you your army and your navy, and infuses into both that liberal obedience, without which your army would be a base rabble, and your navy nothing but rotten timber.

All this, I know well enough, will sound wild and chimerical to the profane herd of those vulgar and mechanical politicians, who have no place among us; a sort of people who think that nothing exists but what is gross and material; and who therefore, far from being qualified to be directors of the great movement of empire, are not fit to turn a wheel in the machine. But to men truly initiated and rightly taught, these ruling and master principles, which, in the opinion of such men as I have mentioned, have no substantial existence, are in truth every thing, and all in all. Magnanimity in politicks is not seldom the truest wisdom; and a great empire and little minds go ill together. If we are conscious of our station, and glow with zeal to fill our places as becomes our situation and ourselves, we ought to auspicate all our public proceedings on America with the old warning of the church, *Sursum corda!* We ought to elevate our minds to the greatness of that trust to which the order of Providence has called us. By adverting to the dignity of this high calling, our ancestors have turned a savage wilderness into a glorious empire; and have made the most extensive, and the only honourable conquests, not by destroying, but by promoting the wealth, the number, the happiness, of the human race. Let us get an American revenue as we have got an American empire. English privileges have made it all that it is; English privileges alone will make it all it can be.

DEMOCRACIES AND REPUBLICS

JAMES MADISON, *The Federalist.* NOS. X, XIV. 1787

THE two great points of difference between a democracy and a republic are: first, the delegation of the government, in the latter, to a small number of citizens elected by the rest; secondly, the greater number of citizens, and greater sphere of country, over which the latter may be extended.

*   *   *   *

In a democracy the people meet and exercise the government in person; in a republic, they assemble and administer it by their representatives and agents. A democracy, consequently, will be confined to a small spot. A republic may be extended over a large region. . . . Under the confusion of names, it has been an easy task to transfer to a republic observations applicable to a democracy only; and among others, the observation that it can never be established but among a small number of people, living within a small compass of territory.

Such a fallacy may have been the less perceived, as most of the popular governments of antiquity were of the democratic species; and even in modern Europe, to which we owe the great principle of representation, no example is seen of a government wholly popular, and founded, at the same time, wholly on that principle. If Europe has the merit of discovering this great mechanical power in government, by the simple agency of which the will of the largest political body may be concentred, and its force directed to any object which the public good requires, America can claim the merit of making the discovery the basis of unmixed and extensive republics.

END OF THE EIGHTEENTH CENTURY

THOMAS CARLYLE, *History of Friedrich II of Prussia.*
Book i. 1858

THE French Revolution may be said to have, for about half a century, quite submerged Friedrich, abolished him from the memories of men; and now on coming to light again, he is found defaced under strange mud-incrustations, and the eyes of mankind look at him from a singularly changed, what we must call oblique and perverse point of vision. This is one of the difficulties in dealing with his History;—especially if you happen to believe both in the French Revolution and in him; that is to say, both that Real Kingship is eternally indispensable, and also that the destruction of Sham Kingship (a frightful process) is occasionally so.

On the breaking out of that formidable Explosion and Suicide of his Century, Friedrich sank into comparative obscurity; eclipsed amid the ruins of that universal earthquake, the very dust of which darkened all the air, and made of day a disastrous midnight. Black midnight, broken only by the blaze of conflagrations;—wherein, to our terrified imaginations, were seen, not men, French and other, but ghastly portents, stalking wrathful, and shapes of avenging gods. It must be owned the figure of Napoleon was titanic; especially to the generation that looked on him, and that waited shuddering to be devoured by him. In general, in that French Revolution, all was on a huge scale; if not greater than anything in human experience, at least more grandiose. All was recorded in bulletins, too, addressed to the shilling-gallery; and there were fellows on the stage with such a breadth of sabre, extent of whiskerage, strength of windpipe, and command of men and gunpowder, as had never been seen before. How they bellowed, stalked and flourished about; counterfeiting Jove's thunder to an amazing degree! Terrific Drawcansir figures, of enormous whiskerage, unlimited command of gunpowder; not without sufficient ferocity, and even a certain heroism, stage-heroism, in them; compared with whom, to the shilling-gallery, and frightened theatre at large, it seemed as if there had been no generals or sovereigns before; as if Friedrich, Gustavus, Cromwell, William Conqueror and Alexander the Great were not worth speaking of henceforth.

All this, however, in half a century is considerably altered. The Drawcansir equipments getting gradually torn off, the natural size is seen better; translated from the bulletin style into that of fact and history, miracles, even to the shilling-gallery, are not so miraculous. It begins to be apparent that there lived great men before the era of bulletins and Agamemnon. Austerlitz and Wagram shot away more gunpowder,— gunpowder probably in the proportion of ten to one, or a hundred to one: but neither of them was tenth-part such a beating to your enemy as that of Rosbach, brought about by strategic art, human ingenuity and intrepidity, and the loss of 165 men. Leuthen, too, the Battle of Leuthen (though so few English readers ever heard of it) may very well hold up its head beside any victory gained by Napoleon or another. For the odds were not far from three to one; the soldiers were of not far from equal quality; and only the General was consummately superior, and the defeat a destruction. Napoleon did indeed, by immense expenditure of men and gunpowder, overrun Europe for a time: but Napoleon never, by husbanding and wisely expending his men and gunpowder, defended a little Prussia against all Europe, year after year for seven years long, till Europe had enough, and gave up the enterprise as one it could not manage. So soon as the Drawcansir equipments are well torn off, and the shilling-gallery got to silence, it will be found that there were great Kings before Napoleon,—and likewise an Art of War, grounded on veracity and human courage and insight, not upon Drawcansir rodomontade, grandiose Dick-Turpinism, revolutionary madness, and unlimited expenditure of men and gunpowder. "You may paint with a very big brush, and yet not be a great painter", says a satirical friend of mine! This is becoming more and more apparent, as the dust-whirlwind, and huge uproar of the last generation, gradually dies away again.

COMMENT ON THE SIEGE OF BADAJOS

SIR WILLIAM FRANCIS PATRICK NAPIER, *History of the War in the Peninsula and in the South of France, 1807–1814.* Vol. IV. 1834

AND why was all this striving in blood against insurmountable difficulties? Why were men sent thus to slaughter, when the application of a just science would have rendered the operation comparatively easy? Because the English ministers, so ready to plunge into war, were quite ignorant of its exigencies; because the English people are warlike without being military, and under the pretence of maintaining a liberty which they do not possess, oppose in peace all useful martial establishments. Expatiating in their schools and colleges, upon Roman discipline and Roman valour, they are heedless of Roman institutions; they desire like that ancient republic, to be free at home and conquerors abroad, but start at perfecting their military system, as a thing incompatible with a constitution, which they yet suffer to be violated by every minister who trembles at the exposure of corruption. In the beginning of each war, England has to seek in blood for the knowledge necessary to insure success, and like the fiend's progress towards Eden, her conquering course is through chaos followed by death!

ADDRESS TO THE REVOLUTIONARIES

EDMUND BURKE, *Reflections on the Revolution in France.* 1790

You will observe, that from Magna Charta to the Declaration of Right, it has been the uniform policy of our constitution to claim and assert our liberties, as an *entailed inheritance* derived to us from our forefathers, and to be transmitted to our posterity; as an estate specially belonging to the people of this kingdom without any reference whatever to any other more general or prior right. By this means our constitution preserves an unity in so great a diversity of its parts. We have an inheritable crown; an inheritable peerage; and an house of commons and a people inheriting privileges, franchises, and liberties, from a long line of ancestors.

This policy appears to me to be the result of profound reflection; or rather the happy effect of following nature, which is wisdom without reflection, and above it. A spirit of innovation is generally the result of a selfish temper and confined views. People will not look forward to posterity, who never look backward to their ancestors. Besides, the people of England well know, that the idea of inheritance furnishes a sure principle of conservation, and a sure principle of transmission; without at all excluding a principle of improvement. It leaves acquisition free; but it secures what it acquires.

Whatever advantages are obtained by a state proceeding on these maxims, are locked fast as in a sort of family settlement; grasped as in a kind of mortmain for ever. By a constitutional policy, working after the pattern of nature, we receive, we hold, we transmit our government and our privileges, in the same manner in which we enjoy and transmit our property and our lives. The institutions of policy, the goods of fortune, the gifts of Providence, are handed down, to us and from us, in the same course and order. Our political system is placed in a just correspondence and symmetry with the order of the world, and with the mode of existence decreed to a permanent body composed of transitory parts; wherein, by the disposition of a stupendous wisdom, moulding together the great mysterious incorporation of the human race, the whole, at one time, is never old, or middle-aged, or young, but in a condition of unchangeable constancy, moves on through the varied tenour of perpetual decay, fall, renovation, and progression. Thus, by preserving the method of nature in the conduct of the state, in what we improve, we are never wholly new; in what we retain we are never wholly obsolete. By adhering in this manner and on those principles to our forefathers, we are guided not by the superstition of antiquarians, but by the spirit of philosophic analogy. In this choice of inheritance we have given to our frame of polity the image of a relation in blood; binding up the constitution of our country with our dearest domestic ties; adopting our fundamental laws into the bosom of our family affections; keeping inseparable, and cherishing with the warmth of all their combined and mutually reflected charities, our state, our hearths, our sepulchres, and our altars.

Through the same plan of a conformity to nature in our artificial institutions, and by calling in the aid of her unerring and powerful instincts, to fortify the fallible and feeble contrivances of our reason, we have derived several other, and those no small benefits, from considering our liberties in the light of an inheritance. Always acting as if in the presence of canonized forefathers, the spirit of freedom, leading in itself to misrule and excess, is tempered with an awful gravity. This idea of a liberal descent inspires us with a sense of habitual native dignity, which prevents that upstart insolence almost inevitably adhering to and disgracing those who are the first acquirers of any distinction. By this means our liberty becomes a noble freedom. It carries an imposing and majestic aspect. It has a pedigree and illustrating ancestors. It has its bearings and its ensigns armorial. It has its gallery of portraits; its monumental inscriptions; its records, evidences, and titles. We procure reverence to our civil institutions on the principle upon which nature teaches us to revere individual men; on account of their age; and on account of those from whom they are descended. All your sophisters cannot produce any thing better adapted to preserve a rational and manly freedom than the course that we have pursued, who have chosen our nature rather than our speculations, our breasts rather than our inventions, for the great conservatories and magazines of our rights and privileges.

WHERE EVERY PROSPECT PLEASES

JOSEPH PRIESTLEY, *Letters to the Right Honourable Edmund Burke*. No. XIV. 1791

How glorious, then, is the prospect, the reverse of all the past, which is now opening upon us, and upon the world. Government, we may now expect to see, not only in theory, and in books, but in actual practice, calculated for the general good, and taking no more upon it than the general good requires; leaving all men the enjoyment of as many of their *natural rights* as possible, and no more interfering with matters of religion, with men's notions concerning God, and a future state, than with philosophy, or medicine.

After the noble example of America, we may expect, in due time, to see the governing powers of all nations confining their attention to the *civil* concerns of them, and consulting their welfare in the present state only; in consequence of which they may all be flourishing and happy. *Truth* of all kinds, and especially *religious truth*, meeting with no obstruction, and standing in no need of heterogeneous supports, will then establish itself by its own evidence; and whatever is *false* and delusive, all the forms of superstition, every corruption of true religion, and all usurpation over the rights of conscience, which have been supported by power or prejudice, will be universally exploded, as they ought to be.

Together with the general prevalence of the true principles of civil government, we may expect to see the extinction of all *national prejudice* and enmity, and the establishment of *universal peace* and good will among all nations. When the affairs of the various societies of mankind shall be conducted by those who shall truly represent them, who shall feel as they feel, and think as they think, who shall really understand, and consult their interests, they will no more engage in those mutually offensive *wars*, which the experience of many centuries has shown to be constantly expensive and ruinous. They will no longer covet what belongs to others, and which they have found to be of no real service to them, but will content themselves with making the most of their own.

The very idea of *distant possessions* will be even ridiculed. The East and the West Indies, and everything *without ourselves* will be disregarded, and wholly excluded from all European systems; and only those divisions of men, and of territory, will take place, which the common convenience requires, and not such as the mad and insatiable ambition of princes demands. No part of America, Africa, or Asia, will be held in subjection to any part of Europe, and all the intercourse that will be kept up among them, will be for their mutual advantage.

The causes of *civil wars*, the most distressing of all others, will likewise cease, as well as those of foreign ones. They are chiefly contentions for *offices*, on account of the power and emoluments annexed to them. But when the *nature* and *uses* of all civil offices shall be well understood, the power and emoluments annexed to them, will not be an object sufficient to produce a war. Is it at all probable, that there will ever be a civil war in America about the presidentship of the *United States*? And when the chief magistracies in other countries shall be reduced to their proper standard, they will be no more worth contending for, than they are in America. If the actual business of a nation be done as well for the small emolument of that presidentship, as the similar business of other nations, there will be no apparent reason why more should be given for doing it.

If there be a superfluity of public money, it will not be employed to augment the profusion, and increase the undue influence, of individuals, but in works of great public utility, which are always wanted, and which nothing but the enormous expenses of government, and of wars, chiefly occasioned by the ambition of kings and courts, have prevented from being carried into execution. The expense of the late American war only would have converted all the waste grounds of this country into gardens. What canals, bridges, and noble roads, what public buildings, public libraries, and public laboratories, &c. &c. would it not have made for us? If the *pride of nations* must be gratified, let it be in such things as these, and not in the idle pageantry of a court, calculated only to corrupt and enslave a nation.

Another cause of civil wars has been an attachment to certain persons and families as possessed of some *inherent right* to kingly power. Such were the bloody wars between the houses of York and Lancaster, in this country. But when, besides the reduction of the power of crowns within their proper bounds (when it will be no greater than the public good requires) that kind of respect for princes which is founded on mere superstition (exactly similar to that which has been attached to priests in all countries) shall vanish, as all superstition certainly will before real knowledge, wise nations will not involve themselves in war for the sake of any particular persons, or families, who have never shewn an equal regard for them. They will consider their own interest more, and that of their *magistrates*, that is their *servants*, less.

Other remaining causes of civil war are different opinions about modes of government, and differences of interests between provinces. But when mankind shall be a little more accustomed to reflection, and consider the miseries of civil war, they will have recourse to any other method of deciding their differences, in preference to that of the sword. It was taken for granted, that the moment America had thrown off the yoke of Great Britain, the different states would go to war among themselves, on some of these accounts. But the event has not verified the prediction, nor is it at all probable that it ever will. The people of that country are wiser than such prophets in this.

If *time* be allowed for the discussion of differences, so great a majority will form one opinion, that the minority will see the necessity of giving way. Thus will *reason* be the umpire in all disputes, and extinguish civil wars as well as foreign ones. The empire of reason will ever be the reign of peace.

THE MODERN STATE

SIR JOHN ROBERT SEELEY, *A Short History of Napoleon the First*. 1886

PERSONALITY exerts a fascinating influence upon us. We perceive far more distinctly, as it were, the deeds we can attribute to a single notable person, than similar deeds of which the responsibility is divided among many persons, of whom some may be obscure and some quite unknown. The enormous character of Napoleon's deeds would not strike us so much if the same deeds had been done by a succession of ordinary French ministries during the same space of time. The best proof of this is that we so seldom remark how the same lawless principles had been gathering head for a very long time in Europe, how many similar acts had been done before in the eighteenth century, how slight is the difference in moral principle, however great the difference in power and opportunity, between Napoleon and other rulers of that age. When we attend to this general character of the age, we come to see that the Napoleonic wars are only the fatal catastrophe towards which Europe had long been madly hurrying, the last paroxysm of the possessed before the evil spirit, which was the spirit of international cynicism, went out of him. We talk of the partition of Poland, but that deed was really not so exceptional, nor should we speak of it as the cause of the demoralisation of Europe, but rather as one among several proofs that Europe was already demoralised.

Professor Stubbs has remarked that in the Middle Ages wars were waged for rights, but in modern times for interests. Till near the end of the seventeenth century, or as long as religion continued to be a leading international influence, it may be said that though there was much disorder and crime, sheer naked cynicism did not yet prevail in the intercourse of nations. But from the war of the Spanish Succession through-out the eighteenth century it may be said that, though there was some improvement in the manner in which war was con-ducted, it was undertaken on more unblushingly immoral grounds than either before or since. The old European system founded on the unity of religion had passed away, and the later system, founded on the struggle of two rival religions, had almost passed away too. On the other hand, the modern system, founded on nationality, only began to show itself at the French Revolution. Hence, whereas our nineteenth century wars are inspired by national patriotism, and the wars of the seventeenth century, even those of Louis XIV, have at least some, if only superficial, varnish of religion, those of the intermediate period—I speak of the Continental wars—are scarcely coloured by any kind of moral pretext. It is the iron age of international relations, the age in which wars are waged simply to round off a territory, to give compactness to a state. The ominous word Partition, pronounced a little earlier in reference to the Spanish Empire, when it was hoped to accomplish by treaty between William III and Louis XIV the settlement which afterwards cost Europe a war, seems to govern the whole century. It would appear that the pre-cedent set in the case of the Spanish Empire demoralised all the politicians of Europe. They saw on the one hand the Bourbon family gain a kingdom in spite of a solemn renuncia-tion; on the other hand, a rearrangement of the map of Europe accomplished by force of arms. Henceforward every great royal demise became the signal for a war on the model of that of the Spanish Succession. Had Louis XV died in childhood, as was expected, there would certainly have been in the twenties a war of the French Succession; there was a war of the Polish Succession in the thirties, and a war of the Austrian Succession in the forties, which last led to a second terrible struggle in the fifties; the seventies witnessed a partition of Poland, and a war of the Bavarian Succession; a partition of Turkey was attempted in the eighties. In the course of these wars kings and ministers accustomed themselves to contemplate rearrangements as large as those made at Utrecht, and to break engagements as sacred as that which had been broken by Louis XIV. This was seen in the eager haste with which so many sovereigns set aside the treaties in which they had pledged themselves to the Pragmatic Sanction. The spectacle then presented by Europe ought to show us that no partition of Poland, occurring thirty years later, was needed to demoralise statesmen....

The principles of '89 had, as it were, made all Frenchmen feel themselves citizens—that is, not so much free, as having an interest in the State. It is not in liberty that the subjects of the Convention or of Napoleon differ from the subjects of Louis XIV, but in the feeling that the Government, however absolute, was *their* Government. So distinct is this from liberty, that in the period when the feeling was fresh it gave a new energy to despotism. For the people took a pride in the strength and severity of the Government which was their own.

Not less great in the history of a people is the moment when it acquires this sense of membership in the State than the moment when it asserts its liberty; not less great, and wholly distinct. Then it ceases to regard Government with sullen dread as an enemy, or with resignation as an incomprehensible superior power, and begins to conceive it as a representative of itself, as the champion of its interests. In no civilised country had the superstitious view prevailed more absolutely than in the France of Louis XIV; all the more inspiring was the change when now the rational view dawned upon the French mind, and the State appeared before their minds as a living organism. We may, perhaps, say that the effect of the Revolution was to make France not free, but *organic*. Parallel cases have occurred in our own age. Italy and Germany in like manner became organic by the abolition of petty, artificial, or foreign Governments, and by the establishment of a harmony between the State and the nation. In both cases the movement appeared to be at the moment rather unfavourable than favourable to the progress of liberty. In both cases the strongest form of government attainable was adopted.

Now it is instructive to observe that in both these cases, also, the earliest instinct of the State thus endowed with organic life was to extend its territory and make war upon its neighbours. The first step towards German unity was marked by an unsuccessful war for Schleswig-Holstein, the second step by a successful one, and the consummation of German unity was, as it were, attested by the conquest of Alsace and Lorraine. The kingdom of Italy could not be content without Rome and Venice, and still raises a wild cry of "Italia Irredenta"....

In the history of Europe it will be said of Napoleon as follows: that at the end of the eighteenth century a movement began by which the great Continental states, which till then had been inorganic, became conscious living organisms; that this change took place in France first; that it gave an extraordinary enlargement and sense of power to the French mind; that, as it was at first peculiar to France, it gave her an immense military advantage over other European states; that the perception of this tempted her into great warlike enterprises; that in these enterprises she found a leader of unrivalled energy, who conducted them with astonishing success—Napoleon.

LIBERTY IN THE MODERN STATE

JOHN EMERICH EDWARD DALBERG-ACTON, LORD ACTON,
Inaugural Lecture on the Study of History. 1895

WHAT do people mean who proclaim that liberty is the palm, and the prize, and the crown, seeing that it is an idea of which there are two hundred definitions, and that this wealth of interpretation has caused more bloodshed than anything, except theology? Is it Democracy as in France, or Federalism as in America, or the national independence which bounds the Italian view, or the reign of the fittest, which is the ideal of the Germans? I know not whether it will ever fall within my sphere of duty to trace the slow progress of that idea through the chequered scenes of our history, and to describe how subtle speculations touching the nature of conscience promoted a nobler and more spiritual conception of the liberty that protects it, until the guardian of rights developed into the guardian of duties which are the cause of rights, and that which had been prized as the material safe-guard for treasures of earth became sacred as security for things that are divine. All that we require is a workday key to history, and our present need can be supplied without pausing to satisfy philosophers. Without inquiring how far Sarasa or Butler, Kant or Vinet, is right as to the infallible voice of God in man, we may easily agree in this, that where absolutism reigned, by irresistible arms, concentrated posses-sions, auxiliary churches, and inhuman laws, it reigns no more; that commerce having risen against land, labour against wealth, the State against the forces dominant in society, the division of power against the State, the thought of individuals against the practice of ages, neither authorities, nor minori-ties, nor majorities can command implicit obedience; and, where there has been long and arduous experience, a rampart of tried conviction and accumulated knowledge, where there is a fair level of general morality, education, courage, and self-restraint, there, if there only, a society may be found that exhibits the condition of life towards which, by elimination of failures, the world has been moving through the allotted space. You will know it by outward signs: Representation, the extinction of slavery, the reign of opinion, and the like; better still by less apparent evidences: the security of the weaker groups and the liberty of conscience, which, effectually secured, secures the rest.

POSSIBILITIES

(i) Hilaire Belloc, *Esto perpetua.* 1906
(ii) William Fiddian Reddaway, *Modern European History. A General Sketch* (1492–1924). Preface. 1924

(i)

Had not our religion suffered the violent schisms which are now so slowly healing, and had not our general life resolved itself for a time into a blind race between the various provinces of Europe, the reconquest of Barbary would have fallen naturally to the nations which regard each its own section of the opposing coast; as in the reconquest of Spain the Asturias advanced upon Leon, the Galicians upon Portugal, and Old Castille upon the southern province to which it extended its own name. Then Italy would have concerned itself with Tunis —with Ifrigya, that is—and with the rare fringe of the Tripolitan and its shallow harbours. The French would have occupied Numidia. The Spaniards would have swept on to re-Christianise the last province of the west from Oran to the Atlantic, and so have completed the task which they let drop after the march upon Granada. Such should have been the natural end of mediæval progress, and that reconstruction of the Empire (which was the nebulous but constant goal towards which the Middle Ages moved) would have been accomplished. But the most sudden and the most inexplicable of our revolutions came in and broke the scheme. The Middle Ages died without a warning. A curious passion for metaphysics seized upon certain districts of the north, which in their exaltation attempted to live alone: the south, in resisting the disruption of Europe, exhausted its energies; and meanwhile the temptation to exploit the Americas and the Indies drained the Mediterranean of adventurers and of navies. Islam in its lethargy acquired new vigour from its latest converts, and the Turks, with none but the Venetians to oppose them, tore away from us the whole of the Levant and rode up the Danube to insult the centre of the continent. The European system flew apart, and its various units moved along separate paths with various careers of hesitation or of fever.

It was not until the Revolution and the reconstitution of sane government among us that the common scheme of the west could reappear.

(ii)

IT is difficult to suppose that Europeans with the smallest perception of their common interest might not in the last four centuries have driven back the Turks, assimilated the Russians, raised themselves to a far higher level of civilization and spread irresistibly over the temperate world.

DEMOCRACY AND PARTY

SIR HENRY SUMNER MAINE, *Popular Government.*
Essay II. 1885

THE delusion that Democracy, when it has once had all things put under its feet, is a progressive form of government, lies deep in the convictions of a particular political school; but there can be no delusion grosser. It receives no countenance either from experience or from probability. Englishmen in the East come into contact with vast populations of high natural intelligence, to which the very notion of innovation is loathsome; and the very fact that such populations exist should suggest that the true difference between the East and the West lies merely in this, that in Western countries there is a larger minority of exceptional persons who, for good reasons or bad, have a real desire for change. All that has made England famous, and all that has made England wealthy, has been the work of minorities, sometimes very small ones. It seems to me quite certain that, if for four centuries there had been a very widely extended franchise and a very large electoral body in this country, there would have been no reformation of religion, no change of dynasty, no toleration of Dissent, not even an accurate Calendar. The threshing-machine, the power-loom, the spinning-jenny, and possibly the steam-engine, would have been prohibited. Even in our day, vaccination is in the utmost danger, and we may say generally that the gradual establishment of the masses in power is of the blackest omen for all legislation founded on scientific opinion, which requires tension of mind to understand it and self-denial to submit to it.

The truth is, that the inherent difficulties of democratic government are so manifold and enormous that, in large and complex modern societies, it could neither last nor work if it were not aided by certain forces which are not exclusively associated with it, but of which it greatly stimulates the energy. Of these forces, the one to which it owes most is unquestionably Party.

No force acting on mankind has been less carefully examined than Party, and yet none better deserves examination. The difficulty which Englishmen in particular feel about it is very like that which men once experienced when they were told that the air had weight. It enveloped them so evenly and pressed on them so equally, that the assertion seemed incredible. Nevertheless it is not hard to show that Party and Party Government are very extraordinary things. Let us suppose it to be still the fashion to write the apologues so dear to the last century, in which some stranger from the East or West, some Persian full of intelligent curiosity, some Huron still unspoilt by civilisation, or some unprejudiced Bonze from India or China, described the beliefs and usages of European countries, just as they struck him, to his kinsmen at the other end of the world. Let us assume that in one of these trifles, by a Voltaire or a Montesquieu, the traveller gave an account of a cultivated and powerful European Commonwealth, in which the system of government consisted in half the cleverest men in the country taking the utmost pains to prevent the other half from governing. Or let us imagine some modern writer, with the unflinching perspicacity of a Machiavelli, analysing the great Party Hero—leader or agitator—as the famous Italian analysed the personage equally interesting and important in his day, the Tyrant or Prince. Like Machiavelli, he would not stop to praise or condemn on ethical grounds: "he would follow the real truth of things rather than an imaginary view of them".* "Many

* *The Prince*, xv (101).

Party Heroes", he would say, "have been imagined, who were never seen or known to exist in reality." But he would describe them as they really were. Allowing them every sort of private virtue, he would deny that their virtues had any effect on their public conduct, except so far as they helped to make men believe their public conduct virtuous. But this public conduct he would find to be not so much immoral as non-moral. He would infer, from actual observation, that the party Hero was debarred by his position from the full practice of the great virtues of veracity, justice, and moral intrepidity. He could seldom tell the full truth; he could never be fair to persons other than his followers and associates; he could rarely be bold except in the interests of his faction. The picture drawn by him would be one which few living men would deny to be correct, though they might excuse its occurrence in nature on the score of moral necessity. And then, a century or two later, when Democracies were as much forgotten as the Italian Princedoms, our modern Machiavelli would perhaps be infamous and his work a proverb of immorality.

A FREE MONARCHY

BENJAMIN DISRAELI, LORD BEACONSFIELD, *Coningsby*. 1844

REPRESENTATION is not necessary, or even in a principal sense, parliamentary. Parliament is not sitting at this moment, and yet the nation is represented in its highest as well as in its most minute interests. Not a grievance escapes notice and redress. I see in the newspaper this morning that a pedagogue has brutally chastised his pupil. It is a fact known all over England. We must not forget that a principle of government is reserved for our days, that we shall not find in our Aristotles, or even in the forests of Tacitus, nor in our Saxon wittenagemotes, nor in our Plantagenet parliaments. Opinion now is supreme, and opinion speaks in print. The representation of the press is far more complete than the representation of parliament. Parliamentary representation was the happy device of a ruder age, to which it was admirably adapted; an age of semi-civilisation, when there was a leading class in the community; but it exhibits many symptoms of desuetude. It is controlled by a system of representation more vigorous and comprehensive; which absorbs its duties and fulfils them more efficiently; and in which discussion is pursued on fairer terms, and often with more depth and information.

And to what power would you intrust the function of taxation?

To some power that would employ it more discreetly than in creating our present amount of debt, and in establishing our present system of imposts.

In a word, true wisdom lies in the policy that would effect its ends by the influence of opinion, and yet by the means of existing forms. Nevertheless if we are forced to revolutions, let us propose to our consideration the idea of a free monarchy, established on fundamental laws, itself the apex of a vast pile of municipal and local government, ruling an educated people, represented by a free and intellectual press. Before such a royal authority, supported by such a national opinion, the sectional anomalies of our country would disappear. Under such a system, where qualification would not be parliamentary, but personal, even statesmen would be educated; we should have no more diplomatists who could not speak French; no more bishops ignorant of theology; no more generals-in-chief who never saw a field.

THE SERVILE STATE

HILAIRE BELLOC, *The Servile State*. 1913

THE future of industrial society, and in particular of English society, left to its own direction, is a future in which subsistence and security shall be guaranteed for the Proletariat, but shall be guaranteed at the expense of the old political freedom and by the establishment of that Proletariat in a status really, though not nominally, servile. At the same time, the Owners will be guaranteed in their profits, the whole machinery of production in the smoothness of its working, and that stability which has been lost under the Capitalist phase of society will be found once more.

The internal strains which have threatened society during its Capitalist phase will be relaxed and eliminated, and the community will settle down upon that Servile basis which was its foundation before the advent of the Christian faith, from which that faith slowly weaned it, and to which in the decay of that faith it naturally returns.

MAGNA EST VERITAS

WILLIAM STUBBS, *The Constitutional History of England in its origin and development.* Vol. III, chap. xxi. 1878

MODERN thought is a little prone to eclecticism in history: it can sympathise with puritanism as an effort after freedom, and put out of sight the fact that puritanism was itself a grinding social tyranny, that wrought out its ends by unscrupulous detraction and by the profane handling of things which should have been sacred even to the fanatic if he really believed in the cause for which he raged. There is little real sympathy with the great object, the peculiar creed that was oppressed; as a struggle for liberty the Quarrel of Puritanism takes its stand besides the Quarrel on Investitures; yet like every other struggle for liberty, it ended in being a struggle for supremacy. On the other hand, the system of Laud and of Charles seems to many minds to contain so much that is good and sacred, that the means by which it was maintained fall into the background. We would not judge between the two theories which have been nursed by the prejudices of ten generations. To one side liberty, to the other law, will continue to outweigh all other considerations of disputed and detailed right or wrong: it is enough for each to look at them as the actors themselves looked at them, or as men look at party questions of their own day, when much of private conviction and personal feeling must be sacrificed to save those broader principles for which only great parties can be made to strive.

The historian looks with actual pain upon many of these things. Especially in quarrels where religion is concerned, the hollowness of the pretension to political honesty becomes a stumblingblock in the way of fair judgment. We know that no other causes have ever created so great and bitter struggles, have brought into the field, whether of war or controversy, greater and more united armies. Yet no truth is more certain than this, that the real motives of religious action do not work on men in masses; and that the enthusiasm which creates Crusaders, Inquisitors, Hussites, Puritans, is not the result of conviction, but of passion provoked by oppression or resistance, maintained by selfwill, or stimulated by the mere desire of victory. And this is a lesson for all time, and for practical life as well as historical judgment. And on the other hand it is impossible to regard this as an adequate solution of the problem: there must be something, even if it be not religion or liberty, for which men will make so great sacrifices.

The best aspect of an age of controversy must be sought in the lives of the best men, whose honesty carries conviction to the understanding, whilst their zeal kindles the zeal of the many. A study of the lives of such men will lead to the conclusion that, in spite of internecine hostility in act, the real and true leaders had far more in common than they knew of; they struggled, in the dark or in the twilight, against the evil which was there, and which they hated with equal sincerity; they fought for the good which was there, and which really was strengthened by the issue of the strife. Their blows fell at random: men perished in arms against one another whose hearts were set on the same end and aim; and that good end and aim which neither of them had seen clearly was the inheritance they left to their children, made possible and realised not so much by the victory of one as by the truth and self-sacrifice of both.

MODERATION

GEORGE SAVILE, MARQUIS OF HALIFAX, *Character of a Trimmer*. 1688

THE want of practice, which repeals the other laws, has no influence upon the law of Truth, because it has root in heaven, and an intrinsic value in itself that can never be impaired: she shows her greatness in this, that her enemies, even when they are successful, are ashamed to own it. Nothing but power full of truth has the prerogative of triumphing, not only after victories, but in spite of them, and to put conquest herself out of countenance. She may be kept under and suppressed, but her dignity still remains with her, even when she is in chains. Falsehood, with all her impudence, has not enough to speak ill of her before her face; such majesty she carries about her, that her most prosperous enemies are fain to whisper their treason; all the power upon the earth can never extinguish her; she has lived in all ages; and let the mistaken zeal of prevailing authority christen an opposition to it with what name they please, she makes it not only an ugly and unmannerly, but a dangerous thing to persist. She has lived very retired indeed, nay, sometimes so buried, that only some few of the discerning parts of mankind could have a glimpse of her; with all that, she has eternity in her, she knows not how to die, and from the darkest clouds that shade and cover her, she breaks from time to time with triumph for her friends, and terror to her enemies.

Our *Trimmer*, therefore, inspired by this divine virtue, thinks fit to conclude with these assertions: that our climate is a *Trimmer*, between that part of the world where men are roasted, and the other where they are frozen; that our church is a *Trimmer*, between the phrenzy of Platonic visions, and the lethargic ignorance of popish dreams; that our laws are *Trimmers*, between the excess of unbounded power, and the extravagance of liberty not enough restrained; that true virtue has ever been thought a *Trimmer*, and to have its dwelling in the middle between the two extremes; that even God Almighty Himself is divided between His two great attributes, His mercy and His justice. In such company, our *Trimmer* is not ashamed of his name, and willingly leaves to the bold champions of either extreme the honour of contending with no less adversaries than nature, religion, liberty, prudence, humanity, and common sense.

CONDUCT OF LIFE

SIR THOMAS MORE, *Utopia.* Preface to Peter Giles. 1516

WHEN I am come home, I must commune with my wife, chat with my children, and talk with my servants. All the which things I reckon and accompt among business, forasmuch as they must of necessity be done: and done they must needs be, unless a man will be stranger in his own house. And in any wise a man must so fashion and order his conditions, and so appoint and dispose himself, that he be merry, jocund and pleasant among them, whom either nature hath provided, or chance hath made, or he himself hath chosen to be the fellows and companions of his life: so that with too much gentle behaviour and familiarity he do not mar them, and by too much sufferance of his servants make them his masters.

UNTIL PHILOSOPHERS ARE KINGS

PLATO, *Republic*, c. 390 B.C. Book V. Translated by Benjamin Jowett. 1871

UNTIL philosophers are kings, or the kings and princes of this world have the spirit and power of philosophy, and political greatness and wisdom meet in one, and those commoner natures who pursue either to the exclusion of the other are compelled to stand aside, cities will never have rest from their evils,—no, nor the human race, as I believe,—and then only will this our State have a possibility of life and behold the light of day.

CITIES OF MEN

To build cities and to live in them properly is the great business of large associations of men.

W. R. LETHABY, 1920

Did we not see from the Delectable Mountains the gate of the city?

JOHN BUNYAN, 1678

BABYLON

HERODOTUS, *History*, c. 446 B.C. Book I. Translated
by George Rawlinson. 1858

THE city stands on a broad plain, and is an exact square, a
hundred and twenty furlongs in length each way, so that the
entire circuit is four hundred and eighty furlongs. While such
is its size, in magnificence there is no other city that approaches
to it. It is surrounded, in the first place, by a broad and deep
moat, full of water, behind which rises a wall fifty royal cubits
in width, and two hundred in height. (The royal cubit is
longer by three fingers' breadth than the common cubit.)

And here I may not omit to tell the use to which the mould
dug out of the great moat was turned, nor the manner wherein
the wall was wrought. As fast as they dug the moat the soil
which they got from the cutting was made into bricks, and
when a sufficient number were completed they baked the
bricks in kilns. Then they set to building, and began with
bricking the borders of the moat, after which they proceeded
to construct the wall itself, using throughout for their cement
hot bitumen, and interposing a layer of wattled reeds at every
thirtieth course of the bricks. On the top, along the edges
of the wall, they constructed buildings of a single chamber
facing one another, leaving between them room for a four-
horse chariot to turn. In the circuit of the wall are a hundred
gates, all of brass, with brazen lintels and side-posts. The
bitumen used in this work was brought to Babylon from the
Is, a small stream which flows into the Euphrates at the point
where the city of the same name stands, eight days' journey
from Babylon. Lumps of bitumen are found in great abundance in this river.

The city is divided into two portions by the river which
runs through the midst of it. This river is the Euphrates, a
broad, deep, swift stream, which rises in Armenia, and empties
itself into the Erythræan sea. The city wall is brought down
on both sides to the edge of the stream: thence, from the

corners of the wall, there is carried along each bank of the river a fence of burnt bricks. The houses are mostly three and four stories high; the streets all run in straight lines, not only those parallel to the river, but also the cross streets which lead down to the water-side. At the river end of these cross streets are low gates in the fence that skirts the stream, which are, like the great gates in the outer wall, of brass, and open on the water.

The outer wall is the main defence of the city. There is, however, a second inner wall, of less thickness than the first, but very little inferior to it in strength. The centre of each division of the town was occupied by a fortress. In the one stood the palace of the kings, surrounded by a wall of great strength and size: in the other was the sacred precinct of Jupiter Belus, a square enclosure two furlongs each way, with gates of solid brass, which was also remaining in my time. In the middle of the precinct there was a tower of solid masonry, a furlong in length and breadth, upon which was raised a second tower, and on that a third, and so on up to eight. The ascent to the top is on the outside, by a path which winds round all the towers. When one is about half-way up, one finds a resting-place and seats, where persons are wont to sit some time on their way to the summit. On the topmost tower there is a spacious temple, and inside the temple stands a couch of unusual size, richly adorned, with a golden table by its side.

TYRE

The Book of the Prophet Ezekiel, c. 570 B.C. Chap. xxvii, 3–25. Revised Version. 1884

O THOU that dwellest at the entry of the sea, which art the merchant of the peoples unto many isles....Thou, O Tyre, hast said, I am perfect in beauty. Thy borders are in the heart of the seas, thy builders have perfected thy beauty.

They have made all thy planks of fir trees from Senir: they have taken cedars from Lebanon to make a mast for thee. Of the oaks of Bashan have they made thine oars; they have made thy benches of ivory inlaid in boxwood, from the isles of Kittim. Of fine linen with broidered work from Egypt was thy sail, that it might be to thee for an ensign; blue and purple from the isles of Elishah was thine awning. The inhabitants of Zidon and Arvad were thy rowers: thy wise men, O Tyre, were in thee, they were thy pilots. The ancients of Gebal and the wise men thereof were in thee thy calkers: all the ships of the sea with their mariners were in thee to occupy thy merchandise.

Persia and Lud and Put were in thine army, thy men of war: they hanged the shield and helmet in thee; they set forth thy comeliness. The men of Arvad with thine army were upon thy walls round about, and the Gammadim were in thy towers: they hanged their shields upon thy walls round about; they have perfected thy beauty.

Tarshish was thy merchant by reason of the multitude of all kinds of riches; with silver, iron, tin, and lead, they traded for thy wares. Javan, Tubal, and Meshech, they were thy traffickers: they traded the persons of men and vessels of brass for thy merchandise. They of the house of Togarmah traded for thy wares with horses and war-horses and mules. The men of Dedan were thy traffickers: many isles were the mart of thine hand: they brought thee in exchange horns of ivory and ebony.

Syria was thy merchant by reason of the multitude of thy handyworks: they traded for thy wares with emeralds, purple, and broidered work, and fine linen, and coral, and rubies. Judah, and the land of Israel, they were thy traffickers: they traded for thy merchandise wheat of Minnith, and pannag, and honey, and oil, and balm. Damascus was thy merchant for the multitude of thy handyworks, by reason of the multitude of all kinds of riches; with the wine of Helbon, and white wool.

Vedan and Javan traded with yarn for thy wares: bright iron, cassia, and calamus, were among thy merchandise. Dedan was thy trafficker in precious cloths for riding. Arabia, and all the princes of Kedar, they were the merchants of thy hand; in lambs, and rams, and goats, in these were they thy

merchants. The traffickers of Sheba and Raamah, they were
thy traffickers: they traded for thy wares with chief of all
spices, and with all precious stones, and gold. Haran and
Canneh and Eden, the traffickers of Sheba, Asshur and
Chilmad, were thy traffickers.

These were thy traffickers in choice wares, in wrappings of
blue and broidered work, and in chests of rich apparel, bound
with cords and made of cedar, among thy merchandise. The
ships of Tarshish were thy caravans for thy merchandise: and
thou wast replenished, and made very glorious in the heart of
the seas.

ATHENS

THUCYDIDES, *History of the Peloponnesian War*, c. 400 B.C.
Book II. Translated by Richard Crawley. 1874.
From the Funeral Speech of Pericles

OUR constitution does not copy the laws of neighbouring
states; we are rather a pattern to others than imitators ourselves. Its administration favours the many instead of the
few; this is why it is called a democracy. If we look to the
laws, they afford equal justice to all in their private differences; if to social standing, advancement in public life falls to
reputation for capacity, class considerations not being allowed
to interfere with merit; nor again does poverty bar the way,
if a man is able to serve the state, he is not hindered by the
obscurity of his condition. The freedom which we enjoy in our
government extends also to our ordinary life. There, far from
exercising a jealous surveillance over each other, we do not
feel called upon to be angry with our neighbour for doing
what he likes, or even to indulge in those injurious looks
which cannot fail to be offensive, although they inflict no
positive penalty. But all this ease in our private relations
does not make us lawless as citizens. Against this fear is our
chief safeguard, teaching us to obey the magistrates and the
laws, particularly such as regard the protection of the injured,
whether they are actually on the statute book, or belong to

that code which, although unwritten, yet cannot be broken without acknowledged disgrace.

Further, we provide plenty of means for the mind to refresh itself from business. We celebrate games and sacrifices all the year round, and the elegance of our private establishments forms a daily source of pleasure and helps to banish the spleen; while the magnitude of our city draws the produce of the world into our harbour, so that to the Athenian the fruits of other countries are as familiar a luxury as those of his own.

If we turn to our military policy, there also we differ from our antagonists. We throw open our city to the world, and never by alien acts exclude foreigners from any opportunity of learning or observing, although the eyes of an enemy may occasionally profit by our liberality; trusting less in system and policy than to the native spirit of our citizens; while in education, where our rivals from their very cradles by a painful discipline seek after manliness, at Athens we live exactly as we please, and yet are just as ready to encounter every legitimate danger. In proof of this it may be noticed that the Lacedæmonians do not invade our country alone, but bring with them all their confederates; while we Athenians advance unsupported into the territory of a neighbour, and fighting upon a foreign soil usually vanquish with ease men who are defending their homes. Our united force was never yet encountered by any enemy, because we have at once to attend to our marine and to despatch our citizens by land upon a hundred different services; so that, wherever they engage with some such fraction of our strength, a success against a detachment is magnified into a victory over the nation, and a defeat into a reverse suffered at the hands of our entire people. And yet if with habits not of labour but of ease, and courage not of art but of nature, we are still willing to encounter danger, we have the double advantage of escaping the experience of hardships in anticipation and of facing them in the hour of need as fearlessly as those who are never free from them.

Nor are these the only points in which our city is worthy of admiration. We cultivate refinement without extravagance and knowledge without effeminacy; wealth we employ more for use than for show, and place the real disgrace of poverty not in owning to the fact but in declining the struggle against it. Our public men have, besides politics, their private affairs to attend to, and our ordinary citizens, though occupied with the pursuits of industry, are still fair judges of public matters; for, unlike any other nation, regarding him who takes no part in these duties not as unambitious but as useless, we Athenians are able to judge at all events if we cannot originate, and instead of looking on discussion as a stumbling-block in the way of action, we think it an indispensable preliminary to any wise action at all. Again, in our enterprises we present the singular spectacle of daring and deliberation, each carried to its highest point, and both united in the same persons; although usually decision is the fruit of ignorance, hesitation of reflection. But the palm of courage will surely be adjudged most justly to those, who best know the difference between hardship and pleasure and yet are never tempted to shrink from danger. In generosity we are equally singular, acquiring our friends by conferring not by receiving favours. Yet, of course, the doer of the favour is the firmer friend of the two, in order by continued kindness to keep the recipient in his debt; while the debtor feels less keenly from the very consciousness that the return he makes will be a payment, not a free gift. And it is only the Athenians who, fearless of consequences, confer their benefits not from calculations of expediency, but in the confidence of liberality.

In short, I say that as a city we are the school of Hellas; while I doubt if the world can produce a man, who where he has only himself to depend upon, is equal to so many emergencies, and graced by so happy a versatility as the Athenian. And that this is no mere boast thrown out for the occasion, but plain matter of fact, the power of the state acquired by these habits proves. For Athens alone of her contemporaries is found when tested to be greater than her reputation, and alone gives no occasion to her assailants to blush at the antagonist by whom they have been worsted, or to her subjects to question her title by merit to rule. Rather, the admiration of the present and succeeding ages will be ours, since we have not left our power without witness, but have shown it by

mighty proofs; and far from needing a Homer for our pane-
gyrist, or other of his craft whose verses might charm for the
moment only for the impression which they gave to melt at
the touch of fact, we have forced every sea and land to be the
highway of our daring, and everywhere, whether for evil or
for good, have left imperishable monuments behind us. Such
is the Athens for which these men, in the assertion of their
resolve not to lose her, nobly fought and died; and well may
every one of their survivors be ready to suffer in her cause.

CARTHAGE

EDWARD AUGUSTUS FREEMAN, "Carthage",
Contemporary Review. 1890

SHE stood alone. She was lady and mistress over her scattered dominions, commanding the resources of lands and
towns, far and near, in every relation of subjection and dependence; but she stood aloof from all, incorporating none
into her own body. She waged her wars by the hands of
strangers. She commanded the services of subjects and dependents; she bought the services of the stoutest barbarians
of the Western world. Her own citizens were but the guiding
spirits of her armies; they never formed their substance and
kernel. It was only in moments of special danger, on her own
soil or on the neighbouring soil of Sicily, that the Sacred Band
went forth to jeopard their lives for the Carthaginian state.
In a Roman army, an army of citizens and kindred allies,
every life was precious. A Carthaginian army might win a
crowning victory, it might undergo a crushing defeat, with
the loss of no lives but such as the gold of Carthage could soon
replace. Here lay her strength and her weakness. A Punic
general could risk his soldiers as even a tyrant could not risk
Greek citizens; but the state of Carthage lived ever in fear of
her hireling swordsmen. The great mutiny of the mercenaries
after the first war with Rome was but the most frightful of
several. It is a ghastly but characteristic tale that Osteôdes,

the Isle of Bones, the modern Ustica, took its name from a mutinous detachment of a Punic army who were left there to perish. A Roman army fought for Rome; a Punic army never fought for Carthage....

All this at once distinguishes Carthage from those ruling cities, Rome the chief of all, which commanded a continuous dominion. That is almost the same thing as saying that her parallels, if she has parallels, must be sought for among sea-faring powers only. The life by sea was the very life of Carthage. When the Romans before the last siege made it a condition of peace that Carthage should be forsaken and some point ten miles from the sea occupied instead, every Carthaginian felt it to be a sentence of death. Athens could not be great without her fleet; but she could live without it. She had for a moment a scattered dominion of somewhat the same kind as the dominion of Carthage; but it was only for a moment. No other city of old Greece, no other city of her own Phœnician stock, comes near enough to her to admit even of contrast. The mediæval world supplies nearer parallels. Among cities of our own race, as we are tempted to call Bern the Teutonic Rome, so are we tempted to call Lübeck the Teutonic Carthage. But neither Lübeck nor any of her Hanseatic sisters fully reproduces the old Phœnician model. They are mighty on the sea, mighty for trade, mighty for warfare; but their special character was to be mighty in both ways, to strike terror and to bear rule, without forming anything which could be called territorial dominion. Far nearer to Carthage are the later seafaring cities of her own Mediterranean waters, Genoa in some measure, Venice in a higher. Venice indeed is the nearest reproduction of Carthage that the world has seen. She too united trade and dominion; she ruled from her islands, as Carthage ruled from her peninsula, over possessions scattered far and wide, fortresses, cities, islands, kingdoms, over all of which she exercised lordship, but none of whom did she or could she incorporate into her own commonwealth....

Among all the great powers of the past, Phœnician Carthage seems to stand alone, in being simply a memory, in having had no direct effect on the later history of the world.... The law of Rome, the tongue and the thoughts of Greece, are essential parts of the civilization of modern Europe. But to Carthage, as far as we can see, we owe nothing. Directly we certainly owe nothing; indirectly Carthage has changed the history of the world in whatever proportion the history of Rome must have been other than what it actually was if Carthage had never been. To Carthage as Carthage, to the great seafaring power of the Western Mediterranean, we owe absolutely nothing.... The Phœnician who founded the elder Carthage has been our master in nothing, save in the warnings, many and grave, which the history of his scattered dominion may give to us into whose hands a dominion of like sort has fallen.

CITIES OF THE ROMAN EMPIRE

EDWARD GIBBON, *Decline and Fall of the Roman Empire.*
Vol. I, chap. ii. 1776

ANCIENT Italy is said to have contained eleven hundred and ninety-seven cities; and for whatsoever era of antiquity the expression might be intended, there is not any reason to believe the country less populous in the age of the Antonines than in that of Romulus. The petty states of Latium were contained within the metropolis of the empire, by whose superior influence they had been attracted. Those parts of Italy which have so long languished under the lazy tyranny of priests and viceroys, had been afflicted only by the more tolerable calamities of war; and the first symptoms of decay which *they* experienced were amply compensated by the rapid improvements of the Cisalpine Gaul. The splendour of Verona may be traced in its remains: yet Verona was less celebrated than Aquileia or Padua, Milan or Ravenna. The spirit of improvement had passed the Alps, and been felt even in the woods of Britain, which were gradually cleared away to open a free space for convenient and elegant habitations. York was the seat of government; London was already enriched by commerce; and Bath was celebrated for the salutary effects of its medicinal waters. Gaul could boast of her twelve hundred cities; and though, in the northern parts, many of them, without excepting Paris itself, were little more than the rude and imperfect townships of a rising people; the southern provinces imitated the wealth and elegance of Italy. Many were the cities of Gaul, Marseilles, Arles, Nismes, Narbonne, Thoulouse, Bourdeaux, Autun, Vienna, Lyons, Langres, and Treves, whose ancient condition might sustain an equal, and perhaps advantageous comparison with their present state. With regard to Spain, that country flourished as a province, and has declined as a kingdom. Exhausted by the abuse of her strength, by America, and by superstition, her pride might possibly be confounded, if we required such a list of three hundred and sixty cities, as Pliny has exhibited under the reign of Vespasian. Three hundred African cities had once acknowledged the authority of Carthage, nor is it likely that their numbers diminished under the administration of the emperors: Carthage itself rose with new splendour from its ashes; and that capital, as well as Capua and Corinth, soon recovered all the advantages which can be separated from independent sovereignty. The provinces of the east present the contrast of Roman magnificence with Turkish barbarism. The ruins of antiquity scattered over uncultivated fields, and ascribed, by ignorance, to the power of magic, scarcely afford a shelter to the oppressed peasant or wandering Arab. Under the reign of the Caesars, the proper Asia alone contained five hundred populous cities, enriched with all the gifts of nature, and adorned with all the refinements of art. Eleven cities of Asia had once disputed the honour of dedicating a temple to Tiberius, and their respective merits were examined by the senate. Four of them were immediately rejected as unequal to the burden; and among these was Laodicea, whose splendour is still displayed in its ruins. Laodicea collected a very considerable revenue from its flocks of sheep, celebrated for the fineness of their wool, and had received, a little before the contest, a legacy of above four hundred thousand pounds by the testament of a generous citizen. If such was the poverty of Laodicea, what must have been the wealth of those cities, whose claim appeared preferable, and particularly of Pergamus, of Smyrna, and of Ephesus, who so long disputed with each other the titular primacy of Asia. The capitals of Syria and Egypt held a still superior rank in the empire: Antioch and Alexandria looked down with disdain on a crowd of dependent cities, and yielded, with reluctance, to the majesty of Rome itself.

THE TOWERS OF JERUSALEM

Flavius Josephus, *Wars of the Jews*, c. a.d. 80. Book v, chap. iv. Translated by William Whiston. 1737

They were many in number, and the steps by which you ascended up to them were every one broad: of these towers, then, the third wall had ninety, and the spaces between them were each two hundred cubits; but in the middle wall were forty towers, and the old wall was parted into sixty, while the whole compass of the city was thirty-three furlongs. Now the third wall was all of it wonderful; yet was the tower Psephinus elevated above it at the north-west corner, and there Titus pitched his own tent: for being seventy cubits high it both afforded a prospect of Arabia at sun-rising as well as it did of the utmost limits of the Hebrew possessions at the sea westward. Moreover, it was an octagon, and over against it was the tower Hippicus, and hard by two others were erected by King Herod in the old wall. These were for largeness, beauty, and strength beyond all that were in the habitable earth; for besides the magnanimity of his nature and his magnificence towards the city on other occasions, he built these after such an extraordinary manner to gratify his own private affections, and dedicated these towers to the memory of those three persons who had been the dearest to him, and from whom he named them. They were his brother, his friend, and his wife. . . . Hippicus, so named from his friend, was square, its length and breadth were each twenty-five cubits and its height thirty, and it had no vacuity in it. Over this solid

building, which was composed of great stones united together, there was a reservoir twenty cubits deep, over which
there was a house of two stories, whose height was twenty-
five cubits, and divided into several parts; over which were
battlements of two cubits, and turrets all round of three
cubits high, insomuch that the entire height added together
amounted to four score cubits. The second tower, which he
named from his brother Phasaelus, had its breadth and its
height equal, each of them forty cubits, over which was its
solid height of forty cubits; over which a cloister went round
about whose height was ten cubits, and it was covered from
enemies by breast-works and bulwarks. There was also built
over that cloister another tower, parted into magnificent
rooms and a place for bathing, so that this tower wanted
nothing that might make it appear to be a royal palace. It
was also adorned with battlements and turrets, more than
was the foregoing, and the entire altitude was about ninety
cubits; the appearance of it resembled the tower of Pharus,
which exhibited a fire to such as sailed to Alexandria, but was
much larger than it in compass. This was now converted to
a house wherein Simon exercised his tyrannical authority.
The third tower was Mariamne, for that was the queen's
name; it was solid as high as twenty cubits; its breadth and
its length were twenty cubits and were equal to each other;
its upper buildings were more magnificent and had greater
variety than the other towers had; for the king thought it
most proper for him to adorn that which was denominated
from his wife better than those denominated from men, as
those were built stronger than this that bore his wife's name.
The entire height of this tower was fifty cubits.

Now as these towers were so very tall they appeared much
taller by the place on which they stood; for that very old
wall wherein they were was built on a high hill, and was itself
a kind of elevation that was still thirty cubits taller, over
which were the towers situated, and thereby were made much
higher to appearance. The largeness also of the stones was
wonderful; for they were not made of common small stones
nor of such large ones only as men could carry, but they were
of white marble cut out of the rock; each stone was twenty

cubits in length, and ten in breadth, and five in depth. They
were so exactly united to one another that each tower looked
like one entire rock of stone, so growing naturally, and afterwards cut by the hands of the artificers into their present
shape and corners; so little or not at all did their joints or
connection appear. Now as these towers were themselves on
the north side of the wall, the king had a palace inwardly
thereto adjoined which exceeds all my ability to describe it;
for it was so very curious as to want no cost nor skill in its
construction, but was entirely walled about to the height of
thirty cubits, and was adorned with towers at equal distances,
and with large bed-chambers that would contain beds for a
hundred guests apiece, in which the variety of the stones is
not to be expressed, for a large quantity of those that were
rare of that kind was collected together. Their roofs were also
wonderful, both for the length of the beams and the splendour
of their ornaments. The number of the rooms was also very
great, and the variety of the figures that were about them was
prodigious; their furniture was complete, and the greatest
part of the vessels that were put in them were of silver and
gold. There were besides many porticoes one beyond another
round about, and in each of those porticoes curious pillars;
yet were all the courts that were exposed to the air everywhere green. There were, moreover, several groves of trees
and long walks through them, with deep canals and cisterns,
that in several parts were filled with brazen statues, through
which the water ran out. There were withal many dove-
courts of tame pigeons about the canals. But indeed it is not
possible to give a complete description of these palaces, and
the very remembrance of them is a torment to one.

ROME

EDWARD GIBBON, *Decline and Fall of the Roman Empire.*
Vol. III, chap. xxxi. 1781

"THE greatness of Rome (such is the language of the historian) was founded on the rare and almost incredible alliance of virtue and of fortune. The long period of her infancy was employed in a laborious struggle against the tribes of Italy, the neighbours and enemies of the rising city. In the strength and ardour of youth she sustained the storms of war, carried her victorious arms beyond the seas and the mountains, and brought home triumphal laurels from every country of the globe. At length, verging towards old age, and sometimes conquering by the terror only of her name, she sought the blessings of ease and tranquillity. The VENERABLE CITY, which had trampled on the necks of the fiercest nations, and established a system of laws, the perpetual guardians of justice and freedom, was content, like a wise and wealthy parent, to devolve on the Caesars, her favourite sons, the care of governing her ample patrimony. A secure and profound peace, such as had been once enjoyed in the reign of Numa, succeeded to the tumults of a republic; while Rome was still adored as the queen of the earth, and the subject nations still reverenced the name of the people and the majesty of the senate. But this native splendour (continues Ammianus) is degraded and sullied by the conduct of some nobles, who, unmindful of their own dignity and of that of their country, assume an unbounded licence of vice and folly. They contend with each other in the empty vanity of titles and surnames, and curiously select or invent the most lofty and sonorous appellations—Reburrus or Fabunius, Pagonius or Tarrasius—which may impress the ears of the vulgar with astonishment and respect. From a vain ambition of perpetuating their memory, they affect to multiply their likeness in statues of bronze and marble; nor are they satisfied unless those statues are covered with plates of gold; an honourable distinction, first granted to Acilius the consul, after he had subdued by his arms and counsels the power of king Antiochus. The ostentation of displaying, of magnifying perhaps, the rent-roll of the estates which they possess in all the provinces, from the rising to the setting sun, provokes the just resentment of every man who recollects that their poor and invincible ancestors were not distinguished from the meanest of the soldiers by the delicacy of their food or the splendour of their apparel. But the modern nobles measure their rank and consequence according to the loftiness of their chariots, and the weighty magnificence of their dress. Their long robes of silk and purple float in the wind; and as they are agitated, by art or accident, they occasionally discover the under garments, the rich tunics, embroidered with the figures of various animals. Followed by a train of fifty servants, and tearing up the pavement, they move along the streets with the same impetuous speed as if they travelled with post-horses; and the example of the senators is boldly imitated by the matrons and ladies, whose covered carriages are continually driving round the immense space of the city and suburbs. Whenever these persons of high distinction condescend to visit the public baths, they assume, on their entrance, a tone of loud and insolent command, and appropriate to their own use the conveniences which were designed for the Roman people. If, in these places of mixed and general resort, they meet any of the infamous ministers of their pleasures, they express their affection by a tender embrace, while they proudly decline the salutations of their fellow-citizens, who are not permitted to aspire above the honour of kissing their hands or their knees. As soon as they have indulged themselves in the refreshment of the bath, they resume their rings and the other ensigns of their dignity, select from their private wardrobe of the finest linen, such as might suffice for a dozen persons, the garments the most agreeable to their fancy, and maintain till their departure the same haughty demeanour, which perhaps might have been excused in the great Marcellus after the conquest of Syracuse. Sometimes indeed these heroes undertake more arduous achievements: they visit their estates in Italy, and procure themselves, by the toil of servile hands, the amusements of the chase. If at any time, but more especially on a hot day, they have courage to sail in their painted galleys from the Lucrine lake to their elegant villas on the sea-coast of Puteoli and Caieta, they compare their own expeditions to the marches of Caesar and Alexander. Yet should a fly presume to settle on the silken folds of their gilded umbrellas, should a sunbeam penetrate through some unguarded and imperceptible chink, they deplore their intolerable hardships, and lament in affected language that they were not born in the land of the Cimmerians, the regions of eternal darkness. In these journeys into the country the whole body of the household marches with their master. In the same manner as the cavalry and infantry, the heavy and the light armed troops, the advanced guard and the rear, are marshalled by the skill of their military leaders, so the domestic officers, who bear a rod as an ensign of authority, distribute and arrange the numerous train of slaves and attendants. The baggage and wardrobe move in the front, and are immediately followed by a multitude of cooks and inferior ministers employed in the service of the kitchens and of the table. The main body is composed of a promiscuous crowd of slaves, increased by the accidental concourse of idle or dependent plebeians. The rear is closed by the favourite band of eunuchs, distributed from age to youth, according to the order of seniority. Their numbers and their deformity excite the horror of the indignant spectators, who are ready to execrate the memory of Semiramis for the cruel art which she invented of frustrating the purposes of nature, and of blasting in the bud the hopes of future generations. In the exercise of domestic jurisdiction the nobles of Rome express an exquisite sensibility for any personal injury, and a contemptuous indifference for the rest of the human species. When they have called for warm water, if a slave has been tardy in his obedience, he is instantly chastised with three hundred lashes; but should the same slave commit a wilful murder, the master will mildly observe that he is a worthless fellow, but that if he repeats the offence he shall not escape punishment. Hospitality was formerly the virtue of the Romans; and every stranger who could plead either merit or misfortune was relieved or rewarded by their generosity. At present, if a foreigner, perhaps of no contemptible rank, is introduced to

one of the proud and wealthy senators, he is welcomed indeed
in the first audience with such warm professions and such kind
inquiries, that he retires enchanted with the affability of his
illustrious friend, and full of regret that he had so long delayed
his journey to Rome, the native seat of manners as well as of
empire. Secure of a favourable reception, he repeats his visit
the ensuing day, and is mortified by the discovery that his
person, his name, and his country are already forgotten. If
he still has resolution to persevere, he is gradually numbered
in the train of dependents, and obtains the permission to pay
his assiduous and unprofitable court to a haughty patron,
incapable of gratitude or friendship, who scarcely deigns to
remark his presence, his departure, or his return. Whenever
the rich prepare a solemn and popular entertainment, whenever they celebrate with profuse and pernicious luxury their
private banquets, the choice of the guests is the subject of
anxious deliberation. The modest, the sober, and the learned
are seldom preferred; and the nomenclators, who are commonly swayed by interested motives, have the address to
insert in the list of invitations the obscure names of the most
worthless of mankind. But the frequent and familiar companions of the great are those parasites who practise the most
useful of all arts, the art of flattery; who eagerly applaud each
word and every action of their immortal patron; gaze with
rapture on his marble columns and variegated pavements,
and strenuously praise the pomp and elegance which he is
taught to consider as a part of his personal merit. At the
Roman tables the birds, the squirrels, or the fish, which appear
of an uncommon size, are contemplated with curious attention; a pair of scales is accurately applied to ascertain their
real weight; and, while the more rational guests are disgusted
by the vain and tedious repetition, notaries are summoned
to attest by an authentic record the truth of such a marvellous
event. Another method of introduction into the houses and
society of the great is derived from the profession of gaming,
or, as it is more politely styled, of play. The confederates
are united by a strict and indissoluble bond of friendship, or
rather of conspiracy; a superior degree of skill in the *Tesse-
rarian* art (which may be interpreted the game of dice and

tables) is a sure road to wealth and reputation. A master of that sublime science, who in a supper or assembly is placed below a magistrate, displays in his countenance the surprise and indignation which Cato might be supposed to feel when he was refused the praetorship by the votes of a capricious people. The acquisition of knowledge seldom engages the curiosity of the nobles, who abhor the fatigue and disdain the advantages of study; and the only books which they peruse are the Satires of Juvenal, and the verbose and fabulous histories of Marius Maximus. The libraries which they have inherited from their fathers are secluded, like dreary sepulchres, from the light of day. But the costly instruments of the theatre, flutes, and enormous lyres, and hydraulic organs, are constructed for their use; and the harmony of vocal and instrumental music is incessantly repeated in the palaces of Rome. In those palaces sound is preferred to sense, and the care of the body to that of the mind. It is allowed as a salutary maxim, that the light and frivolous suspicion of a contagious malady is of sufficient weight to excuse the visits of the most intimate friends; and even the servants who are despatched to make the decent inquiries are not suffered to return home till they have undergone the ceremony of a previous ablution. Yet this selfish and unmanly delicacy occasionally yields to the more imperious passion of avarice. The prospect of gain will urge a rich and gouty senator as far as Spoleto; every sentiment of arrogance and dignity is subdued by the hopes of an inheritance, or even of a legacy; and a wealthy childless citizen is the most powerful of the Romans. The art of obtaining the signature of a favourable testament, and sometimes of hastening the moment of its execution, is perfectly understood; and it has happened that in the same house, though in different apartments, a husband and a wife, with the laudable design of overreaching each other, have summoned their respective lawyers, to declare at the same time their mutual but contradictory intentions. The distress which follows and chastises extravagant luxury often reduces the great to the use of the most humiliating expedients. When they desire to borrow, they employ the base and supplicating style of the slave in the comedy; but when they are called upon to pay, they assume the royal and tragic declamation of the grandsons of Hercules. If the demand is repeated, they readily procure some trusty sycophant, instructed to maintain a charge of poison, or magic, against the insolent creditor, who is seldom released from prison till he has signed a discharge of the whole debt. These vices, which degrade the moral character of the Romans, are mixed with a puerile superstition that disgraces their understanding. They listen with confidence to the predictions of haruspices, who pretend to read in the entrails of victims the signs of future greatness and prosperity; and there are many who do not presume either to bathe or to die, or to appear in public, till they have diligently consulted, according to the rules of astrology, the situation of Mercury and the aspect of the moon. It is singular enough that this vain credulity may often be discovered among the profane sceptics who impiously doubt or deny the existence of a celestial power...."

As early as the time of Hadrian it was the just complaint of the ingenuous natives that the capital had attracted the vices of the universe and the manners of the most opposite nations. The intemperance of the Gauls, the cunning and levity of the Greeks, the savage obstinacy of the Egyptians and Jews, the servile temper of the Asiatics, and the dissolute, effeminate prostitution of the Syrians, were mingled in the various multitude, which, under the proud and false denomination of Romans, presumed to despise their fellow-subjects, and even their sovereigns, who dwelt beyond the precincts of the ETERNAL CITY.

Yet the name of that city was still pronounced with respect: the frequent and capricious tumults of its inhabitants were indulged with impunity; and the successors of Constantine, instead of crushing the last remains of the democracy by the strong arm of military power, embraced the mild policy of Augustus, and studied to relieve the poverty and to amuse the idleness of an innumerable people. For the convenience of the lazy plebeians, the monthly distributions of corn were converted into a daily allowance of bread; a great number of ovens were constructed and maintained at the public expense; and at the appointed hour, each citizen, who was furnished with a ticket, ascended the flight of steps which had been assigned to his peculiar quarter or division, and received, either as a gift or at a very low price, a loaf of bread of the weight of three pounds for the use of his family. The forests of Lucania, whose acorns fattened large droves of wild hogs, afforded, as a species of tribute, a plentiful supply of cheap and wholesome meat. During five months of the year a regular allowance of bacon was distributed to the poorer citizens; and the annual consumption of the capital, at a time when it was much declined from its former lustre, was as-certained, by an edict of Valentinian the Third, at three millions six hundred and twenty-eight thousand pounds. In the manners of antiquity the use of oil was indispensable for the lamp as well as for the bath, and the annual tax which was imposed on Africa for the benefit of Rome amounted to the weight of three millions of pounds, to the measure, per-haps, of three hundred thousand English gallons. The anxiety of Augustus to provide the metropolis with sufficient plenty of corn was not extended beyond that necessary article of human subsistence; and when the popular clamour accused the dearness and scarcity of wine, a proclamation was issued by the grave reformer to remind his subjects that no man could reasonably complain of thirst, since the aqueducts of Agrippa had introduced into the city so many copious streams of pure and salubrious water. This rigid sobriety was insensibly relaxed; and, although the generous design of Aurelian does not appear to have been executed in its full extent, the use of wine was allowed on very easy and liberal terms. The ad-ministration of the public cellars was delegated to a magistrate of honourable rank; and a considerable part of the vintage of Campania was reserved for the fortunate inhabitants of Rome.

The stupendous aqueducts, so justly celebrated by the praises of Augustus himself, replenished the *Thermae*, or baths, which had been constructed in every part of the city with Imperial magnificence. The baths of Antoninus Cara-calla, which were open, at stated hours, for the indiscriminate service of the senators and the people, contained above six-teen hundred seats of marble; and more than three thousand were reckoned in the baths of Diocletian. The walls of the lofty apartments were covered with curious mosaics, that imitated the art of the pencil in the elegance of design and the variety of colours. The Egyptian granite was beautifully encrusted with the precious green marble of Numidia; the perpetual stream of hot water was poured into the capacious basins through so many wide mouths of bright and massy silver; and the meanest Roman could purchase, with a small copper coin, the daily enjoyment of a scene of pomp and luxury which might excite the envy of the kings of Asia. From these stately palaces issued a swarm of dirty and ragged plebeians, without shoes and without a mantle; who loitered away whole days in the streets or Forum to hear news and to hold disputes; who dissipated in extravagant gaming the miserable pittance of their wives and children; and spent the hours of the night in obscure taverns and brothels in the indulgence of gross and vulgar sensuality.

But the most lively and splendid amusement of the idle multitude depended on the frequent exhibition of public games and spectacles. The piety of Christian princes had suppressed the inhuman combats of gladiators; but the Roman people still considered the Circus as their home, their temple, and the seat of the republic. The impatient crowd rushed at the dawn of day to secure their places, and there were many who passed a sleepless and anxious night in the adjacent porticoes. From the morning to the evening, careless of the sun or of the rain, the spectators, who sometimes amounted to the number of four hundred thousand, remained in eager attention; their eyes fixed on the horses and charioteers, their minds agitated with hope and fear for the success of the *colours* which they espoused; and the happiness of Rome appeared to hang on the event of a race. The same immoderate ardour inspired their clamours and their applause as often as they were entertained with the hunting of wild beasts and the various modes of theatrical representation. These representations in modern capitals may deserve to be considered as a pure and elegant school of taste, and perhaps of virtue. But the Tragic and Comic Muse of the Romans, who seldom aspired beyond the imitation of Attic genius, had been almost

totally silent since the fall of the republic; and their place was
unworthily occupied by licentious farce, effeminate music,
and splendid pageantry. The pantomimes, who maintained
their reputation from the age of Augustus to the sixth century,
expressed, without the use of words, the various fables of the
gods and heroes of antiquity; and the perfection of their art,
which sometimes disarmed the gravity of the philosopher,
always excited the applause and wonder of the people. The
vast and magnificent theatres of Rome were filled by three
thousand female dancers, and by three thousand singers, with
the masters of the respective choruses. Such was the popular
favour which they enjoyed, that, in a time of scarcity, when
all strangers were banished from the city, the merit of con-
tributing to the public pleasures exempted *them* from a law
which was strictly executed against the professors of the
liberal arts.

It is said that the foolish curiosity of Elagabalus attempted
to discover, from the quantity of spiders' webs, the number of
the inhabitants of Rome. A more rational method of inquiry
might not have been undeserving of the attention of the wisest
princes, who could easily have resolved a question so important for the Roman government and so interesting to succeeding ages. The births and deaths of the citizens were duly
registered; and if any writer of antiquity had condescended
to mention the annual amount, or the common average, we
might now produce some satisfactory calculation which would
destroy the extravagant assertions of critics, and perhaps
confirm the modest and probable conjectures of philosophers.
The most diligent researches have collected only the following
circumstances, which, slight and imperfect as they are, may
tend in some degree to illustrate the question of the populousness of ancient Rome. When the capital of the empire was besieged by the Goths, the circuit of the walls was accurately
measured by Ammonius, the mathematician, who found it
equal to twenty-one miles. It should not be forgotten that the
form of the city was almost that of a circle, the geometrical
figure which is known to contain the largest space within any
given circumference. The architect Vitruvius, who flourished
in the Augustan age, and whose evidence, on this occasion,

has peculiar weight and authority, observes that the innumerable habitations of the Roman people would have
spread themselves far beyond the narrow limits of the city;
and that the want of ground, which was probably contracted
on every side by gardens and villas, suggested the common,
though inconvenient, practice of raising the houses to a considerable height in the air. But the loftiness of these buildings,
which often consisted of hasty work and insufficient materials,
was the cause of frequent and fatal accidents; and it was
repeatedly enacted by Augustus, as well as by Nero, that the
height of private edifices within the walls of Rome should not
exceed the measure of seventy feet from the ground. Juvenal
laments, as it should seem from his own experience, the hardships of the poorer citizens, to whom he addresses the salutary
advice of emigrating, without delay, from the smoke of
Rome, since they might purchase in the little towns of Italy
a cheerful, commodious dwelling at the same price which they
annually paid for a dark and miserable lodging. House-rent
was therefore immoderately dear: the rich acquired, at an
enormous expense, the ground, which they covered with
palaces and gardens; but the body of the Roman people was
crowded into a narrow space; and the different floors and
apartments of the same house were divided, as it is still the
custom of Paris and other cities, among several families of
plebeians. The total number of houses in the fourteen regions
of the city is accurately stated in the description of Rome
composed under the reign of Theodosius, and they amount to
forty-eight thousand three hundred and eighty-two. The two
classes of *domus* and of *insulae*, into which they are divided,
include all the habitations of the capital, of every rank and
condition, from the marble palace of the Anicii, with a
numerous establishment of freedmen and slaves, to the lofty
and narrow lodging-house where the poet Codrus and his wife
were permitted to hire a wretched garret immediately under
the tiles. If we adopt the same average which, under similar
circumstances, has been found applicable to Paris, and indifferently allow about twenty-five persons for each house, of
every degree, we may fairly estimate the inhabitants of Rome
at twelve hundred thousand: a number which cannot be

thought excessive for the capital of a mighty empire, though it exceeds the populousness of the greatest cities of modern Europe.

Such was the state of Rome under the reign of Honorius, at the time when the Gothic army formed the siege, or rather the blockade, of the city.

ALEXANDRIA

EDWARD GIBBON, *Decline and Fall of the Roman Empire*. Vol. I, chap. x. 1776.

THE foundation of Alexandria was a noble design, at once conceived and executed by the son of Philip. The beautiful and regular form of that great city, second only to Rome itself, comprehended a circumference of fifteen miles; it was peopled by three hundred thousand free inhabitants, besides at least an equal number of slaves. The lucrative trade of Arabia and India flowed through the port of Alexandria to the capital and provinces of the empire. Idleness was unknown. Some were employed in blowing of glass, others in weaving of linen, others again manufacturing the papyrus. Either sex, and every age, was engaged in the pursuits of industry, nor did even the blind or the lame want occupations suited to their condition. But the people of Alexandria, a various mixture of nations, united the vanity and inconstancy of the Greeks with the superstition and obstinacy of the Egyptians. The most trifling occasion, a transient scarcity of flesh or lentils, the neglect of an accustomed salutation, a mistake of precedency in the public baths, or a religious dispute, were at any time sufficient to kindle a sedition among that vast multitude, whose resentments were furious and implacable.

CONSTANTINOPLE

EDWARD GIBBON, *Decline and Fall of the Roman Empire.*
Vol. II, chap. xvii. 1781

SITUATED in the forty-first degree of latitude, the Imperial city commanded, from her seven hills, the opposite shores of Europe and Asia; the climate was healthy and temperate, the soil fertile, the harbour secure and capacious, and the approach on the side of the continent was of small extent and easy defence. The Bosphorus and the Hellespont may be considered as the two gates of Constantinople, and the prince who possessed those important passages could always shut them against a naval enemy and open them to the fleets of commerce. The preservation of the eastern provinces may, in some degree, be ascribed to the policy of Constantine, as the barbarians of the Euxine, who in the preceding age had poured their armaments into the heart of the Mediterranean, soon desisted from the exercise of piracy, and despaired of forcing this insurmountable barrier. When the gates of the Hellespont and Bosphorus were shut, the capital still enjoyed within their spacious enclosure every production which could supply the wants or gratify the luxury of its numerous inhabitants. The sea-coasts of Thrace and Bithynia, which languish under the weight of Turkish oppression, still exhibit a rich prospect of vineyards, of gardens, and of plentiful harvests; and the Propontis has ever been renowned for an inexhaustible store of the most exquisite fish, that are taken in their stated seasons, without skill, and almost without labour. But when the passages of the straits were thrown open for trade, they alternately admitted the natural and artificial riches of the north and south, of the Euxine and of the Mediterranean. Whatever rude commodities were collected in the forests of Germany and Scythia, as far as the sources of the Tanais and the Borysthenes; whatsoever was manufactured by the skill of Europe or Asia; the corn of Egypt, and the gems and spices of the farthest India, were brought by the varying winds into the port of Constantinople, which, for many ages, attracted the commerce of the ancient world....

The master of the Roman world, who aspired to erect an eternal monument of the glories of his reign, could employ in the prosecution of that great work the wealth, the labour, and all that yet remained of the genius, of obedient millions. Some estimate may be formed of the expense bestowed with Imperial liberality on the foundation of Constantinople by the allowance of about two millions five hundred thousand pounds for the construction of the walls, the porticoes, and the aqueducts. The forests that overshadowed the shores of the Euxine, and the celebrated quarries of white marble in the little island of Proconnesus, supplied an inexhaustible stock of materials, ready to be conveyed, by the convenience of a short water-carriage, to the harbour of Byzantium. A multitude of labourers and artificers urged the conclusion of the work with incessant toil; but the impatience of Constantine soon discovered that, in the decline of the arts, the skill as well as numbers of his architects bore a very unequal proportion to the greatness of his designs. The magistrates of the most distant provinces were therefore directed to institute schools, to appoint professors, and, by the hopes of rewards and privileges, to engage in the study and practice of architecture a sufficient number of ingenious youths who had received a liberal education. The buildings of the new city were executed by such artificers as the reign of Constantine could afford; but they were decorated by the hands of the most celebrated masters of the age of Pericles and Alexander. To revive the genius of Phidias and Lysippus surpassed indeed the power of a Roman emperor; but the immortal productions which they had bequeathed to posterity were exposed without defence to the rapacious vanity of a despot. By his commands the cities of Greece and Asia were despoiled of their most valuable ornaments. The trophies of memorable wars, the objects of religious veneration, the most finished statues of the gods and heroes, of the sages and poets of ancient times, contributed to the splendid triumph of Constantinople; and gave occasion to the remark of the historian Cedrennus, who observes, with some enthusiasm, that nothing seemed wanting except the souls of the illustrious men whom these admirable monuments were intended to represent. But it is not in the city of Constantine, nor in the declining period of an empire, when the human mind was depressed by civil and religious slavery, that we should seek for the souls of Homer and of Demosthenes.

During the siege of Byzantium the conqueror had pitched his tent on the commanding eminence of the second hill. To perpetuate the memory of his success, he chose the same advantageous position for the principal Forum, which appears to have been of a circular or rather elliptical form. The two opposite entrances formed triumphal arches; the porticoes, which enclosed it on every side, were filled with statues, and the centre of the Forum was occupied by a lofty column, of which a mutilated fragment is now degraded by the appellation of the *burnt pillar*. This column was erected on a pedestal of white marble twenty feet high, and was composed of ten pieces of porphyry, each of which measured about ten feet in height, and about thirty-three in circumference. On the summit of the pillar, above one hundred and twenty feet from the ground, stood the colossal statue of Apollo. It was of bronze, had been transported either from Athens or from a town of Phrygia, and was supposed to be the work of Phidias. The artist had represented the god of day, or, as it was afterwards interpreted, the emperor Constantine himself, with a sceptre in his right hand, the globe of the world in his left, and a crown of rays glittering on his head. The Circus, or Hippodrome, was a stately building about four hundred paces in length, and one hundred in breadth. The space between the two *metae* or goals was filled with statues and obelisks; and we may still remark a very singular fragment of antiquity, the bodies of three serpents twisted into one pillar of brass. Their triple heads had once supported the golden tripod which, after the defeat of Xerxes, was consecrated in the temple of Delphi by the victorious Greeks. The beauty of the Hippodrome has been long since defaced by the rude hands of the Turkish conquerors, but, under the similar appellation of Atmeidan, it still serves as a place of exercise for their horses. From the throne, whence the Emperor viewed the Circensian games, a winding staircase descended to the palace; a magnificent edifice, which scarcely yielded to the residence of Rome itself, and which, together with the dependent courts, gardens, and porticoes, covered a considerable extent of ground upon the banks of the Propontis, between the Hippodrome and the church of St Sophia. We might likewise celebrate the baths, which still retained the name of Zeuxippus, after they had been enriched by the munificence of Constantine, with lofty columns, various marbles, and above threescore statues of bronze. But we should deviate from the design of this history if we attempted minutely to describe the different buildings or quarters of the city. It may be sufficient to observe that whatever could adorn the dignity of a great capital, or contribute to the benefit or pleasure of its numerous inhabitants, was contained within the walls of Constantinople. A particular description, composed about a century after its foundation, enumerates a capitol or school of learning, a circus, two theatres, eight public and one hundred and fifty-three private baths, fifty-two porticoes, five granaries, eight aqueducts or reservoirs of water, four spacious halls for the meetings of the senate or courts of justice, fourteen churches, fourteen palaces, and four thousand three hundred and eighty-eight houses which, for their size or beauty, deserved to be distinguished from the multitude of plebeian habitations.

VENICE

EDWARD GIBBON, *Decline and Fall of the Roman Empire.*
Vol. VI, chap. lx. 1788

IN the invasion of Italy by Attila, I have mentioned the flight of the Venetians from the fallen cities of the continent, and their obscure shelter in the chain of islands that line the extremity of the Adriatic Gulf. In the midst of the waters, free, indigent, laborious, and inaccessible, they gradually coalesced into a republic: the first foundations of Venice were

laid in the island of Rialto; and the annual election of the
twelve tribunes was superseded by the permanent office of
a duke or doge. On the verge of the two empires, the Venetians exult in the belief of primitive and perpetual independence. Against the Latins their antique freedom has been
asserted by the sword, and may be justified by the pen.
Charlemagne himself resigned all claims of sovereignty to the
islands of the Adriatic Gulf: his son Pepin was repulsed in the
attacks of the *lagunas* or canals, too deep for the cavalry, and
too shallow for the vessels; and in every age, under the
German Cæsars, the lands of the republic have been clearly
distinguished from the kingdom of Italy. But the inhabitants
of Venice were considered by themselves, by strangers, and
by their sovereigns, as an inalienable portion of the Greek
empire: in the ninth and tenth centuries the proofs of their
subjection are numerous and unquestionable; and the vain
titles, the servile honours, of the Byzantine court, so ambi-
tiously solicited by their dukes, would have degraded the
magistrates of a free people. But the bands of this dependence, which was never absolute or rigid, were imperceptibly
relaxed by the ambition of Venice and the weakness of Constantinople. Obedience was softened into respect, privilege
ripened into prerogative, and the freedom of domestic
government was fortified by the independence of foreign
dominion. The maritime cities of Istria and Dalmatia bowed
to the sovereigns of the Adriatic; and when they armed against
the Normans in the cause of Alexius, the emperor applied,
not to the duty of his subjects, but to the gratitude and
generosity of his faithful allies. The sea was their patrimony:
the western parts of the Mediterranean, from Tuscany to
Gibraltar, were indeed abandoned to their rivals of Pisa and
Genoa; but the Venetians acquired an early and lucrative
share of the commerce of Greece and Egypt. Their riches increased with the increasing demand of Europe: their manufactures of silk and glass, perhaps the institution of their
bank, are of high antiquity; and they enjoyed the fruits of
their industry in the magnificence of public and private life.
To assert her flag, to avenge her injuries, to protect the freedom of navigation, the republic could launch and man a fleet

of a hundred galleys; and the Greeks, and Saracens, and the Normans were encountered by her naval arms. The Franks of Syria were assisted by the Venetians in the reduction of the sea-coast; but their zeal was neither blind nor disinterested; and in the conquest of Tyre they shared the sovereignty of a city, the first seat of the commerce of the world. The policy of Venice was marked by the avarice of a trading, and the insolence of a maritime power; yet her ambition was prudent: nor did she often forget that, if armed galleys were the effect and safeguard, merchant vessels were the cause and supply, of her greatness. In her religion she avoided the schism of the Greeks, without yielding a servile obedience to the Roman pontiff; and a free intercourse with the infidels of every clime appears to have allayed betimes the fever of superstition. Her primitive government was a loose mixture of democracy and monarchy: the doge was elected by the votes of the general assembly; as long as he was popular and successful, he reigned with the pomp and authority of a prince; but in the frequent revolutions of the state, he was deposed, or banished, or slain, by the justice or injustice of the multitude. The twelfth century produced the first rudiments of the wise and jealous aristocracy, which has reduced the doge to a pageant, and the people to a cipher.

THE ITALIAN COMMUNES

John Addington Symonds, *Renaissance in Italy.*
Vol. i. 1875

After a first glance into Italian history the student recoils as from a chaos of inscrutable confusion. To fix the moment of transition from ancient to modern civilisation seems impossible. There is no formation of a new people, as in the case of Germany or France or England, to serve as starting-point. Differ as the Italian races do in their original type; Gauls, Ligurians, Etruscans, Umbrians, Latins, Iapygians, Greeks have been fused together beneath the stress of Roman rule into a nation that survives political mutations and the disasters of barbarian invasions. Goths, Lombards, and Franks blend successively with the masses of this complex population, and lose the outlines of their several personalities. The Western Empire melts imperceptibly away. The Roman Church grows no less imperceptibly, and forms the Holy Roman Empire as the equivalent of its own spiritual greatness in the sphere of secular authority. These two institutions, the crowning monuments of Italian creative genius, dominate the Middle Ages, powerful as facts, but still more powerful as ideas. Yet neither of them controls the evolution of Italy in the same sense as France was controlled by the monarchical, and Germany by the federative, principle. The forces of the nation, divided and swayed from side to side by this commanding dualism, escaped both influences in so far as either Pope or Emperor strove to mould them into unity. Meanwhile the domination of Byzantine Greeks in the southern provinces, the kingdom of the Goths at Ravenna, the kingdom of the Lombards and Franks at Pavia, the incursions of Huns and Saracens, the kingdom of the Normans at Palermo, formed but accidents and moments in a national development which owed important modifications to each successive episode, but was not finally determined by any of them. When the Communes emerge into prominence, shaking off the supremacy of the Greeks in the South, vindicating their liberties against the Empire in the North, jealously guarding their independence from Papal encroachment in the centre, they have already assumed shapes of marked distinctness and bewildering diversity. Venice, Milan, Genoa, Florence, Bologna, Siena, Perugia, Amalfi, Lucca, Pisa, to mention only a few of the more notable, are indiscriminately called Republics. Yet they differ in their internal type no less than in external conditions. Each wears from the first and preserves a physiognomy that justifies our thinking and speaking of the town as an incarnate entity. The cities of Italy, down to the very smallest, bear the attributes of individuals. The mutual attractions and repulsions that presided over their growth have given them specific qualities which they will never lose, which will be reflected in their architecture, in their customs, in their language, in their policy, as well as in the institutions of their government. We think of them involuntarily as persons, and reserve for them epithets that mark the permanence of their distinctive characters. To treat of them collectively is almost impossible. Each has its own biography, and plays a part of consequence in the great drama of the nation. Accordingly the study of Italian politics, Italian literature, Italian art, is not really the study of one national genius, but of a whole family of cognate geniuses, grouped together, conscious of affinity, obeying the same general conditions, but issuing in markedly divergent characteristics. Democracies, oligarchies, aristocracies spring into being by laws of natural selection within the limits of a single province. Every municipality has a separate nomenclature for its magistracies, a somewhat different method of distributing administrative functions. In one place there is a Doge appointed for life; in another the government is put into commission among officers elected for a period of months. Here we find a Patrician, a Senator, a Tribune; there Consuls, Rectors, Priors, Ancients, Buonuomini, Conservatori. At one period and in one city the Podestà seems paramount; across the border a Captain of the People or a Gonfaloniere di Giustizia is supreme. Vicars of the Empire, Exarchs, Catapans, Rectors for the Church, Legates, Commissaries, succeed each other with dazzling rapidity. Councils are multiplied and called by names that have their origin and meaning buried in the dust of archæology. Consigli del Popolo, Credenza, Consiglio del Comune, Senato, Gran Consiglio, Pratiche, Parlamenti, Monti, Consiglio de' Savi, Arti, Parte Guelfa, Consigli di Dieci, di Tre, I Novo, Gli Otto, I Cento— such are a few of the titles chosen at random from the constitutional records of different localities.

Not one is insignificant. Not one but indicates some moment of importance in the social evolution of the state. Not one but speaks of civil strife, whereby the burgh in question struggled into individuality and defined itself against its neighbour. Like fossils in geological strata, these names survive long after their old uses have been forgotten, to guide the explorer in his reconstruction of a buried past. While one town appears to respect the feudal lordship of great families, another pronounces nobility to be a crime, and forces on its citizens the reality or the pretence of labour. Some recognise the supremacy of ecclesiastics. Others, like Venice, resist the least encroachment of the Church, and stand aloof from Roman Christianity in jealous isolation. The interests of one class are maritime, of another military, of a third industrial, of a fourth financial, of a fifth educational. Amalfi, Pisa, Genoa, and Venice depend for power upon their fleets and colonies; the little cities of Romagna and the March supply the Captains of adventure with recruits; Florence and Lucca live by manufacture; Milan by banking; Bologna, Padua, Vicenza, owe their wealth to students attracted by their universities. Foreign alliances or geographical affinities connect one centre with the Empire of the East, a second with France, a third with Spain. The North is overshadowed by Germany; the South is disquieted by Islam. The types thus formed and thus discriminated are vital, and persist for centuries with the tenacity of physical growths. Each differentiation owes its origin to causes deeply rooted in the locality. The freedom and apparent waywardness of nature, when she sets about to form crystals of varying shapes and colours, that shall last and bear her stamp for ever, have governed their uprising and their progress to maturity. At the same time they exhibit the keen jealousies and mutual hatreds of rival families in the animal kingdom. Pisa destroys Amalfi; Genoa, Pisa; Venice, Genoa; with ruthless and remorseless egotism in the conflict of commercial interests. Florence enslaves Pisa because she needs a way to the sea. Siena and Perugia, upon their inland altitudes, consume themselves in brilliant but unavailing efforts to expand. Milan engulfs the lesser towns of Lombardy. Verona absorbs Padua and Treviso. Venice extends dominion over the Friuli and the Veronese conquests. Strife and covetousness reign from the Alps to the Ionian Sea. But it is a strife of living energies, the covetousness of impassioned and puissant units. Italy as a whole is almost invisible to the student by reason of the many-sided, combative, self-centred crowd of numberless Italian communities. Proximity foments hatred and stimulates hostility. Fiesole looks down and threatens Florence. Florence returns frown for frown, and does not rest till she has made her neighbour of the hills a slave. Perugia and Assisi turn the Umbrian plain into a wilderness of wolves by their recurrent warfare. Scowling at one another across the Valdichiana, Perugia rears a tower against Chiusi, and Chiusi builds her Becca Questa in responsive menace. The tiniest burgh upon the Arno receives from Dante, the poet of this internecine strife and fierce town-rivalry, its stigma of immortalising satire and insulting epithet, for no apparent reason but that its dwellers dare to drink of the same water and to breathe the same air as Florence. It would seem as though the most ancient furies of antagonistic races, enchained and suspended for centuries by the magic of Rome, had been unloosed; as though the indigenous populations of Italy, tamed by antique culture, were reverting to their primal instincts, with all the discords and divisions introduced by the military system of the Lombards, the feudalism of the Franks, the alien institutions of the Germans, superadded to exasperate the passions of a nation blindly struggling against obstacles that block the channel of continuous progress. Nor is this the end of the perplexity. Not only are the cities at war with one another, but they are plunged in ceaseless strife within the circuit of their ramparts. The people with the nobles, the burghs with the castles, the plebeians with the burgher aristocracy, the men of commerce with the men of arms and ancient lineage, Guelfs and Ghibellines, clash together in persistent fury. One half the city expels the other half. The exiles roam abroad, cement alliances, and return to extirpate their conquerors. Fresh proscriptions and new expulsions follow. Again alliances are made and revolutions accomplished, till the ancient feuds of the towns are crossed, recrossed, and tangled in a web of madness that defies analysis.

THE NETHERLAND CITIES

JOHN LOTHROP MOTLEY, *Rise of the Dutch Republic.*
Vol. I. 1855

COMMERCE, the mother of Netherland freedom, and, eventually, its destroyer—even as in all human history the vivifying becomes afterwards the dissolving principle—commerce changes insensibly and miraculously the aspect of society. Clusters of hovels become towered cities; the green and gilded Hanse of commercial republicanism coils itself around the decaying trunk of feudal despotism. Cities leagued with cities throughout and beyond Christendom—empire within empire —bind themselves closer and closer in the electric chain of human sympathy and grow stronger and stronger by mutual support. Fishermen and river raftsmen become ocean adventurers and merchant princes. Commerce plucks up half-drowned Holland by the locks and pours gold into her lap. Gold wrests power from iron. Needy Flemish weavers become mighty manufacturers. Armies of workmen, fifty thousand strong, tramp through the swarming streets. Silkmakers, clothiers, brewers become the gossips of kings, lend their royal gossips vast sums, and burn the royal notes of hand in fires of cinnamon wood. Wealth brings strength, strength confidence. Learning to handle cross-bow and dagger, the burghers fear less the baronial sword, finding that their own will cut as well, seeing that great armies—flowers of chivalry —can ride away before them fast enough at battles of spurs and other encounters. Sudden riches beget insolence, tumults, civic broils. Internecine quarrels, horrible tumults stain the streets with blood, but education lifts the citizens more and more out of the original slough. They learn to tremble as little at priestcraft as at swordcraft, having acquired something of each. Gold in the end, unsanctioned by right divine, weighs up the other forces, supernatural as they are. And so, struggling along their appointed path, making cloth, making money, making treaties with great kingdoms, making war by land and sea, ringing great bells, waving great banners, they, too—these insolent, boisterous burghers—

accomplish their work....Sometimes by bargains, sometimes by blood, by gold, threats, promises, or good hard blows they extorted their charters. Their codes, statutes, joyful entrances, and other constitutions were dictated by the burghers and sworn to by the monarch. They were concessions from above; privileges—private laws; fragments indeed of a larger liberty, but vastly better than the slavery for which they had been substituted; solid facts instead of empty abstractions, which, in those practical and violent days, would have yielded little nutriment; but they still rather sought to reconcile themselves, by a rough, clumsy fiction, with the hierarchy which they had invaded, than to overturn the system. Thus the cities, not regarding themselves as representatives or aggregations of the people, became fabulous personages, bodies without souls, corporations which had acquired vitality and strength enough to assert their existence. As persons, therefore—gigantic in-dividualities—they wheeled into the feudal ranks and as-sumed feudal powers and responsibilities. The city of Dort, of Middleburg, of Ghent, of Louvain, was a living being, doing fealty, claiming service, bowing to its lord, struggling with its equals, trampling upon its slaves....

Ghent was, in all respects, one of the most important cities in Europe....The activity and wealth of its burghers was pro-verbial. The bells were rung daily, and the drawbridges over the many arms of the river intersecting the streets were raised, in order that all business might be suspended, while the armies of workmen were going to or coming from their labours. As early as the fourteenth century, the age of the Arteveldes, Froissart estimated the number of fighting men whom Ghent could bring into the field at eighty thousand. The city, by its jurisdiction over many large but subordinate towns, disposed of more than its own immediate population, which has been reckoned as high as two hundred thousand.

Placed in the midst of well-cultivated plains, Ghent was surrounded by strong walls, the external circuit of which measured nine miles. Its streets and squares were spacious and elegant, its churches and other public buildings numerous and splendid. The sumptuous church of Saint John or Saint Bavon, where Charles the Fifth had been baptized, the ancient castle whither Baldwin Bras de Fer had brought the daughter of Charles the Bald, the city hall with its graceful Moorish front, the well-known belfry, where for three centuries had perched the dragon sent by the Emperor Baldwin of Flanders from Constantinople, and where swung the famous Roland, whose iron tongue had called the citizens, generation after generation, to arms, whether to win battles over foreign kings at the head of their chivalry, or to plunge their swords in each other's breasts, were all conspicuous in the city and celebrated in the land....

The chief city of the Netherlands, the commercial capital of the world, was Antwerp. In the North and East of Europe, the Hanseatic league had withered with the revolution in commerce. At the South, the splendid marble channels, through which the overland India trade had been conducted from the Mediterranean by a few stately cities, were now dry, the great aqueducts ruinous and deserted. Verona, Venice, Nuremberg, Augsburg, Bruges, were sinking, but Antwerp with its deep and convenient river, stretched its arm to the ocean and caught the golden prize, as it fell from its sister-cities' grasp....It had now become the principal entrepôt and exchange of Europe. The Fuggers, Velsens, Ostetts of Germany, the Gualterotti and Bonvisi of Italy, and many other great mercantile houses, were there established. No city, except Paris, surpassed it in population, none approached it in commercial splendour....

The city itself was one of the most beautiful in Europe. Placed upon a plain along the banks of the Scheldt, shaped like a bent bow with the river for its string, it enclosed within its walls some of the most splendid edifices in Christendom. The world-renowned church of Nôtre-Dame, the stately Exchange where five thousand merchants daily congregated, prototype of all similar establishments throughout the world, the capacious mole and port where twenty-five hundred vessels were often seen at once, and where five hundred made their daily entrance or departure, were all establishments which it would have been difficult to rival in any other part of the world.

* * * *

The gay capital of Brabant—of that province which rejoiced in the liberal constitution known by the cheerful title of the "joyful entrance", was worthy to be the scene of the imposing show.* Brussels had been a city for more than five centuries, and, at that day, numbered about one hundred thousand inhabitants. Its walls, six miles in circumference, were already two hundred years old. Unlike most Netherland cities, lying usually upon extensive plains, it was built along the sides of an abrupt promontory. A wide expanse of living verdure, cultivated gardens, shady groves, fertile corn-fields, flowed round it like a sea. The foot of the town was washed by the little river Senne, while the irregular but picturesque streets rose up the steep sides of the hill like the semi-circles and stairways of an amphitheatre. Nearly in the heart of the place rose the audacious and exquisitely embroidered tower of the town-house, three hundred and sixty-six feet in height, a miracle of needlework in stone, rivalling in its intricate carving the cobweb tracery of that lace which has for centuries been synonymous with the city, and rearing itself above a façade of profusely decorated and brocaded architecture. The crest of the elevation was crowned by the towers of the old ducal palace of Brabant, with its extensive and thickly-wooded park on the left, and by the stately mansions of Orange, Egmont, Aremburg, Culemburg, and other Flemish grandees, on the right. The great forest of Soignies, dotted with monasteries and convents, swarming with every variety of game, whither the citizens made their summer pilgrimages, and where the nobles chased the wild boar and the stag, extended to within a quarter of a mile of the city walls. The population, as thrifty, as intelligent, as prosperous as that of any city in Europe, was divided into fifty-two guilds of artisans, among which the most important were the armourers, whose suits of mail would turn a musket-ball; the gardeners, upon whose gentler creations incredible sums were annually lavished; and the tapestry-workers, whose gorgeous fabrics were the wonder of the world.

*   *   *   *

* The public abdication of Charles V, 1555.

Thus fifteen ages have passed away, and in the place of a horde of savages living among swamps and thickets, swarm three millions of people, the most industrious, the most prosperous, perhaps the most intelligent under the sun. Their cattle, grazing on the bottom of the sea, are the finest in Europe, their agricultural products of more exchangeable value than if nature had made their land to overflow with wine and oil. Their navigators are the boldest, their mercantile marine the most powerful, their merchants the most enterprising in the world. Holland and Flanders, peopled by one race, vie with each other in the pursuits of civilization. The Flemish skill in the mechanical and in the fine arts is unrivalled. Belgian musicians delight and instruct other nations, Belgian pencils have, for a century, caused the canvas to glow with colours and combinations never seen before. Flemish fabrics are exported to all parts of Europe, to the East and West Indies, to Africa. The splendid tapestries, silks, linens, as well as the more homely and useful manufactures of the Netherlands, are prized throughout the world. Most ingenious, as they had already been described by the keen-eyed Caesar, in imitating the arts of other nations, the skilful artificers of the country at Louvain, Ghent, and other places, reproduce the shawls and silks of India with admirable accuracy....

Within the little circle which encloses the seventeen provinces are 208 walled cities, many of them among the most stately in Christendom, 150 chartered towns, 6,300 villages, with their watch-towers and steeples, besides numerous other more insignificant hamlets; the whole guarded by a belt of sixty fortresses of surpassing strength.

LONDON

John Stow, *Survey of London.* 1598

Of orders and customs in this city of old time, Fitzstephen
saith as followeth: "Men of all trades, sellers of all sorts of
wares, labourers in every work, every morning are in their
distinct and several places: furthermore, in London, upon the
river side, between the wine in ships and the wine to be sold
in taverns, is a common cookery, or cooks' row; there daily,
for the season of the year, men might have meat, roast, sod,
or fried; fish, flesh, fowls, fit for rich and poor. If any come
suddenly to any citizen from afar, weary, and not willing to
tarry till the meat be bought and dressed, while the servant
bringeth water for his master's hands, and fetcheth bread, he
shall have immediately from the river's side all viands whatsoever he desireth: what multitude soever, either of soldiers
or strangers, do come to the city, whatsoever hour, day or
night, according to their pleasures may refresh themselves;
and they which delight in delicateness may be satisfied with
as delicate dishes there as may be found elsewhere. And this
Cooke's row is very necessary to the city; and, according to
Plato in Gorgius, next to physic, is the office of cooks, as part
of a city.

"Without one of the gates is a plain field, both in name and
deed, where every Friday, unless it be a solemn bidden holy
day, is a notable show of horses to be sold; earls, barons,
knights, and citizens repair thither to see or to buy; there
may you of pleasure see amblers pacing it delicately; there
may you see trotters fit for men of arms, sitting more hardly;
there may you have notable young horses, not yet broken;
there may you have strong steeds, well limbed geldings,
whom the buyers do specially regard for pace and swiftness;
the boys which ride these horses, sometimes two, sometimes
three, do run races for wagers, with a desire of praise, or hope
of victory. In another part of that field are to be sold all implements of husbandry, as also fat swine, milch kine, sheep,

and oxen; there stand also mares and horses fit for ploughs and teams, with their young colts by them. At this city, merchant strangers of all nations had their keys and wharfs; the Arabians sent gold; the Sabians spice and frankincense; the Scythian armour, Babylon oil, Indian purple garments, Egypt precious stones, Norway and Russia amber-greece and sables, and the Frenchmen wine. According to the truth of Chronicles, this city is ancienter than Rome, built of the ancient Troyans and of Brute, before that was built by Romulus and Rhemus; and therefore useth the ancient customs of Rome. This city, even as Rome, is divided into wards; it hath yearly sheriffs instead of consuls; it hath the dignity of senators in aldermen. It hath under officers, common sewers, and conduits in streets; according to the quality of causes, it hath general courts and assemblies upon appointed days. I do not think that there is any city wherein are better customs, in frequenting the churches, in serving God, in keeping holy days, in giving alms, in entertaining strangers, in solemnising marriages, in furnishing banquets, celebrating funerals, and burying dead bodies.

"The only plagues of London are immoderate quaffing among the foolish sort, and often casualties by fire. Most part of the bishops, abbots, and great lords of the land have houses there, whereunto they resort, and bestow much when they are called to parliament by the king, or to council by their metropolitan, or otherwise by their private business."

Thus far Fitzstephen, of the estate of things in his time, whereunto may be added the present, by conference whereof the alteration will easily appear.

Men of trades and sellers of wares in this city have oftentimes since changed their places, as they have found their best advantage. For whereas mercers and haberdashers used to keep their shops in West Cheape, of later time they held them on London Bridge, where partly they yet remain. The goldsmiths of Gutheron's lane and Old Exchange are now for the most part removed into the south side of West Cheape, the peperers and grocers of Soper's lane are now in Bucklesberrie, and other places dispersed. The drapers of Lombard street and of Cornehill are seated in Candlewick street and

Watheling street; the skinners from St Marie Pellipers, or at the Axe, into Budge row and Walbrooke; the stock fishmongers in Thames street; wet fishmongers in Knightriders street and Bridge street; the ironmongers, of Ironmongers' lane and Old Jurie, into Thames street; the vintners from the Vinetree into divers places. But the brewers for the more part remain near to the friendly water of Thames; the butchers in Eastcheape, St Nicholas shambles, and the Stockes market; the hosiers of old time in Hosier lane, near unto Smithfield, are since removed into Cordwayner street, the upper part thereof by Bow church, and last of all into Birchoveris lane by Cornehill; the shoe-makers and curriers of Cordwayner street removed the one to St Martin's le Grand, the other to London wall near unto Mooregate; the founders remain by themselves in Lothberie; cooks, or pastelars, for the more part in Thames street, the other dispersed into divers parts; poulters of late removed out of the Poultrie, betwixt the Stockes and the great Conduit in Cheape, into Grasse street and St Nicholas shambles; bowyers, from Bowyers' row by Ludgate into divers places, and almost worn out with the fletchers; pater noster makers of old time, or bead-makers, and text-writers, are gone out of Pater noster row, and are called stationers of Paule's churchyard; patten-makers, of St Margaret, Pattens' lane, clean worn out; labourers every work-day are to be found in Cheape, about Soper's land end; horse-coursers and sellers of oxen, sheep, swine, and such like, remain in their old market of Smithfield, etc.

That merchants of all nations had their keys and wharfs at this city, whereunto they brought their merchandises before and in the reign of Henry II, mine author wrote of his own knowledge to be true, though for the antiquity of the city he took the common opinion. Also that this city was in his time and afore divided into wards, had yearly sheriffs, aldermen, general courts, and assemblies, and such like notes by him set down, in commendation of the citizens; whereof there is no question, he wrote likewise of his own experience, as being born and brought up amongst them.

TYPES: ANCIENT

Revelation of St John the Divine, c. A.D. 95.
Chap. xxi. 10–21. R.V. 1881

AND he carried me away in the Spirit to a mountain great
and high, and shewed me the holy city Jerusalem, coming
down out of heaven from God, having the glory of God: her
light was like unto a stone most precious, as it were a jasper
stone, clear as crystal: having a wall great and high; having
twelve gates, and at the gates twelve angels; and names written
thereon, which are the names of the twelve tribes of the
children of Israel: on the east were three gates; and on the
north three gates; and on the south three gates; and on the
west three gates. And the wall of the city had twelve foundations, and on them twelve names of the twelve apostles of the
Lamb. And he that spake with me had for a measure a golden
reed to measure the city, and the gates thereof, and the wall
thereof. And the city lieth foursquare, and the length thereof
is as great as the breadth: and he measured the city with the
reed, twelve thousand furlongs: the length and the breadth
and the height thereof are equal. And he measured the wall
thereof, a hundred and forty and four cubits, according to the
measure of a man, that is, of an angel. And the building of
the wall thereof was jasper: and the city was pure gold, like
unto pure glass. The foundations of the wall of the city were
adorned with all manner of precious stones. The first foundation was jasper; the second, sapphire; the third, chalcedony;
the fourth, emerald; the fifth, sardonyx; the sixth, sardius;
the seventh, chrysolite; the eighth, beryl; the ninth, topaz;
the tenth, chrysoprase; the eleventh, jacinth; the twelfth,
amethyst. And the twelve gates were twelve pearls; each one
of the several gates was of one pearl; and the street of the city
was pure gold, as it were transparent glass.

TYPES: MEDIEVAL

JOHN BUNYAN, *Pilgrim's Progress*. 1678

T H E N I saw in my Dream, that when they were got out of the
Wilderness, they presently saw a Town before them, and the
name of that Town is *Vanity*; and at the town there is a *Fair*
kept, called *Vanity-Fair*: It is kept all the year long; it beareth
the name of *Vanity-Fair*, because the Town where 'tis kept, *is
lighter than* Vanity; and also, because all that is there sold, or
that cometh thither, is *Vanity*. As is the saying of the wise,
All that cometh is Vanity.

This Fair is no new erected business, but a thing of ancient
standing; I will show you the original of it.

Almost five thousand years agone, there were Pilgrims
walking to the Cœlestial City, as these two honest persons are:
and *Beelzebub, Apollyon,* and *Legion,* with their Companions,
perceiving by the path that the Pilgrims made, that their way
to the City lay through *this Town* of *Vanity,* they contrived
here to set up a Fair; a Fair wherein should be sold *all sorts of
Vanity,* and that it should last all the year long. Therefore at
this Fair are all such Merchandise sold, as Houses, Lands,
Trades, Places, Honours, Preferments, Titles, Countries, Kingdoms, Lusts, Pleasures and Delights of all sorts, as Whores,
Bawds, Wives, Husbands, Children, Masters, Servants, Lives,
Blood, Bodies, Souls, Silver, Gold, Pearls, Precious Stones, and
what not.

And, moreover, at this Fair there is at all times to be seen
Juggling, Cheats, Games, Plays, Fools, Apes, Knaves, and
Rogues, and that of every kind.

Here are to be seen, too, and that for nothing, Thefts,
Murders, Adulteries, False-swearers, and that of a blood-red
colour.

And as in other fairs of less moment, there are the several
Rows and Streets, under their proper names, where such and
such Wares are vended: So here likewise, you have the proper
Places, Rows, Streets (*viz.* Countreys and Kingdoms), where the
Wares of this Fair are soonest to be found: Here is the *Britain*
Row, the *French* Row, the *Italian* Row, the *Spanish* Row, the
German Row, where several sorts of Vanities are to be sold.

TYPES: MODERN

SINCLAIR LEWIS, *Babbitt*. Chap. i. 1922

THE towers of Zenith aspired above the morning mist; austere towers of steel and cement and limestone, sturdy as cliffs and delicate as silver rods. They were neither citadels nor churches, but frankly and beautifully office-buildings.

The mist took pity on the fretted structures of earlier generations: the Post Office with its shingle-tortured mansard, the red brick minarets of hulking old houses, factories with stingy and sooted windows, wooden tenements coloured like mud. The city was full of such grotesqueries, but the clean towers were thrusting them from the business centre, and on the farther hills were shining new houses, homes—they seemed—for laughter and tranquillity.

Over a concrete bridge fled a limousine of long sleek hood and noiseless engine. These people in evening clothes were returning from an all-night rehearsal of a Little Theatre play, an artistic adventure considerably illuminated by champagne. Below the bridge curved a railway, a maze of green and crimson lights. The New York Flyer boomed past, and twenty lines of polished steel leaped into the glare.

In one of the skyscrapers the wires of the Associated Press were being closed. The telegraph operators wearily raised their celluloid eye-shades after a night of talking with Paris and Peking. Through the building crawled the charwomen, yawning, their old shoes slapping. The dawn mist spun away. Queues of men with lunch-boxes clumped towards the immensity of new factories, sheets of glass and hollow tile, glittering shops where five thousand men worked beneath one roof, pouring out the honest wares that would be sold up the Euphrates and across the veldt. The whistles rolled out in greeting a chorus cheerful as the April dawn; the song of labour in a city built—it seemed—for giants.

TYPES: EASTERN

Sir RICHARD FRANCIS BURTON, *Pilgrimage to Al-Madinah and Meccah*. Part I, chap. V. 1855

ALL is squalor in the brilliancy of noon-day. In darkness you see nothing but a silhouette. When, however, the moon is high in the heavens, and the summer stars rain light upon God's world, there is something not of earth in the view. A glimpse at the strip of pale blue sky above scarcely reveals three ells of breadth: in many places the interval is less: here the copings meet, and there the outriggings of the houses seem to inter-lace. Now they are parted by a pencil of snowy sheen, then by a flood of silvery splendour; while under the projecting cornices and the huge hanging balcony-windows of fantastic wood-work, supported by gigantic brackets and corbels, and under deep verandahs, and gateways, vast enough for Behe-moth to pass through, and in blind wynds and long cul-de-sacs, lie patches of thick darkness, made visible by the dim-mest of oil lamps. The arch is a favourite feature: in one place you see it a mere skeleton-rib opening into some huge deserted hall; in another the ogre is full of fretted stone and wood carved like lace-work. Not a line is straight, the tall dead walls of the Mosques slope over their massy buttresses, and the thin minarets seem about to fall across your path. The cornices project crookedly from the houses, while the great gables stand merely by force of cohesion. And that the Line of Beauty may not be wanting, the graceful bending form of the palm, on whose topmost feathers, quivering in the cool night breeze, the moonbeam glistens, springs from a gloomy mound, or from the darkness of a mass of houses almost level with the ground. Briefly, the whole view is so strange, so fantastic, so ghostly, that it seems preposterous to imagine that in such places human beings like ourselves can be born, and live through life, and carry out the command "increase and multiply", and die.

WAR AND PEACE

And the king said unto Cushi, Is the young man Ab-
salom safe? And Cushi answered, The enemies of my
lord the king, and all that rise against thee to do thee hurt,
be as that young man is. And the king was much moved,
and went up to the chamber over the gate, and wept: and
as he went, thus he said, O my son Absalom, my son, my
son Absalom! would God I had died for thee, O Ab-
salom, my son, my son!

II SAMUEL xviii. 32, 33. A.V.

WARFARE BY EASY PAYMENTS

Adam Smith, *Wealth of Nations.* Book v, chap. iii. 1776

The ordinary expense of the greater part of modern governments, in time of peace, being equal, or nearly equal, to their
ordinary revenue, when war comes, they are both unwilling
and unable to increase their revenue in proportion to the increase of their expense. They are unwilling, for fear of offending the people, who, by so great and so sudden an increase of
taxes, would soon be disgusted with the war; and they are
unable, from not well knowing what taxes would be sufficient
to produce the revenue wanted. The facility of borrowing
delivers them from the embarrassment which this fear and
inability would otherwise occasion. By means of borrowing
they are enabled, with a very moderate increase of taxes, to
raise, from year to year, money sufficient for carrying on the
war; and by the practice of perpetual funding, they are
enabled, with the smallest possible increase of taxes, to raise
annually the largest possible sum of money. In great empires,
the people who live in the capital, and in the provinces remote
from the scene of action, feel, many of them, scarce any in-
conveniency from the war, but enjoy, at their ease, the amusement of reading in the newspapers the exploits of their own
fleets and armies. To them this amusement compensates the
small difference between the taxes which they pay on account
of the war, and those which they had been accustomed to pay
in time of peace. They are commonly dissatisfied with the
return of peace, which puts an end to their amusement, and
to a thousand visionary hopes of conquest and national glory,
from a longer continuance of the war.

COMMONSENSE ABOUT WAR

SAMUEL JOHNSON, *Thoughts on the late Transactions respecting Falkland's Islands.* 1771

As war is the last of remedies, *cuncta prius tentanda,* all lawful expedients must be used to avoid it. As war is the extremity of evil, it is surely the duty of those whose station intrusts them with the care of nations, to avert it from their charge. There are diseases of animal nature which nothing but amputation can remove; so there may, by the depravation of human passions, be sometimes a gangrene in collective life, for which fire and the sword are the necessary remedies; but in what can skill or caution be better shewn than preventing such dreadful operations, while there is yet room for gentler methods?

It is wonderful with what coolness and indifference the greater part of mankind see war commenced. Those that hear of it at a distance, or read of it in books, but have never presented its evils to their minds, consider it as little more than a splendid game, a proclamation, an army, a battle, and a triumph. Some indeed must perish in the most successful field; but they die upon the bed of honour, "resign their lives amidst the joys of conquest, and filled with England's glory, smile in death".

The life of a modern soldier is ill represented by heroic fiction. War has means of destruction more formidable than the cannon and the sword. Of the thousands and ten thousands that perished in our late conquests with France and Spain, a very small part ever felt the stroke of an enemy; the rest languished in tents and ships, amidst damps and putrefaction; pale, torpid, spiritless and helpless; gasping and groaning, unpitied among men, made obdurate by long continuance of hopeless misery; and were at last whelmed in pits, or heaved into the ocean, without notice and without remembrance. By incommodious encampments and unwholesome stations, where courage is useless, and enterprise impracticable, fleets are silently dispeopled, and armies sluggishly melted away.

Thus is a people gradually exhausted, for the most part, with little effect. The wars of civilized nations make very slow changes in the system of empire. The public perceives scarcely any alteration but an increase of debt; and the few individuals who are benefited, are not supposed to have the clearest right to their advantages. If he that shared the danger enjoyed the profit, and after bleeding in the battle, grew rich by the victory, he might shew his gains without envy. But at the conclusion of a ten years' war, how are we recompensed for the death of multitudes and the expense of millions, but by contemplating the sudden glories of paymasters and agents, contractors and commissaries, whose equipages shine like meteors, and whose palaces rise like exhalations?

These are the men who, without virtue, labour, or hazard, are growing rich as their country is impoverished; they rejoice when obstinacy or ambition adds another year to slaughter and devastation; and laugh from their desks at bravery and science, while they are adding figure to figure, and cipher to cipher, hoping for a new contract from a new armament, and computing the profits of a siege or tempest.

VIRTUE

Marcus Tullius Cicero, *De Officiis*, 44 b.c. Book i.
Translated by Roger L'Estrange. 1680

I n the undertaking of a war there should be such a prospect as if the only end of it were peace. It is the part of a valiant and a resolute man not to be discomposed in disasters, or to make a bustle, and be put beside himself, but to maintain a presence of mind and judgment without departing from reason. As this is the mark and effect of a great courage, so is the other of an excellent understanding, to forecast in our thoughts the events of things to come, and to weigh beforehand the good and the bad, and what's to be done when it happens without being put to the foolish exclamation of,

Who would have thought it? These are the works of an elevated soul that supports itself upon prudence and judgment; but he that rashly thrusts himself into dangers without fear or wit, and engages an enemy hand over head, this is only brutality and outrage; but yet when the time comes, and necessity requires it, let a man fight with his sword in his hand, and rather lose his life than his honour and freedom.

HONOUR

WILLIAM SHAKESPEARE, *First Part of King Henry the Fourth*. Act v, Sc. i

Falstaff. Hal, if thou see me down in the battle, and bestride me, so; 'tis a point of friendship.

Prince Henry. Nothing but a colossus can do thee that friendship. Say thy prayers, and farewell.

Falstaff. I would it were bed-time, Hal, and all well.

Prince Henry. Why, thou owest God a death.   [*Exit.*

Falstaff. 'Tis not due yet: I would be loath to pay him before his day. What need I be so forward with him that calls not on me? Well, 'tis no matter; honour pricks me on. Yea, but how if honour prick me off when I come on? how then? Can honour set to a leg? No. Or an arm? No. Or take away the grief of a wound? No. Honour hath no skill in surgery then? No. What is honour? a word. What is that word, honour? Air. A trim reckoning! Who hath it? he that died o' Wednesday. Doth he feel it? No. Doth he hear it? No. It is insensible, then? Yea, to the dead. But will it not live with the living? No. Why? Detraction will not suffer it. Therefore I'll none of it: honour is a mere scutcheon; and so ends my catechism.   [*Exit.*

MERCENARIES: ASSYRIAN

Second Book of the Kings, c. 560 B.C.
Chap. xix. 10–12, 23, 24. A.V. 1611

THUS shall ye speak to Hezekiah king of Judah, saying, Let not thy God in whom thou trustest deceive thee, saying, Jerusalem shall not be delivered into the hand of the king of Assyria. Behold, thou hast heard what the kings of Assyria have done to all lands, by destroying them utterly: and shalt thou be delivered? Have the gods of the nations delivered them which my fathers have destroyed; as Gozan, and Haran, and Rezeph, and the children of Eden which were in Thelasar?...

With the multitude of my chariots I am come up to the height of the mountains, to the sides of Lebanon, and will cut down the tall cedar trees thereof, and the choice fir trees thereof: and I will enter into the lodgings of his borders, and into the forest of his Carmel. I have digged and drunk strange waters, and with the sole of my feet have I dried up all the rivers of besieged places.

MERCENARIES: PERSIAN

HERODOTUS, *History,* c. 446 B.C. Book VII, chaps liv–lvi.
Translated by George Rawlinson. 1858

ALL that day the preparations for the passage continued; and on the morrow they burnt all kinds of spices upon the bridges, and strewed the way with myrtle-boughs, while they waited anxiously for the sun, which they hoped to see as he rose. And now the sun appeared; and Xerxes took a golden goblet and poured from it a libation into the sea, praying the while with his face turned to the sun, "that no misfortune might befall him such as to hinder his conquest of Europe, until he had penetrated to its uttermost boundaries". After he had prayed, he cast the golden cup into the Hellespont, and with it a golden bowl, and a Persian sword of the kind which they call *acinaces*.[1] I cannot say for certain whether it was as an offering to the sun-god that he threw these things into the deep, or whether he had repented of having scourged the Hellespont, and thought by his gifts to make amends to the sea for what he had done.

When, however, his offerings were made, the army began to cross; and the foot-soldiers, with the horsemen, passed over by one of the bridges—that (namely) which lay towards the Euxine—while the sumpter-beasts and the camp-followers passed by the other, which looked on the Ægean. Foremost went the Ten Thousand Persians, all wearing garlands upon their heads; and after them a mixed multitude of many nations. These crossed upon the first day.

On the next day the horsemen began the passage; and with them went the soldiers who carried their spears with the point downwards, garlanded, like the Ten Thousand;—then came the sacred horses and the sacred chariot; next Xerxes with his lancers and the thousand horse; then the rest of the army. At the same time the ships sailed over to the opposite shore....

As soon as Xerxes had reached the European side, he stood to contemplate his army as they crossed under the lash. And the crossing continued during seven days and seven nights, without rest or pause.

MERCENARIES: GREEK

XENOPHON, *Anabasis, or The Expedition of Cyrus*, chap. v. c. 375 B.C. Translated by John Selby Watson. 1854

THE next day it was thought necessary to march away as fast as possible, before the enemy's force should be re-assembled, and get possession of the pass. Collecting their baggage at once, therefore, they set forward through a deep snow, taking with them several guides; and, having the same day passed the height on which Tiribazus had intended to

---

[1] A short straight sword.

attack them, they encamped. Hence they proceeded three days' journey through a desert tract of country, a distance of fifteen parasangs, to the river Euphrates, and passed it without being wet higher than the middle. The sources of the river were said not to be far off. From hence they advanced three days' march, through much snow and a level plain, a distance of fifteen parasangs; the third day's march was extremely troublesome, as the north wind blew full in their faces, completely parching up everything and benumbing the men. One of the augurs, in consequence, advised that they should sacrifice to the wind; and a sacrifice was accordingly offered; when the vehemence of the wind appeared to every one manifestly to abate. The depth of the snow was a fathom; so that many of the baggage-cattle and slaves perished, with about thirty of the soldiers. They continued to burn fires through the whole night, for there was plenty of wood at the place of encampment. But those who came up late could get no wood; those therefore who had arrived before, and had kindled fires, would not admit the late comers to the fire unless they gave them a share of the corn or other provisions that they had brought. Thus they shared with each other what they respectively had. In the places where the fires were made, as the snow melted, there were formed large pits that reached down to the ground; and here there was accordingly opportunity to measure the depth of the snow.

From hence they marched through the snow the whole of the following day, and many of the men contracted the *bulimia*. Xenophon, who commanded in the rear, finding in his way such of the men as had fallen down with it, knew not what disease it was. But as one of those acquainted with it, told him that they were evidently affected with *bulimia*, and that they would get up if they had something to eat, he went round among the baggage, and, wherever he saw anything eatable, he gave it out, and sent such as were able to run to distribute it among those diseased, who, as soon as they had eaten, rose up and continued their march. As they proceeded, Cheirisophus came, just as it grew dark, to a village, and found, at a spring in front of the rampart, some women and girls belonging to the place fetching water. The women asked

him who they were; and the interpreter answered, in the
Persian language, that they were people going from the king
to the satrap. They replied that he was not there, but about
a parasang off. However, as it was late, they went with the
water-carriers within the rampart, to the head man of the
village; and here Cheirisophus, and as many of the troops as
could come up, encamped; but of the rest, such as were unable to get to the end of the journey, spent the night on the
way without food or fire; and some of the soldiers lost their
lives on that occasion. Some of the enemy too, who had
collected themselves into a body, pursued our rear, and seized
any of the baggage-cattle that were unable to proceed, fighting
with one another for the possession of them. Such of the
soldiers, also, as had lost their sight from the effects of the
snow, or had had their toes mortified by the cold, were left
behind.

MERCENARIES: CARTHAGINIAN

Titus Livius Patavinus, *History of Rome*, c. 20 b.c. Book xxi,
35–37. Translated by Alfred John Church and William
Jackson Brodribb. 1883

Next day, as the barbarians were less active in their attacks,
the army was again united, and fought its way through the
pass, but not without loss, which, however, fell more heavily
on the beasts of burden than on the men. From this point the
mountaineers became less numerous; hovering round more
like brigands than soldiers, they threatened now the van, now
the rear, whenever the ground gave them a chance, or
stragglers in advance or behind offered an opportunity. The
elephants, though it was a tedious business to drive them
along the narrow precipitous passes, at least protected the
troops from the enemy wherever they went, inspiring as they
did, a peculiar fear in all who were unused to approach them.

On the ninth day they reached the top of the Alps, passing
for the most part over trackless steeps, and by devious ways,

into which they were led by the treachery of their guides. Two days they encamped on the height, and the men, worn out with hardships and fighting, were allowed to rest. Some beasts of burden too which had fallen down among the crags, found their way to the camp by following the army's track. The men were already worn out and wearied with their many miseries, when a fall of snow coming with the setting of the Pleiades added to their sufferings a terrible fear. At daybreak the march commenced, and as the army moved wearily over ground all buried in snow, languor and despair were visibly written on every face, when Hannibal stepped to the front, and having ordered a halt on a peak which commanded a wide and distant prospect, pointed to Italy and to the plains round the Po, as they lay beneath the heights of the Alps, telling his men, "'Tis the walls not of Italy only but of Rome itself that you are now scaling. What remains," he added, "will be a smooth descent; in one, or at the most, in two battles we shall have the citadel and capital of Italy in our grasp and power".

The army then began to advance, and now even the enemy attempted nothing but some stealthy ambuscades, as opportunity offered. The remainder, however, of the march proved far more difficult than the ascent, as the Alps for the most part on the Italian side have a shorter and therefore a steeper slope. In fact the whole way was precipitous, narrow, and slippery, so much so that they could not keep themselves from falling, nor could those who had once stumbled retain their foothold. Thus they tumbled one over another and the beasts of burden over the men.

Next they came to a much narrower pass with walls of rock so perpendicular that a light-armed soldier could hardly let himself down by feeling his way, and grasping with his hands the bushes and roots sticking out around him. The place of old was naturally precipitous, and now by a recent landslip it had been broken away sheer to a depth of a thousand feet. Here the cavalry halted, as if it must be the end of their route, and Hannibal wondering what delayed the march, was told that the rock was impassable. Then he went himself to examine the spot. There seemed to be no doubt that he must lead his army round by pathless and hitherto untrodden slopes, however tedious might be the circuit. This route, however, was impracticable; while indeed on last season's still unmelted snow lay a fresh layer of moderate depth. The foot of the first comer found a good hold on the soft and not very deep drift, but when it had been once trampled down under the march of such a host of men and beasts, they had to walk on the bare ice beneath, and the liquid mud from the melting snow. Here there was a horrible struggle. The slippery ice allowed no firm foothold, and indeed betrayed the foot all the more quickly on the slope, so that whether a man helped himself to rise by his hands or knees, his supports gave way, and he fell again. And here there were no stalks or roots to which hand or foot could cling. Thus there was incessant rolling on nothing but smooth ice or slush of snow. The beasts broke through, occasionally treading down even to the very lowest layer of snow, and when they fell, as they wildly struck out with their hoofs in their efforts to rise, they cut clean to the bottom, till many of them stuck fast in the hard and deep frozen ice, as if caught in a trap.

At last, when both men and beasts were worn out with fruitless exertion, they encamped on a height, in a spot which with the utmost difficulty they had cleared; so much snow had to be dug out and removed. The soldiers were then marched off to the work of making a road through the rock, as there only was a passage possible. Having to cut into the stone, they heaped up a huge pile of wood from great trees in the neighbourhood, which they had felled and lopped. As soon as there was strength enough in the wind to create a blaze they lighted the pile, and melted the rocks, as they heated, by pouring vinegar on them. The burning stone was cleft open with iron implements, and then they relieved the steepness of the slopes by gradual winding tracks, so that even the elephants as well as the other beasts could be led down. Four days were spent in this rocky pass, and the beasts almost perished of hunger, as the heights generally are quite bare, and such herbage as grows is buried in snow. Amid the lower slopes were valleys, sunny hills too, and streams, and woods beside them, and spots now at last more worthy to be

the habitations of man. Here they sent the beasts to feed,
and the men worn out with the toil of road making, were
allowed to rest. In the next three days they reached level
ground, and now the country was less wild, as was also the
character of the inhabitants.

MERCENARIES: ROMAN

CAIUS CORNELIUS TACITUS, *Annals*, c. A.D. 115. Book IV,
chap. v. Translated by Arthur Murphy. 1793

THE chief strength of the empire was on the Rhine, consisting
of eight legions, to bridle at once the Germans and the Gauls.
Spain, lately subdued, was held in subjection by three legions.
Juba reigned in Mauritania, deriving his title from the favour of
Rome. The rest of Africa was kept in awe by two legions. A
like number served in Egypt. In that vast extent of country,
which stretches from Syria to the Euphrates, bordering on
the confines of Iberia, Albania, and other states under the
protection of the Roman arms, four legions maintained the
rights of the empire. Thrace was governed by Rhæmetalces
and the sons of Cotys. The banks of the Danube were secured
by four legions, two in Pannonia, and two in Mæsia. Two
more were stationed in Dalmatia, in a situation, if a war broke
out at their back, to support the other legions; or, if a sudden
emergence required their presence, ready to advance by rapid
marches into Italy.

MERCENARIES: BYZANTINE

EDWARD GIBBON, *Decline and Fall of the Roman
Empire*. Vol. v, chap. lv. 1788

WHEN the Scandinavian chiefs had struck a deep and permanent root into the soil, they mingled with the Russians
in blood, religion, and language, and the first Waladimir had
the merit of delivering his country from these foreign mer-

cenaries. They had seated him on the throne; his riches were insufficient to satisfy their demands; but they listened to his pleasing advice, that they should seek, not a more grateful, but a more wealthy, master; that they should embark for Greece, where, instead of the skins of squirrels, silk and gold would be the recompense of their service. At the same time the Russian prince admonished his Byzantine ally to disperse and employ, to recompense and restrain, these impetuous children of the North. Contemporary writers have recorded the introduction, name, and character of the *Varangians*: each day they rose in confidence and esteem; the whole body was assembled at Constantinople to perform the duty of guards; and their strength was recruited by a numerous band of their countrymen from the island of Thule. On this occasion the vague appellation of Thule is applied to England; and the new Varangians were a colony of English and Danes who fled from the yoke of the Norman conqueror. The habits of pilgrimage and piracy had approximated the countries of the earth; the exiles were entertained in the Byzantine court; and they preserved, till the last age of the empire, the inheritance of spotless loyalty, and the use of the Danish or English tongue. With their broad and double-edged battle-axes on their shoulders, they attended the Greek emperor to the temple, the senate, and the hippodrome; he slept and feasted under their trusty guard; and the keys of the palace, the treasury, and the capital, were held by the firm and faithful hands of the Varangians.

MERCENARIES: ISLAMIC

EDWARD GIBBON, *Decline and Fall of the Roman Empire*. Vol. VI, chap. lxiv. 1788

THE vizir of Amurath reminded his sovereign that, according to the Mohammedan law, he was entitled to a fifth part of the spoil and captives; and that the duty might easily be levied, if vigilant officers were stationed at Gallipoli, to watch the passage, and to select for his use the stoutest and most beautiful of the Christian youth. The advice was followed: the edict was proclaimed; many thousands of the European captives were educated in religion and arms; and the new militia was consecrated and named by a celebrated dervish. Standing in the front of their ranks, he stretched the sleeve of his gown over the head of the foremost soldier, and his blessing was delivered in these words: "Let them be called Janizaries (*Yengi cheri*, or new soldiers); may their countenance be ever bright! their hand victorious! their sword keen! may their spear always hang over the heads of their enemies; and wheresoever they go, may they return with a *white face*!" Such was the origin of these haughty troops, the terror of the nations, and sometimes of the sultans themselves.

MERCENARIES: PLANTAGENET

Sir JOHN FROISSART, *Chronicles* (1326–1340). Vol. I, chap. ccxxxiv. Translated by Lord Berners. 1523

BETWEEN Saint-John's de Pied-de-Port and the city of Pampelone under the mountains there are straits and perilous passages, for there is a hundred places on the same passages that a hundred men may keep a passage against all the world. Also it was at the same season very cold, for it was about the month of February when they passed. But or they passed, they took wise counsel how or by what means they should pass; for it was shewed them plainly that they could not pass all at once, and therefore they ordained that they should pass in three battles three sundry days, as the Monday, Tuesday and Wednesday; the Monday the vaward, whereof was captain the duke of Lancaster, and in his company the constable of Acquitaine sir John Chandos, who had twelve hundred pennons of his arms, the field silver, a sharp pile gules, and with him was the two marshals of Acquitaine, as sir Guichard d'Angle and sir Stephen Cosington, and with them was the pennon of Saint George. There was also sir William Beauchamp, son to the earl

of Warwick, sir Hugh Hastings, and the lord Nevill, who
served sir John Chandos with thirty spears in that viage at
his own charge because of the taking of the battle of Auray;
and also there was the lord d'Aubeterre, sir Garsis of the
Castle, sir Richard of Tanton, sir Robert Cheyne, sir Robert
Briquet, John Creswey, Amery of the Rochechouart, Gaillard
of la Motte, William of Clifton, Willekos the Butler and Pen-
neriel. All these were there with their pennons under sir John
Chandos' rule: they were to the number of ten thousand
horses, and all these passed the Monday, as is before said.

The Tuesday passed the prince of Wales and king don Peter,
and also the king of Navarre, who was come again to the
prince to bear him company and to ensign him the ready
passage. And with the prince there was sir Louis of Harcourt,
the viscount of Chatelleraut, the viscount of Rochechouart,
the lord of Partenay, the lord of Poyane, the lord of Tannay-
Bouton, and all the Poitevins, sir Thomas Felton, great
seneschal of Acquitaine, sir William his brother, sir Eustace
d'Aubrecicourt, the seneschal of Saintonge, the seneschal of
Rochelle, the seneschal of Quercy, the seneschal of Limousin,
the seneschal of Agenois, the seneschal of Bigorre, sir Richard
of Pontchardon, sir Niel Loring, sir d'Aghorisses, sir Thomas
Banaster, sir Louis of Melval, sir Raymond of Mareuil, the
lord of Pierrebuffiere, and to the number of four thousand
men of arms, and they were a ten thousand horses. The same
Tuesday they had evil passage because of wind and snow:
howbeit they passed forth and lodged in the country of Pampelone, and the king of Navarre brought the prince and the
king don Peter into the city of Pampelone to supper and
made them great cheer.

The Wednesday passed the king James of Mallorca and the
earl of Armagnac, the earl d'Albret his nephew, sir Bernard
d'Albret, lord of Geronde, the earl of Perigord, the viscount
of Caraman, the earl of Comminges, the captal of Buch, the
lord of Clisson, the three brethren of Pommiers, sir John, sir
Elie and sir Aymenion, the lord of Caumont, the lord of Mussi-
dan, sir Robert Knolles, the lord Lesparre, the lord of Condom,
the lord of Rauzan, sir Petiton of Curton, sir Amery of Tastes,
the lord de la Barthe, sir Bertram of Tastes, the lord of Puy-

cornet, sir Thomas of Winstanley, sir Perducas d'Albret, the
bourg of Breteuil, Naudan of Bageran, Bernard de la Salle,
Ortingo, l'Amit and all the other of the companions, and they
were a ten thousand horse. They had more easy passage than
those that passed the day before; and so all the whole host
lodged in the county of Pampelone, abiding each other,
refreshing them and their horses.

MERCENARIES: ITALIAN

THOMAS BABINGTON, Lord MACAULAY, "Essay on
Machiavelli", *Edinburgh Review*. 1827

WHEN the princes and commonwealths of Italy began to
use hired troops, their wisest course would have been to form
separate military establishments. Unhappily this was not
done. The mercenary warriors of the Peninsula, instead of
being attached to the service of different powers, were regarded as the common property of all. The connection between
the state and its defenders was reduced to the most simple
and naked traffic. The adventurer brought his horse, his
weapons, his strength, and his experience, into the market.
Whether the King of Naples, or the Duke of Milan, the Pope
or the Signory of Florence, struck the bargain, was to him a
matter of perfect indifference. He was for the highest wages
and the longest term. When the campaign for which he had
contracted was finished, there was neither law nor punctilio
to prevent him from instantly turning his arms against his
late masters. The soldier was altogether disjoined from the
citizen and from the subject.

The natural consequences followed. Left to the conduct of
men who neither loved those whom they defended, nor hated
those whom they opposed, who were often bound by stronger
ties to the army against which they fought than to the state
which they served, who lost by the termination of the conflict, and gained by its prolongation, war completely changed
its character. Every man came into the field of battle

impressed with the knowledge that, in a few days, he might be taking the pay of the power against which he was then employed, and fighting by the side of his enemies against his associates. The strongest interests and the strongest feelings concurred to mitigate the hostility of those who had lately been brethren in arms, and who might soon be brethren in arms once more. Their common profession was a bond of union not to be forgotten even when they were engaged in the service of contending parties. Hence it was that operations, languid and indecisive beyond any recorded in history, marches, and counter-marches, pillaging expeditions and blockades, bloodless capitulations and equally bloodless combats, make up the military history of Italy during the course of nearly two centuries. Mighty armies fight from sunrise to sunset. A great victory is won. Thousands of prisoners are taken; and hardly a life is lost. A pitched battle seems to have been really less dangerous than an ordinary civil tumult.

MERCENARIES: BRITISH

Colonel GEORGE FRANCIS ROBERT HENDERSON,
The Science of War. Chap. xiv. 1905

IT was more than ever true, at the end of the nineteenth century, that the morning drum-beat of Great Britain goes round the world. The regiments of the regular army had quarters in every continent except Australasia. They held the islands of the sea; their bayonets glittered on the furthest frontiers of civilisation; and on the coasts of the seven seas their sentries looked down on the still waters of many harbours....

A man must have been east of Malta before he is qualified to sit in judgment on the regular army of Great Britain. The beardless regiments of Aldershot or the Curragh can no more compare with the masses of strong men, horse, foot and artillery, soldiers of whom no conscript army has seen the like, who hold India and Egypt, than the lazy routine of English quarters can compare with the vigilance and stir of

the restless East. It is in those far regions, where the menace
of peril is always present, that the British army is seasoned
for war. It is there, on the great training-ground, amid strife
and turmoil, that the character of its officers is developed,
their fibre hardened, their observation quickened, their re-
sourcefulness called into action. It was there, on the wild
frontiers of the Empire, that the Sepoy generals, who caused
the author of that felicitous phrase such an infinity of discomfort, who established the Pax Britannica in the vast
jungles of Burma, who saved India in the time of the Great
Mutiny, and who planted the Union Jack on the ruins of
Khartoum, were fashioned out of the same material that was
the sport of criticism at home.

BATTLE IN THE GREAT HARBOUR, 413 B.C.

THUCYDIDES, *History of the Peloponnesian War*, c. 400 B.C.
Book VII, chap. xxiii. Translated by Richard Crawley. 1874

THE Syracusans and their allies had already put out with
about the same number of ships as before, a part of which kept
guard at the outlet, and the remainder all round the rest of
the harbour, in order to attack the Athenians on all sides at
once; while the land forces held themselves in readiness at
the points at which the vessels might put into the shore. The
Syracusan fleet was commanded by Sicanus and Agatharchus,
who had each a wing of the whole force, with Pythen and the
Corinthians in the centre. When the rest of the Athenians
came up to the barrier, with the first shock of their charge
they overpowered the ships stationed there, and tried to undo
the fastenings; after this, as the Syracusans and allies bore
down upon them from all quarters, the action spread from the
barrier over the whole harbour, and was more obstinately
disputed than any of the preceding ones. On either side the
rowers showed great zeal in bringing up their vessels at the
boatswains' orders, and the helmsmen great skill in ma-
nœuvring, and great emulation one with another; while the

ships once alongside, the soldiers on board did their best not to
let the service on deck be outdone by the others; in short, every
man strove to prove himself the first in his particular department. And as many ships were engaged in a small compass
(for these were the largest fleets fighting in the narrowest space
ever known, being together little short of two hundred), the
regular attacks with the beak were few, there being no opportunity of backing water or of breaking the line; while the
collisions caused by one ship chancing to run foul of another,
either in flying from or attacking a third, were more frequent.
So long as a vessel was coming up to the charge the men on the
decks rained darts and arrows and stones upon her; but once
alongside, the heavy infantry tried to board each other's vessel,
fighting hand to hand. In many quarters also it happened,
by reason of the narrow room, that a vessel was charging an
enemy on one side and being charged herself on another, and
that two, or sometimes more ships had perforce got entangled
round one, obliging the helmsman to attend to defence here,
offence there, not to one thing at once, but to many on
all sides; while the huge din caused by the number of ships
crashing together not only spread terror, but made the orders
of the boatswains inaudible. The boatswains on either side
in the discharge of their duty and in the heat of the conflict
shouted incessantly orders and appeals to their men; the
Athenians they urged to force the passage out, and now if ever
to show their mettle and lay hold of a safe return to their
country; to the Syracusans and their allies they cried that it
would be glorious to prevent the escape of the enemy, and
conquering, to exalt the countries that were theirs. The
generals, moreover, on either side, if they saw any in any part
of the battle backing ashore without being forced to do so,
called out to the captain by name and asked him—the
Athenians, whether they were retreating because they
thought the thrice hostile shore more their own than that sea
which had cost them so much labour to win; the Syracusans,
whether they were flying from the flying Athenians, whom
they well knew to be eager to escape in whatever way they
could.

Meanwhile the two armies on shore, while victory hung in

the balance, were a prey to the most agonising and conflicting emotions; the natives thirsting for more glory than they had already won, while the invaders feared to find themselves in even worse plight than before. The all of the Athenians being set upon their fleet, their fear for the event was like nothing they had ever felt; while their view of the struggle was necessarily as chequered as the battle itself. Close to the scene of action and not all looking at the same point at once, some saw their friends victorious and took courage, and fell to calling upon heaven not to deprive them of salvation, while others who had their eyes turned upon the losers, wailed and cried aloud, and, although spectators, were more overcome than the actual combatants. Others, again, were gazing at some spot where the battle was evenly disputed; as the strife was protracted without decision, their swaying bodies reflected the agitation of their minds, and they suffered the worst agony of all, ever just within reach of safety or just on the point of destruction. In short, in that one Athenian army as long as the sea-fight remained doubtful there was every sound to be heard at once, shrieks, cheers, "*We win*", "*We lose*", and all the other manifold exclamations that a great host would necessarily utter in great peril; and with the men in the fleet it was nearly the same; until at last the Syracusans and their allies, after the battle had lasted a long while, put the Athenians to flight, and with much shouting and cheering chased them in open rout to the shore.

IN THE TEUTOBURGERWALD

GAIUS CORNELIUS TACITUS, *Annals*, c. A.D. 115. Book I, chaps. lx–lxii. Translated by Arthur Murphy. 1793

THE Romans were now at a small distance from the forest of Teutoburgium, where the bones of Varus and his legions were said to be still unburied.

Touched by this affecting circumstance, Germanicus resolved to pay the last human office to the relics of that unfortunate commander and his slaughtered soldiers. The same tender sentiment diffused itself through the army: some felt the touch of nature for their relations, others for their friends; and all lamented the disasters of war, and the wretched lot of human kind. Cæcina was sent forward to explore the woods; where the waters were out, to throw up bridges; and, by heaping loads of earth on the swampy soil, to secure a solid footing. The army marched through a gloomy solitude. The place presented an awful spectacle, and the memory of a tragical event increased the horror of the scene. The first camp of Varus appeared in view. The extent of the ground, and the three different enclosures for the eagles, still distinctly seen, left no doubt but that the whole was the work of the three legions. Farther on were traced the ruins of a rampart, and the hollow of a ditch well nigh filled up. This was supposed to be the spot where the few, who escaped the general massacre, made their last effort, and perished in the attempt. The plains around were white with bones, in some places thinly scattered, in others lying in heaps, as the men happened to fall in flight, or in a body resisted to the last. Fragments of javelins, and the limbs of horses, lay scattered about the field. Human skulls were seen upon the trunks of trees. In the adjacent woods stood the savage altars where the tribunes and principal centurions were offered up a sacrifice with barbarous rites. Some of the soldiers who survived that dreadful day, and afterwards broke their chains, related circumstantially several particulars. "Here the commanders of the legions were put to the sword: on that spot the eagles were seized. There Varus received his first wound; and this the place where he gave himself the mortal stab, and died by his own sword. Yonder mound was the tribunal from which Arminius harangued his countrymen: here he fixed his gibbets; there he dug the funeral trenches; and in that quarter he offered every mark of scorn and insolence to the colours and the Roman eagles."

Six years had elapsed since the overthrow of Varus; and now, on the same spot, the Roman army collected the bones of their slaughtered countrymen. Whether they were burying the remains of strangers, or of their own friends, no man knew: all, however, considered themselves as performing the last obsequies to their kindred, and their brother-soldiers. While employed in this pious office, their hearts were torn with contending passions; by turns oppressed with grief, and burning for revenge. A monument to the memory of the dead was raised with turf. Germanicus with his own hand laid the first sod; discharging at once the tribute due to the legions, and sympathising with the rest of the army.

JERUSALEM DELIVERED

EDWARD GIBBON, *Decline and Fall of the Roman Empire.*
Vol. VI, chap. lviii. 1788

GODFREY of Bouillon erected his standard on the first swell of Mount Calvary: to the left, as far as St. Stephen's gate, the line of attack was continued by Tancred and the two Roberts; and Count Raymond established his quarters from the citadel to the foot of Mount Sion, which was no longer included within the precincts of the city. On the fifth day the crusaders made a general assault, in the fanatic hope of battering down the walls without engines, and of scaling them without ladders. By the dint of brutal force they burst the first barrier, but they were driven back with shame and slaughter to the camp: the influence of vision and prophecy was deadened by the too frequent abuse of those pious stratagems; and time and labour were found to be the only means of victory. The time of the siege was indeed fulfilled in forty days, but they were forty days of calamity and anguish. A repetition of the old complaint of famine may be imputed in some degree to the voracious or disorderly appetite of the Franks; but the stony soil of Jerusalem is almost destitute of water; the scanty springs and hasty torrents were dry in the summer season: nor was the thirst of the besiegers relieved, as in the city, by the artificial supply of cisterns and aqueducts. The circumjacent country is equally destitute of trees for the uses of shade or building; but some large beams were discovered

in a cave by the crusaders: a wood near Sichem, the enchanted grove of Tasso, was cut down: the necessary timber
was transported to the camp by the vigour and dexterity of
Tancred; and the engines were framed by some Genoese
artists, who had fortunately landed in the harbour of Jaffa.
Two movable turrets were constructed at the expense, and
in the stations, of the duke of Lorraine and the count of
Toulouse, and rolled forwards with devout labour, not to the
most accessible, but to the most neglected, parts of the fortification. Raymond's tower was reduced to ashes by the fire
of the besieged, but his colleague was more vigilant and
successful; the enemies were driven by his archers from the
rampart; the drawbridge was let down; and on a Friday, at
three in the afternoon, the day and hour of the Passion, Godfrey of Bouillon stood victorious on the walls of Jerusalem.
His example was followed on every side by the emulation of
valour; and about four hundred and sixty years after the
conquest of Omar, the holy city was rescued from the Mohammedan yoke. In the pillage of public and private wealth,
the adventurers had agreed to respect the exclusive property
of the first occupant; and the spoils of the great mosque,
seventy lamps and massy vases of gold and silver, rewarded
the diligence, and displayed the generosity, of Tancred. A
bloody sacrifice was offered by his mistaken votaries to the
God of the Christians: resistance might provoke, but neither
age nor sex could mollify, their implacable rage: they indulged
themselves three days in a promiscuous massacre; and the
infection of the dead bodies produced an epidemical disease.
After seventy thousand Moslems had been put to the sword,
and the harmless Jews had been burnt in their synagogue,
they could still reserve a multitude of captives whom interest
or lassitude persuaded them to spare. Of these savage heroes
of the cross, Tancred alone betrayed some sentiments of com-
passion; yet we may praise the more selfish lenity of Raymond, who granted a capitulation and safe-conduct to the
garrison of the citadel. The holy sepulchre was now free; and
the bloody victors prepared to accomplish their vow. Bare-
headed and barefoot, with contrite hearts and in a humble
posture, they ascended the hill of Calvary, amidst the loud

anthems of the clergy; kissed the stone which had covered the Saviour of the world; and bedewed with tears of joy and penitence the monument of their redemption.

FALL OF CONSTANTINOPLE

EDWARD GIBBON, *Decline and Fall of the Roman Empire.*
Vol. VI, chap. lxviii. 1788

At daybreak, without the customary signal of the morning gun, the Turks assaulted the city by sea and land; and the similitude of a twined or twisted thread has been applied to the closeness and continuity of their line of attack. The foremost ranks consisted of the refuse of the host, a voluntary crowd who fought without order or command; of the feebleness of age or childhood, of peasants and vagrants, and of all who had joined the camp in the blind hope of plunder and martyrdom. The common impulse drove them onwards to the wall; the most audacious to climb were instantly precipitated; and not a dart, nor a bullet, of the Christians, was idly wasted on the accumulated throng. But their strength and ammunition were exhausted in this laborious defence: the ditch was filled with the bodies of the slain; they supported the footsteps of their companions; and of this devoted vanguard the death was more serviceable than the life. Under their respective bashaws and sanjaks, the troops of Anatolia and Romania were successively led to the charge: their progress was various and doubtful; but, after a conflict of two hours, the Greeks still maintained and improved their advantage; and the voice of the emperor was heard, encouraging his soldiers to achieve, by a last effort, the deliverance of their country. In that fatal moment the Janizaries arose, fresh, vigorous, and invincible. The sultan himself on horseback, with an iron mace in his hand, was the spectator and judge of their valour; he was surrounded by ten thousand of his domestic troops, whom he reserved for the decisive occasion; and the tide of battle was directed and impelled by his voice

and eye. His numerous ministers of justice were posted
behind the line, to urge, to restrain, and to punish; and if
danger was in the front, shame and inevitable death were in
the rear, of the fugitives. The cries of fear and of pain were
drowned in the martial music of drums, trumpets, and atta-
balls; and experience has proved that the mechanical operations of sounds, by quickening the circulation of the blood and
spirits, will act on the human machine more forcibly than the
eloquence of reason and honour. From the lines, the galleys,
and the bridge, the Ottoman artillery thundered on all sides;
and the camp and city, the Greeks and the Turks, were involved in a cloud of smoke, which could only be dispelled by
the final deliverance or destruction of the Roman empire. The
single combats of the heroes of history or fable amuse our
fancy and engage our affections: the skilful evolutions of war
may inform the mind, and improve a necessary, though pernicious, science. But in the uniform and odious pictures of
a general assault, all is blood and horror, and confusion; nor
shall I strive, at the distance of three centuries and a thousand
miles, to delineate a scene at which there could be no spectators, and of which the actors themselves were incapable of
forming any just or adequate idea.

The immediate loss of Constantinople may be ascribed to
the bullet, or arrow, which pierced the gauntlet of John
Justiniani. The sight of his blood, and the exquisite pain,
appalled the courage of the chief, whose arms and counsels
were the firmest rampart of the city. As he withdrew from
his station in quest of a surgeon, his flight was perceived
and stopped by the indefatigable emperor. "Your wound",
exclaimed Palæologus, "is slight; the danger is pressing: your
presence is necessary; and whither will you retire?"—"I will
retire", said the trembling Genoese, "by the same road which
God has opened to the Turks"; and at these words he hastily
passed through one of the breaches of the inner wall. By this
pusillanimous act he stained the honours of a military life;
and the few days which he survived in Galata, or the isle of
Chios, were embittered by his own and the public reproach.
His example was imitated by the greatest part of the Latin
auxiliaries, and the defence began to slacken when the attack

was pressed with redoubled vigour. The number of the Ottomans was fifty, perhaps a hundred, times superior to that of
the Christians; the double walls were reduced by the cannon
to a heap of ruins: in a circuit of several miles some places
must be found more easy of access, or more feebly guarded;
and if the besiegers could penetrate in a single point, the
whole city was irrecoverably lost. The first who deserved the
sultan's reward was Hassan the Janizary, of gigantic stature
and strength. With his scimitar in one hand and his buckler in
the other, he ascended the outward fortification: of the thirty
Janizaries who were emulous of his valour, eighteen perished
in the bold adventure. Hassan and his twelve companions
had reached the summit: the giant was precipitated from the
rampart: he rose on one knee, and was again oppressed by
a shower of darts and stones. But his success had proved that
the achievement was possible: the walls and towers were instantly covered with a swarm of Turks; and the Greeks, now
driven from the vantage ground, were overwhelmed by increasing multitudes. Amidst these multitudes, the emperor,
who accomplished all the duties of a general and a soldier,
was long seen and finally lost. The nobles, who fought round
his person, sustained, till their last breath, the honourable
names of Palæologus and Cantacuzene: his mournful exclamation was heard, "Cannot there be found a Christian to
cut off my head?" and his last fear was that of falling alive
into the hands of the infidels. The prudent despair of Constantine cast away the purple: amidst the tumult he fell by an
unknown hand, and his body was buried under a mountain
of the slain. After his death resistance and order were no
more: the Greeks fled towards the city; and many were
pressed and stifled in the narrow pass of the gate of St. Ro-
manus. The victorious Turks rushed through the breaches of
the inner wall; and as they advanced into the streets, they
were soon joined by their brethren, who had forced the gate
Phenar on the side of the harbour. In the first heat of the
pursuit about two thousand Christians were put to the sword;
but avarice soon prevailed over cruelty; and the victors acknowledged that they should immediately have given quarter,
if the valour of the emperor and his chosen bands had not

prepared them for a similar opposition in every part of the capital. It was thus, after a siege of fifty-three days, that Constantinople, which had defied the power of Chosroes, the Chagan, and the caliphs, was irretrievably subdued by the arms of Mohammed the Second.

LANDEN

THOMAS BABINGTON, LORD MACAULAY, *History of England.* Chap. xx. 1855

AT length Luxemburg formed his decision. A last attempt must be made to carry Neerwinden; and the invincible household troops, the conquerors of Steinkirk, must lead the way.

The household troops came on in a manner worthy of their long and terrible renown. A third time Neerwinden was taken. A third time William tried to retake it. At the head of some English regiments he charged the guards of Lewis with such fury that, for the first time in the memory of the oldest warrior, that far famed band gave way. It was only by the strenuous exertions of Luxemburg, of the Duke of Chartres, and of the Duke of Bourbon, that the broken ranks were rallied. But by this time the centre and left of the allied army had been so much thinned for the purpose of supporting the conflict at Neerwinden that the entrenchments could no longer be defended on other points. A little after four in the afternoon the whole line gave way. All was havoc and confusion. Solmes had received a mortal wound, and fell, still alive, into the hands of the enemy. The English soldiers, to whom his name was hateful, accused him of having in his sufferings shown pusillanimity unworthy of a soldier. The Duke of Ormond was struck down in the press; and in another moment he would have been a corpse, had not a rich diamond on his finger caught the eye of one of the French guards, who justly thought that the owner of such a jewel would be a valuable prisoner. The Duke's life was saved; and he was speedily exchanged for Berwick. Ruvigny, animated by the true refugee hatred of the country which had cast him out, was taken fighting in the thickest of the battle. Those into whose hands he had fallen knew him well, and knew that, if they carried him to their camp, his head would pay for that treason to which persecution had driven him. With admirable generosity they pretended not to recognise him, and suffered him to make his escape in the tumult.

It was only on such occasions as this that the whole greatness of William's character appeared. Amidst the rout and uproar, while arms and standards were flung away, while multitudes of fugitives were choking up the bridges and fords of the Gette or perishing in its waters, the King, having directed Talmash to superintend the retreat, put himself at the head of a few brave regiments, and by desperate efforts arrested the progress of the enemy. His risk was greater than that which others ran. For he could not be persuaded either to encumber his feeble frame with a cuirass, or to hide the ensigns of the garter. He thought his star a good rallying point for his own troops, and only smiled when he was told that it was a good mark for the enemy. Many fell on his right hand and on his left. Two led horses, which in the field always closely followed his person, were struck dead by cannon shots. One musket ball passed through the curls of his wig, another through his coat: a third bruised his side and tore his blue riband to tatters. Many years later greyheaded old pensioners who crept about the arcades and alleys of Chelsea Hospital used to relate how he charged at the head of Galway's horse, how he rallied one corps which seemed to be shrinking: "That is not the way to fight, gentlemen. You must stand close up to them. Thus, gentlemen, thus". "You might have seen him,"—an eyewitness wrote, only four days after the battle,—"with his sword in his hand, throwing himself upon the enemy. It is certain that, one time, among the rest, he was seen at the head of two English regiments, and that he fought seven with these two in sight of the whole army, driving them before him above a quarter of an hour. Thanks be to God that preserved him." The enemy pressed on him so close that it was with difficulty that he at length made his way over the Gette.

A small body of brave men, who shared his peril to the last, could hardly keep off the pursuers as he crossed the bridge.

Never, perhaps, was the change which the progress of civilisation has produced in the art of war more strikingly illustrated than on that day. Ajax beating down the Trojan leader with a rock which two ordinary men could scarcely lift, Horatius defending the bridge against an army, Richard the Lionhearted spurring along the whole Saracen line without finding an enemy to stand his assault, Robert Bruce crushing with one blow the helmet and head of Sir Henry Bohun in sight of the whole array of England and Scotland, such are the heroes of a dark age. In such an age bodily vigour is the most indispensable qualification of a warrior. At Landen two poor sickly beings, who, in a rude state of society, would have been regarded as too puny to bear any part in combats, were the souls of two great armies. In some heathen countries they would have been exposed while infants. In Christendom they would, six hundred years earlier, have been sent to some quiet cloister. But their lot had fallen on a time when men had discovered that the strength of the muscles is far inferior in value to the strength of the mind. It is probable that, among the hundred and twenty thousand soldiers who were marshalled round Neerwinden under all the standards of Western Europe, the two feeblest in body were the hunchbacked dwarf who urged forward the fiery onset of France, and the asthmatic skeleton who covered the slow retreat of England.

The French were victorious: but they had bought their victory dear. More than ten thousand of the best troops of Lewis had fallen. Neerwinden was a spectacle at which the oldest soldiers stood aghast. The streets were piled breast high with corpses. Among the slain were some great lords and some renowned warriors. Montchevreuil was there, and the mutilated trunk of the Duke of Uzes, first in order of precedence among the whole aristocracy of France. Thence too Sarsfield was borne desperately wounded to a pallet from which he never rose again. The Court of Saint Germains had conferred on him the empty title of Earl of Lucan: but history knows him by the name which is still dear to the most un-

fortunate of nations. The region, renowned in history as the
battle field, during many ages, of the greatest powers of
Europe, has seen only two more terrible days, the day of
Malplaquet and the day of Waterloo. During many months
the ground was strewn with skulls and bones of men and
horses, and with fragments of hats and shoes, saddles and
holsters. The next summer the soil, fertilised by twenty
thousand corpses, broke forth into millions of poppies. The
traveller who, on the road from Saint Tron to Tirlemont, saw
that vast sheet of rich scarlet spreading from Landen to Neerwinden, could hardly help fancying that the figurative prediction of the Hebrew prophet was literally accomplished,
that the earth was disclosing her blood, and refusing to cover
the slain.

INFANTRY AT FONTENOY

HON. SIR JOHN WILLIAM FORTESCUE, *History of the
British Army*. Vol. II. 1899

IN the first line, counting from right to left, stood a battalion
of the First Guards, another of the Coldstream, and another
of the Scots Guards, the First, Twenty-first, Thirty-first, Eighth,
Twenty-fifth, Thirty-third, and Nineteenth; in the second line
the Buffs occupied the post of honour on the right, and next
to them came in succession the Twenty-third, Thirty-second,
Eleventh, Twenty-eighth, Thirty-fourth, and Twentieth.
Certain Hanoverian battalions joined them on the extreme
left. The drums beat, the men shouldered arms, and the
detachments harnessed themselves to the two light field-guns
that accompanied each battalion. Ingoldsby saw what was
going forward and aligned his battalions with them on the
right. Then the word was given to advance, and the two lines
moved off with the slow and measured step for which they
were famous in Europe.

Forward tramped the ranks of scarlet, silent and stately as
if on parade. Full half a mile of ground was to be traversed

before they could close with the invisible enemy that awaited
them in the entrenchments over the crest of the slope, and
the way was marked clearly by the red flashes and puffs of
white smoke that leaped from Fontenoy and the Redoubt
d'Eu on either flank. The shot plunged fiercely and more
fiercely into the serried lines as they advanced into that
murderous cross-fire, but the gaping ranks were quietly closed,
the perfect order was never lost, the stately step was never
hurried. Only the Hanoverians in the second line, finding that
they were cramped for space, dropped back quietly and de-
corously, and marched on in third line behind the British.
Silent and inexorable the scarlet lines strode on. They came
abreast of village and redoubt, and the shot which had hitherto swept away files now swept away ranks. Then the first line
passed beyond redoubt and village, and the French cannon
took it in reverse. The gaps grew wider and more frequent,
the front grew narrower as the men closed up, but still the
proud battalions advanced, strewing the sward behind them
with scarlet, like some mass of red blossom that floats down
a lazy stream and sheds its petals as it goes.

At last the crest of the ridge was gained and the ranks of the
French battalions came suddenly into view little more than
a hundred yards distant, their coats alone visible behind the
breastwork. Next to the forest of Barry, and exposed to the
extreme right of the British, a line of red showed the presence
of the Swiss Guards; next to them stood a line of blue, the
four battalions of the French Guards, and next to the Guards
a line of white, the regiments of Courtin, Aubeterre, and of the
King, the choicest battalions of the French Army. Closer and
closer came the British, still with arms shouldered, always
silent, always with the same slow, measured tread, till they
had advanced to within fifty yards of the French. Then at
length Lord Charles Hay of the First Guards stepped forward
with flask in hand, and doffing his hat drank politely to his
enemies. "I hope, gentlemen," he shouted, "that you are
going to wait for us to-day and not swim the Scheldt as you
swam the Main at Dettingen. Men of the King's company,"
he continued, turning round to his own people, "these are the
French Guards, and I hope you are going to beat them to-

day"; and the English Guards answered with a cheer. The French officers hurried to the front, for the appearance of the British was a surprise to them, and called for a cheer in reply, but only a half-hearted murmur came from the French ranks, which quickly died away and gave place to a few sharp words of command; for the British were now within thirty yards. "For what we are about to receive may the Lord make us truly thankful", murmured an English Guardsman as he looked down the barrels of the French muskets, but before his comrades round him had done laughing the French Guards had fired; and the turn of the British had come at last.

For despite of that deadly march through the cross-fire of the French batteries to the muzzles of the French muskets, the scarlet ranks still glared unbroken through the smoke; and now the British muskets, so long shouldered, were levelled, and with crash upon crash the volleys rang out from end to end of the line, first the First Guards, then the Scots, then the Coldstreams, and so through brigade after brigade, two battalions loading while the third fired, a ceaseless, rolling, infernal fire. Down dropped the whole of the French front rank, blue coats, red coats, and white, before the storm. Nineteen officers and six hundred men of the French and Swiss Guards fell at the first discharge; regiment Courtin was crushed out of existence; regiment Aubeterre, striving hard to stem the tide, was swept aside by a single imperious volley which laid half of its men on the ground. The British infantry were perfectly in hand; their officers could be seen coolly tapping the muskets of the men with their canes so that every discharge might be low and deadly; while the battalion-guns also poured in round after round of grape with terrible effect. The first French line was utterly shattered and broken. Even while the British were advancing, Saxe had brought up additional troops to meet them and had posted regiments Couronne and Soissonois in rear of the King's regiment, and the Brigade Royal in rear of the French Guards; but all alike went down before the irresistible volleys. The red-coats continued their triumphant advance for full three hundred yards into the heart of the French camp, and old Ligonier's heart leaped within him, for he thought that the battle was won.

FUZILEERS AT ALBUERA, 1811

Sir William Francis Patrick Napier, *History of the War in the Peninsula and in the South of France*, 1807–1814. Vol. iii. 1831

The fourth division had only two brigades in the field; the one Portuguese under general Harvey, the other British, commanded by sir W. Myers and composed of the seventh and twenty-third regiments, was called the fuzileer brigade. General Cole directed the Portuguese to move between Lumley's dragoons and the hill, where they were immediately charged by some of the French horsemen, but beat them off with great loss: meanwhile he led the fuzileers in person up the height.

At this time six guns were in the enemy's possession, the whole of Werlé's reserves were coming forward to reinforce the front column of the French, and the remnant of Houghton's brigade could no longer maintain its ground; the field was heaped with carcasses, the lancers were riding furiously about the captured artillery on the upper part of the hill, and on the lower slopes, a Spanish and an English regiment in mutual error were exchanging volleys: behind all, general Hamilton's Portuguese, in withdrawing from the heights above the bridge, appeared to be in retreat. The conduct of a few brave men soon changed this state of affairs. Colonel Robert Arbuthnot, pushing between the double fire of the mistaken troops, arrested that mischief, while Cole, with the fuzileers, flanked by a battalion of the Lusitanian legion under colonel Hawkshawe, mounted the hill, dispersed the lancers, recovered the captured guns, and appeared on the right of Houghton's brigade exactly as Abercrombie passed it on the left.

Such a gallant line, issuing from the midst of the smoke and rapidly separating itself from the confused and broken multitude, startled the enemy's heavy masses, which were increasing and pressing onwards as to an assured victory: they wavered, hesitated, and then vomiting forth a storm of fire, hastily endeavoured to enlarge their front, while a fearful discharge of grape from all their artillery whistled through the British ranks. Myers was killed; Cole and the three colonels, Ellis, Blakeney, and Hawkshawe, fell wounded, and the fuzileer battalions, struck by the iron tempest, reeled and staggered like sinking ships. Suddenly and sternly recovering, they closed on their terrible enemies, and then was seen with what a strength and majesty the British soldier fights. In vain did Soult, by voice and gesture, animate his Frenchmen; in vain did the hardiest veterans, extricating themselves from the crowded columns, sacrifice their lives to gain time for the mass to open out on such a fair field; in vain did the mass itself bear up, and fiercely striving, fire indiscriminately upon friends and foes, while the horsemen hovering on the flank threatened to charge the advancing line. Nothing could stop that astonishing infantry. No sudden burst of undisciplined valour, no nervous enthusiasm, weakened the stability of their order; their flashing eyes were bent on the dark columns in their front; their measured tread shook the ground; their dreadful volleys swept away the head of every formation; their deafening shouts overpowered the dissonant cries that broke from all parts of the tumultuous crowd, as foot by foot and with a horrid carnage it was driven by the incessant vigour of the attack to the farthest edge of the hill. In vain did the French reserves, joining with the struggling multitude, endeavour to sustain the fight; their efforts only increased the irremediable confusion, and the mighty mass giving way like a loosened cliff, went headlong down the ascent. The rain flowed after in streams discoloured with blood, and fifteen hundred unwounded men, the remnant of six thousand unconquerable British soldiers, stood triumphant on the fatal hill!

MOVEMENT OF CAVALRY SUPPORTS

ALEXANDER WILLIAM KINGLAKE, *The Invasion of the Crimea.*
"The Battle of Balaclava." Vol. v, chap. i, sect. 10. 1875

THROUGHOUT their whole course down the valley the officers and the men of the 11th Hussars, the 4th Light Dragoons, and the 8th Hussars never judged themselves to be absolved from the hard task of maintaining their formation, and patiently enduring to see their ranks torn, without having means for the time of even trying to harm their destroyers. These three regiments, moreover, were subjected to another kind of trial from which the first line was exempt; for men not only had (as had had the first line) to see numbers torn out of their ranks, and then close up and pass on, but were also compelled to be witnesses of the havoc that battle had been making with their comrades in front. The ground they had to pass over was thickly strewn with men and horses lying prostrate in death, or from wounds altogether disabling; but these were less painful to see than the maimed officers or soldiers, still able to walk or to crawl, and the charger moving horribly with three of his limbs, whilst dragging the wreck of the fourth, or convulsively labouring to rise from the ground by the power of the forelegs when the quarters had been shattered by round-shot.

And, although less distressing to see, the horses which had just lost their riders without being themselves disabled, were formidable disturbers of any regiment which had to encounter them. The extent to which a charger can apprehend the perils of a battle-field may be easily underrated by one who confines his observation to horses still carrying their riders; for, as long as a troop-horse in action feels the weight and the hand of a master, his deep trust in man keeps him seemingly free from great terror, and he goes through the fight, unless wounded, as though it were a field-day at home; but the moment that death or a disabling wound deprives him of his rider, he seems all at once to learn what a battle is —to perceive its real dangers with the clearness of a human being, and to be agonised with horror of the fate he may incur for want of a hand to guide him. Careless of the mere thunders of guns he shows plainly enough that he more or less knows the dread accent that is used by missiles of war whilst cutting their way through the air, for as often as these sounds disclose to him the near passage of bullet or round-shot, he shrinks and cringes. His eyeballs protrude. Wild with fright, he still does not most commonly gallop home into camp. His instinct seems rather to tell him that what safety, if any, there is for him must be found in the ranks; and he rushes at the first squadron he can find, urging piteously, yet with violence, that he too by right is a troop-horse—that he too is willing to charge, but not to be left behind—that he must and he will "fall in". Sometimes a riderless charger thus bent on aligning with his fellows, will not be content to range himself on the flank of the line, but dart at some point in the squadron which he seemingly judges to be his own rightful place, and strive to force himself in. Riding, as it is usual for the commander of a regiment to do, some way in advance of his regiment, Lord George Paget was especially tormented and pressed by the riderless horses which chose to turn round and align with him. At one time there were three or four of these horses advancing close abreast of him on one side, and as many as five on the other. Impelled by terror, by gregarious instinct, and by their habit of ranging in line, they so "closed" in upon Lord George as to besmear his overalls with blood from the gory flanks of the nearest intruders, and oblige him to use his sword.

BATTLE OF NATIONS: LEIPZIG, 1813

John Holland Rose, *Life of Napoleon I.*
Vol. II, chap. xxxv. 1901

They had Napoleon in their power, as he surmised. Late on that Sunday, he withdrew his drenched and half-starved troops nearer to Leipzig; for Blücher had gained ground on the north and threatened the French line of retreat. Why the

Emperor did not retreat during the night must remain a mystery. All the peoples of Europe were now closing in on him. On the north were Prussians, Russians, Swedes, and a few British troops. To the south-east were the dense masses of the allied Grand Army drawn from all the lands between the Alps and the Urals; and among Bennigsen's array on the east of Leipzig were to be seen the Bashkirs of Siberia, whose bows and arrows gained them from the French soldiery the sobriquet of *les Amours*.

To this ring of 300,000 fighters Napoleon could oppose scarcely half as many. Yet the French fought on, if not for victory, yet for honour; and, under the lead of Prince Ponia-towski, whose valour on the 16th had gained him the coveted rank of a Marshal of France, the Poles once more clutched desperately at the wraith of their national independence. Napoleon took his stand with his staff on a hill behind Probstheyde near a half-ruined windmill, fit emblem of his fortunes; while, further south, the three allied monarchs watched from a higher eminence the vast horse-shoe of smoke slowly draw in towards the city. In truth, this immense conflict baffles all description. On the north-east, the Crown Prince of Sweden gradually drove his columns across the Parthe, while Blücher hammered at the suburbs.

Near the village of Paunsdorf, the allies found a weak place in the defence, where Reynier's Saxons showed signs of disaffection. Some few went over to the Russians in the forenoon, and about 3 p.m. others marched over with loud hurrahs. They did not exceed 3,000 men, with 19 cannon, but these pieces were at once effectively used against the French. Napoleon hurried towards the spot with part of his Guards, who restored the fight on that side. But it was only for a time. The defence was everywhere overmatched.

Even the inspiration of his presence and the desperate efforts of Murat, Poniatowski, Victor, Macdonald, and thou-sands of nameless heroes, barely held off the masses of the allied Grand Army. On the north and north-east, Marmont and Ney were equally overborne. Worst of all, the supply of cannon balls was running low. With pardonable exaggera-tion the Emperor afterwards wrote to Clarke: "If I had then had 30,000 rounds, I should to-day be the master of the world".

At nightfall, the chief returned weary and depressed to the windmill, and instructed Berthier to order the retreat. Then, beside a watch-fire, he sank down on a bench into a deep slumber, while his generals looked on in mournful silence. All around them there surged in the darkness the last cries of battle, the groans of the wounded, and the dull rumble of a retreating host. After a quarter of an hour he awoke with a start and threw an astonished look on his staff; then, re-collecting himself, he bade an officer repair to the King of Saxony and tell him the state of affairs.

Early next morning, he withdrew into Leipzig, and, after paying a brief visit to the King, rode away towards the western gate. It was none too soon. The conflux of his still mighty forces streaming in by three high roads, produced in all the streets of the town a crush which thickened every hour. The Prussians and Swedes were breaking into the northern suburbs, while the white-coats drove in the defenders on the south. Slowly and painfully the throng of fugitives struggled through the town towards the western gate. On that side the confusion became ever worse, as the shots of the allies began to whiz across the arches and causeway that led over the Pleisse and the Elster, while the hurrahs of the Russians drew near on the north. Ammunition wagons, gendarmes, women, grenadiers and artillery, cavalry and cattle, the wounded, the dying, Marshals and sutlers, all were wedged into an indis-tinguishable throng that fought for a foothold on that narrow road of safety; and high above the din came the clash of merry bells from the liberated suburbs, bells that three days before had rung forced peals of triumph at Napoleon's orders, but now bade farewell for ever to French domination. To in-crease the rout, a temporary bridge thrown over the Elster broke down under the crush; and the rush for the roadway became more furious. In despair of reaching it, hundreds threw themselves into the flooded stream, but few reached the further shore: among the drowned was that flower of Polish chivalry, Prince Poniatowski.

But this mishap was soon to be outdone. A corporal of

engineers, in the absence of his chief, had received orders to blow up the bridge outside the western gate, as soon as the pursuers were at hand; but, alarmed by the volleys of Sacken's Russians, whom Blücher had sent to work round by the river courses north-west of the town, the bewildered subaltern fired the mine while the rearguard and a great crowd of stragglers were still on the eastern side. This was the climax of this day of disaster, which left in the hands of the allies as many as thirty generals, including Lauriston and Reynier, and 33,000 of the rank and file, along with 260 cannon and 870 ammunition wagons. From the village of Lindenau Napoleon gazed back at times over the awesome scene, but in general he busied himself with reducing to order the masses that had struggled across. The Old Guard survived, staunch as ever, and had saved its 120 cannon, but the Young Guard was reduced to a mere wreck. Amidst all the horrors of that day, the Emperor maintained a stolid composure, but observers saw that he was bathed in sweat. Towards evening, he turned and rode away westwards; and from the weary famished files, many a fierce glance and muttered curse shot forth as he passed by. Men remembered that it was exactly a year since the Grand Army broke up from Moscow.

TWO KINDS OF WAR

JOHN RICHARD GREEN, *A Short History of the English People*. Vol. IV. 1874

During the earlier years of the war, indeed, the increase of wealth had been enormous. England was sole mistress of the seas. The war gave her possession of the colonies of Spain, of Holland, and of France; and if her trade was checked for a time by the Berlin Decree, the efforts of Napoleon were soon rendered fruitless by the vast smuggling system which sprang up along the southern coasts and the coast of North Germany. English exports had nearly doubled since the opening of the century. Manufactures profited by the discoveries of Watt and

Arkwright; and the consumption of raw cotton in the mills of Lancashire rose during the same period from fifty to a hundred millions of pounds. The vast accumulation of capital, as well as the vast increase of the population at this time, told upon the land, and forced agriculture into a feverish and unhealthy prosperity. Wheat rose to famine prices, and the value of land rose in proportion with the price of wheat. Inclosures went on with prodigious rapidity; the income of every landowner was doubled, while the farmers were able to introduce improvements into the processes of agriculture which changed the whole face of the country. But if the increase of wealth was enormous, its distribution was partial. During the fifteen years which preceded Waterloo, the number of the population rose from ten to thirteen millions, and this rapid increase kept down the rate of wages, which would naturally have advanced in a corresponding degree with the increase in the national wealth. Even manufactures, though destined in the long run to benefit the labouring classes, seemed at first rather to depress them; for one of the earliest results of the introduction of machinery was the ruin of a number of small trades which were carried on at home, and the pauperization of families who relied on them for support. In the winter of 1811 the terrible pressure of this transition from handicraft to machinery was seen in the Luddite, or machine-breaking, riots which broke out over the northern and midland counties, and which were only suppressed by military force. While labour was thus thrown out of its older grooves, and the rate of wages kept down at an artificially low figure by the rapid increase of population, the rise in the price of wheat, which brought wealth to the landowner and the farmer, brought famine and death to the poor, for England was cut off by the war from the vast cornfields of the Continent or of America, which nowadays redress from their abundance the results of a bad harvest. Scarcity was followed by a terrible pauperization of the labouring classes. The amount of the poor-rate rose fifty per cent.; and with the increase of poverty followed its inevitable result, the increase of crime.

The natural relation of trade and commerce to the general wealth of the people at large was thus disturbed by the peculiar circumstances of the time. The war enriched the land-owner, the farmer, the merchant, the manufacturer; but it impoverished the poor. It is indeed from these fatal years which lie between the Peace of Luneville and Waterloo that we must date the war of classes, that social severance between employers and employed, which still forms the main difficulty of English politics.

A GENERAL PEACE

WILLIAM PENN, *The Peace of Europe.* 1693

IN my first section, I showed the desirableness of peace; in my next, the truest means of it; to wit, justice not war. And in my last, that this justice was the fruit of government, as government itself was the result of society which first came from a reasonable design in men of peace. Now if the sovereign princes of Europe, who represent that society, or independent state of men that was previous to the obligations of society, would for the same reason that engaged men first into society, viz., love of peace and order, agree to meet by their stated deputies in a general diet, estates, or parliament, and there establish rules of justice for sovereign princes to observe one to another; and thus to meet yearly, or once in two or three years at farthest, or as they shall see cause, and to be styled, the Sovereign or Imperial Diet, Parliament, or State of Europe; before which sovereign assembly should be brought all differences depending between one sovereign and another that cannot be made up by private embassies before the sessions begin; and that if any of the sovereignties that constitute these imperial states shall refuse to submit their claim or pretensions to them, or to abide and perform the judgment thereof, and seek their remedy by arms, or delay their compliance beyond the time prefixed in their resolutions, all the other sovereignties, united as one strength, shall compel the submission and performance of the sentence, with damages to the suffering party, and charges to the sovereignties that obliged their submission. To be sure, Europe would quietly obtain the so much desired and needed peace to her harassed inhabitants; no sovereignty in Europe having the power and therefore cannot show the will to dispute the conclusion; and, consequently, peace would be procured and continued in Europe.

INEVITABILITY OF WAR

Francis, Lord Jeffrey, *Edinburgh Review*. February, 1813

Men delight in war, in spite of the pains and miseries which it entails upon them and their fellows, because it exercises all the talents, and calls out all the energies of their nature—because it holds them out conspicuously as the objects of public sentiment and general sympathy—because it gratifies their pride of art, and gives them a lofty sentiment of their own power, worth, and courage,—but principally because it sets the game of existence upon a higher stake, and dispels, by its powerful interest, those feelings of *ennui* which steal upon every condition from which hazard and anxiety are excluded, and drive us into danger and suffering as a relief. While human nature continues to be distinguished by those attributes, we do not see any chance of war being superseded by the increase of wisdom and morality.

GOOD NEWS

(i) *Joel*, c. 800 B.C. Chap. ii, 21–27. A.V. 1611
(ii) *St Luke's Gospel*, c. A.D. 70. Chap. ii, 8–17. A.V. 1611

(i)

Fear not, O land; be glad and rejoice: for the Lord will do great things. Be not afraid, ye beasts of the field: for the pastures of the wilderness do spring, for the tree beareth her fruit, the fig tree and the vine do yield their strength. Be glad then, ye children of Zion, and rejoice in the Lord your God: for he hath given you the former rain moderately, and he will cause to come down for you the rain, the former rain, and the latter rain in the first month. And the floors shall be full of wheat, and the fats shall overflow with wine and oil. And I will restore to you the years that the locust hath eaten, the cankerworm, and the caterpiller, and the palmerworm, my great army which I sent among you. And ye shall eat in plenty, and be satisfied, and praise the name of the Lord your God, that hath dealt wondrously with you: and my people shall never be ashamed. And ye shall know that I am in the midst of Israel, and that I am the Lord your God, and none else: and my people shall never be ashamed.

(ii)

AND there were in the same country shepherds abiding in the field, keeping watch over their flock by night. And, lo, the angel of the Lord came upon them, and the glory of the Lord shone round about them: and they were sore afraid. And the angel said unto them, Fear not: for, behold, I bring you good tidings of great joy, which shall be to all people. For unto you is born this day in the city of David a Saviour, which is Christ the Lord. And this shall be a sign unto you; Ye shall find the babe wrapped in swaddling clothes, lying in a manger. And suddenly there was with the angel a multitude of the heavenly host praising God, and saying, Glory to God in the highest, and on earth peace, good will toward men. And it came to pass, as the angels were gone away from them into heaven, the shepherds said one to another, Let us now go even unto Bethlehem, and see this thing which is come to pass, which the Lord hath made known unto us. And they came with haste, and found Mary, and Joseph, and the babe lying in a manger. And when they had seen it, they made known abroad the saying which was told them concerning this child.

ADMIRALTY

He pointed with his wand to all the knowen Seas, Gulfs, Bayes, Straights, Capes, Rivers, Empires, Kingdomes, Dukedomes, and Territories of ech part, with declaration also of their speciall commodities, & particular wants, which by the benefit of trafficke, & entercourse of merchants, are plentifully supplied. From the Mappe he brought me to the Bible, and turning to the 107 Psalme, directed mee to the 23 & 24 verses, which I read, that they which go downe to the sea in ships, and occupy by the great waters, they see the works of the Lord, and his woonders in the deepe, &c.

RICHARD HAKLUYT, 1589

THE NAVIES OF GREECE

THUCYDIDES, *History of the Peloponnesian War*, c. 400 B.C.
Book I, chap. i. Translated by Richard Crawley. 1874

T HE first person known to us by tradition as having established a navy is Minos. He made himself master of what
is now called the Hellenic sea, and ruled over the Cyclades,
into most of which he sent the first colonies, expelling the
Carians and appointing his own sons governors; and thus did
his best to put down piracy in those waters, a necessary step
to secure the revenues for his own use.

For in early times the Hellenes and the barbarians of the
coast and islands, as communications by sea became more
common, were tempted to turn pirates, under the conduct of
their most powerful men; the motives being to serve their own
cupidity and to support the needy. They would fall upon a
town unprotected by walls, and consisting of a mere collection
of villages, and would plunder it; indeed, this came to be the
main source of their livelihood, no disgrace being yet attached
to such an achievement, but even some glory. . . .

With respect to their towns, later on, at an era of increased
facilities of navigation and a greater supply of capital, we
find the shores becoming the site of walled towns, and the
isthmuses being occupied for the purposes of commerce, and
defence against a neighbour. But the old towns, on account of
the great prevalence of piracy, were built away from the sea,
whether on the islands or the continent, and still remain in
their old sites. For the pirates used to plunder one another,
and indeed all coast populations, whether seafaring or not.

The islanders, too, were great pirates. These islanders were
Carians and Phœnicians, by whom most of the islands were
colonised, as was proved by the following fact. During the
purification of Delos by Athens in this war all the graves in
the island were taken up, and it was found that above half
their inmates were Carians: they were identified by the
fashion of the arms buried with them, and by the method of

interment, which was the same as the Carians still follow. But as soon as Minos had formed his navy, communication by sea became easier, as he colonised most of the islands, and thus expelled the malefactors. The coast populations now began to apply themselves more closely to the acquisition of wealth, and their life became more settled; some even began to build themselves walls on the strength of their newly-acquired riches. For the love of gain would reconcile the weaker to the dominion of the stronger, and the possession of capital enabled the more powerful to reduce the smaller towns to subjection. And it was at a somewhat later stage of this development that they went on the expedition against Troy.

What enabled Agamemnon to raise the armament was more, in my opinion, his superiority in strength, than the oaths of Tyndareus, which bound the Suitors to follow him.... He had also a navy far stronger than his contemporaries, so that, in my opinion, fear was quite as strong an element as love in the formation of the confederate expedition. The strength of his navy is shown by the fact that his own was the largest contingent, and that of the Arcadians was furnished by him; this at least is what Homer says, if his testimony is deemed sufficient. Besides, in his account of the transmission of the sceptre, he calls him

"Of many an isle, and of all Argos king".

Now Agamemnon's was a continental power; and he could not have been master of any except the adjacent islands (and these would not be many), but through the possession of a fleet....

But as the power of Hellas grew, and the acquisition of wealth became more an object, the revenues of the states increasing, tyrannies were by their means established almost everywhere,—the old form of government being hereditary monarchy with definite prerogatives,—and Hellas began to fit out fleets and apply herself more closely to the sea. It is said that the Corinthians were the first to approach the modern style of naval architecture, and that Corinth was the first place in Hellas where galleys were built; and we have

Ameinocles, a Corinthian shipwright, making four ships for the Samians. Dating from the end of this war, it is nearly three hundred years ago that Ameinocles went to Samos. Again, the earliest sea-fight in history was between the Corinthians and Corcyræans; this was about two hundred and sixty years ago, dating from the same time. Planted on an isthmus, Corinth had from time out of mind been a commercial emporium; as formerly almost all communication between the Hellenes within and without Peloponnese was carried on overland, and the Corinthian territory was the highway through which it travelled. She had consequently great money resources, as is shown by the epithet "wealthy" bestowed by the old poets on the place, and this enabled her, when traffic by sea became more common, to procure her navy and put down piracy; and as she could offer a mart for both branches of the trade, she acquired for herself all the power which a large revenue affords. Subsequently the Ionians attained to great naval strength in the reign of Cyrus, the first king of the Persians, and of his son Cambyses, and while they were at war with the former commanded for a while the Ionian sea. Polycrates also, the tyrant of Samos, had a powerful navy in the reign of Cambyses with which he reduced many of the islands, and among them Rhenea, which he consecrated to the Delian Apollo. About this time also the Phocæans, while they were founding Marseilles, defeated the Carthaginians in a sea-fight. These were the most powerful navies. And even these, although so many generations had elapsed since the Trojan war, seem to have been principally composed of the old fifty-oars and long-boats, and to have counted few galleys among their ranks. Indeed it was only shortly before the Persian war and the death of Darius the successor of Cambyses, that the Sicilian tyrants and the Corcyræans acquired any large number of galleys. For after these there were no navies of any account in Hellas till the expedition of Xerxes; Ægina, Athens, and others may have possessed a few vessels, but they were principally fifty-oars. It was quite at the end of this period that the war with Ægina and the prospect of the barbarian invasion enabled Themistocles to persuade the Athenians to build the fleet with which they fought at Salamis; and even these vessels had not complete decks.

The navies, then, of the Hellenes during the period we have traversed were what I have described. All their insignificance did not prevent their being an element of the greatest power to those who cultivated them, alike in revenue and in dominion. They were the means by which the islands were reached and reduced, those of the smallest area falling the easiest prey. Wars by land there were none, none at least by which power was acquired; we have the usual border contests, but of distant expeditions with conquest for object we hear nothing among the Hellenes.

THE CAPE DOUBLED, c. 612 b.c.

HERODOTUS, *History*, c. 446 B.C.   Book IV, chap. xlii.
Translated by George Rawlinson.   1858

As for Libya, we know it to be washed on all sides by the sea, except where it is attached to Asia. This discovery was first made by Necôs, the Egyptian king, who on desisting from the canal which he had begun between the Nile and the Arabian Gulf, sent to sea a number of ships manned by Phœnicians, with orders to make for the Pillars of Hercules, and return to Egypt through them, and by the Mediterranean. The Phœnicians took their departure from Egypt by way of the Erythræan Sea, and so sailed into the southern ocean. When autumn came, they went ashore, wherever they might happen to be, and having sown a tract of land with corn, waited until the grain was fit to cut. Having reaped it, they again set sail; and thus it came to pass that two whole years went by, and it was not till the third year that they doubled the Pillars of Hercules, and made good their voyage home. On their return, they declared—I for my part do not believe them, but perhaps others may—that in sailing round Libya they had the sun upon their right hand. In this way was the extent of Libya first discovered.

THE FIRST PUNIC WAR, 264–241 B.C.

POLYBIUS OF MEGALOPOLIS, *Histories*, c. 150 B.C. Book I, chap. lxiii. Translated by Evelyn Shirley Shuckburgh. 1889

IT was at once the longest, most continuous, and most severely contested war known to us in history. Apart from the other battles fought and the preparations made, which I have described in my previous chapters, there were two sea-fights, in one of which the combined numbers of the two fleets exceeded five hundred quinqueremes, in the other nearly approached seven hundred. In the course of the war, counting what were destroyed by shipwreck, the Romans lost seven hundred quinqueremes, the Carthaginians five hundred. Those therefore who have spoken with wonder of the sea-battles of an Antigonus, a Ptolemy, or a Demetrius, and the greatness of their fleets, would we may well believe have been overwhelmed with astonishment at the hugeness of these proportions if they had had to tell the story of this war. If, further, we take into consideration the superior size of the quinqueremes, compared with the triremes employed by the Persians against the Greeks, and again by the Athenians and Lacedaemonians in their wars with each other, we shall find that never in the whole history of the world have such enormous forces contended for mastery at sea.

These considerations will establish my original observation, and show the falseness of the opinion entertained by certain Greeks. It was *not* by mere chance or without knowing what they were doing that the Romans struck their bold stroke for universal supremacy and dominion, and justified their boldness by its success. No: it was the natural result of discipline gained in the stern school of difficulty and danger.

FORTUNE AND ANTONY

PLUTARCH OF CHAERONEIA, *Lives of the Noble Greeks and Romans*, c. A.D. 80. Translated by Sir Thomas North. 1579

WHEN Antonius had determined to fight by sea, he set all the other ships on fire, but three-score ships of Egypt, and reserved only but the best and greatest galleys, from three banks, unto ten banks of oars. Into them he put two-and-twenty thousand fighting men, with two thousand darters and slingers....All that day and the three days following, the sea rose so high and was so boisterous, that the battell was put off. The fift day the storm ceased, and the sea calmed again and then they rowed with force of oars in battell one against the other. Antonius leading the right wing with Publicola, and Cælius the left, and Marcus Octavius, and Marcus Justeius the midst. Octavius Cæsar on the other side, had placed Agrippa in the left wing of his army, and had kept the right wing for himself. For the armies by land, Canidius was general of Antonius' side, and Taurus of Cæsar's side: who kept their men in battell ray the one before the other, upon the seaside, without stirring one against the other. Further, touching both the chieftains: Antonius being in a swift pinnace, was carried up and down by force of oars through his army, and spake to his people to encourage them to fight valiantly, as if they were on mainland, because of the steadiness and heaviness of their ships: and commanded the pilots and maisters of the galleys, that they should not stir, none otherwise than if they were at anker, and so receive the first charge of their enemies, and that they should not go out of the strait of the gulf. Cæsar betimes in the morning going out of his tent, to see his ships throughout....When he had visited the order of his army throughout, he took a little pinnace, and went to the right wing, and wondered when he saw his enemies lie still in the strait, and stirred not. For discerning them afar off, men would have thought they had been ships riding at anker, and a good while he was so persuaded. So he kept his galleys eight furlong from his enemies: about noon there rose a little gale of wind from the sea, and then Antonius' men waxing angry with tarrying so long, and trusting to the greatness and height of their ships, as if they had been invincible: they began to march forward with their left wing. Cæsar seeing that, was a glad man and began a little to give back from the right wing, to allure them to come farther out of the strait and gulf, to the end that he might with his light ships well manned with watermen, turn and environ the galleys of the enemies, the which were heavy of yarage, both for their bigness, as also for lack of watermen to row them. When the skirmish began, and that they came to join, there was no great hurt at the first meeting, neither did the ships vehemently hit one against the other, as they do commonly in fight by sea. For on the one side, Antonius' ships for their heaviness, could not have the strength and swiftness to make their blows of any force: and Cæsar's ships on the other side took great heed, not to rush and shock with the forecastles of Antonius' ships, whose prows were armed with great brazen spurs. Furthermore they durst not flank them, because their points were easily broken, which way so ever they came to set upon his ships, that were made of great main square pieces of timber, bound together with great iron pins: so that the battell was much like to a battell by land, or to speak more properly to the assault of a city. For there were always three or four of Cæsar's ships about one of Antonius' ships, and the soldiers fought with their pikes, halberds and darts, and threw pots and darts with fire. Antonius' ships on the other side bestowed among them, with their cross-bows and engines of battery, great store of shot from their high towers of wood, that were upon their ships. Now Publicola seeing Agrippa put forth his left wing of Cæsar's army, to compass Antonius' ships that fought: he was driven also to loose off to have more room, and going a little at one side, to put those farther off that were afraid, and in the middest of the battell. For they were sore distressed by Antonius. Howbeit the battell was yet of even hand, and the victory doubtful, being indifferent to both: when suddenly they saw the three-score ships of Cleopatra busy about their yard-masts, and hoising sail to fly. So they fled through the midst of them that were in fight, for they had been placed behind the great ships, and did marvellously disorder the other ships. For the enemies themselves wondered much to see them sail in that sort, with full sail towards Peloponnesus. There Antonius shewed plainly, that he had not only lost the courage and heart of an emperor, but also of a valiant man, and that he was not his own man: (proving that true which an old man spake in mirth, that the soul of a lover lived in another body, and not in his own) he was so carried away with the vain love of this woman, as if he had been glued to her, and that she could not have removed without moving of him also. For when he saw Cleopatra's ship under sail, he forgot, forsook, and betrayed them that fought for him, and embarked upon a galley with five banks of oars, to follow her that was already begun to overthrow him, and would in the end be his utter destruction. When she knew his galley afar off, she lift up a sign in the poop of her ship, and so Antonius coming to it, was pluckt up where Cleopatra was, howbeit he saw her not at his first coming, nor she him, but went and sat down alone in the prow of his ship, and said never a word, clapping his head between both his hands....And thus it stood with Antonius. Now for his army by sea, that fought before the head or foreland of Actium: they held out a long time, and nothing troubled them more than a great boisterous wind that rose full in the prows of their ships and yet with much ado, his navy was at length overthrown, five hours within night.

A WRECK

Acts of the Apostles, c. A.D. 70. Chaps. xxvii–xxviii. A.V. 1611

AND when it was determined that we should sail into Italy, they delivered Paul and certain other prisoners unto one named Julius, a centurion of Augustus' band. And entering into a ship of Adramyttium, we launched, meaning to sail by the coasts of Asia; one Aristarchus, a Macedonian of Thessalonica, being with us. And the next day we touched at Sidon. And Julius courteously entreated Paul, and gave him liberty to go unto his friends to refresh himself. And when we had launched from thence, we sailed under Cyprus, because the winds were contrary. And when we had sailed over the sea of Cilicia and Pamphylia, we came to Myra, a city of Lycia. And there the centurion found a ship of Alexandria sailing into Italy; and he put us therein.

And when we had sailed slowly many days, and scarce were come over against Cnidus, the wind not suffering us, we sailed under Crete, over against Salmone; and, hardly passing it, came unto a place which is called The fair havens; nigh whereunto was the city of Lasea. Now when much time was spent, and when sailing was now dangerous, because the fast was now already past, Paul admonished them, and said unto them, Sirs, I perceive that this voyage will be with hurt and much damage, not only of the lading and ship, but also of our lives. Nevertheless the centurion believed the master and the owner of the ship, more than those things which were spoken by Paul. And because the haven was not commodious to winter in, the more part advised to depart thence also, if by any means they might attain to Phenice, and there to winter; which is an haven of Crete, and lieth toward the south west and north west.

And when the south wind blew softly, supposing that they had obtained their purpose, loosing thence, they sailed close by Crete. But not long after there arose against it a tempestuous wind, called Euroclydon. And when the ship was caught, and could not bear up into the wind, we let her drive. And running under a certain island which is called Clauda, we had much work to come by the boat: which when they had taken up, they used helps, undergirding the ship; and, fearing lest they should fall into the quicksands, strake sail, and so were driven. And we being exceedingly tossed with a tempest, the next day they lightened the ship; and the third day we cast out with our own hands the tackling of the ship. And when neither sun nor stars in many days appeared, and no small tempest lay on us, all hope that we should be saved was then taken away.

But after long abstinence Paul stood forth in the midst of them, and said, Sirs, ye should have hearkened unto me, and not have loosed from Crete, and to have gained this harm and loss. And now I exhort you to be of good cheer: for there shall be no loss of any man's life among you, but of the ship. For there stood by me this night the angel of God, whose I am, and whom I serve, saying, Fear not, Paul; thou must be brought before Cæsar: and, lo, God hath given thee all them that sail with thee. Wherefore, sirs, be of good cheer: for I believe God, that it shall be even as it was told me. Howbeit we must be cast upon a certain island.

But when the fourteenth night was come, as we were driven up and down in Adria, about midnight the shipmen deemed that they drew near to some country; and sounded, and found it twenty fathoms: and when they had gone a little further, they sounded again, and found it fifteen fathoms. Then fearing lest we should have fallen upon rocks, they cast four anchors out of the stern, and wished for the day. And as the shipmen were about to flee out of the ship, when they had let down the boat into the sea, under colour as though they would have cast anchors out of the foreship, Paul said to the centurion and to the soldiers, Except these abide in the ship, ye cannot be saved. Then the soldiers cut off the ropes of the boat, and let her fall off.

And while the day was coming on, Paul besought them all to take meat, saying, This day is the fourteenth day that ye have tarried and continued fasting, having taken nothing. Wherefore I pray you to take some meat: for this is for your health: for there shall not an hair fall from the head of any of you. And when he had thus spoken, he took bread, and gave thanks to God in presence of them all: and when he had broken it, he began to eat. Then were they all of good cheer, and they also took some meat. And we were in all in the ship two hundred threescore and sixteen souls. And when they had eaten enough, they lightened the ship, and cast out the wheat into the sea.

And when it was day, they knew not the land: but they discovered a certain creek with a shore, into the which they were minded, if it were possible, to thrust in the ship. And when they had taken up the anchors, they committed themselves unto the sea, and loosed the rudder bands, and hoised up the mainsail to the wind, and made toward shore. And falling into a place where two seas met, they ran the ship aground; and the forepart stuck fast, and remained unmoveable, but the hinder part was broken with the violence of the waves. And the soldiers' counsel was to kill the prisoners, lest any of them should swim out, and escape. But the centurion, willing to save Paul, kept them from their purpose; and commanded that they which could swim should cast themselves first into the sea, and get to land: and the rest, some on boards, and some on broken pieces of the ship. And so it came to pass, that they escaped all safe to land. And when they were escaped, then they knew that the island was called Melita. And the barbarous people shewed us no little kindness: for they kindled a fire, and received us every one, because of the present rain, and because of the cold.

THE VANDALS

EDWARD GIBBON, *Decline and Fall of the Roman Empire.*
Vol. III, chap. xxxvi. 1781

THE Vandals and Alani, who followed the successful standard of Genseric, had acquired a rich and fertile territory, which stretched along the coast above ninety days' journey from Tangier to Tripoli; but their narrow limits were pressed and confined, on either side, by the sandy desert and the Mediterranean. The discovery and conquest of the Black nations, that might dwell beneath the torrid zone, could not tempt the rational ambition of Genseric; but he cast his eyes towards the sea; he resolved to create a naval power, and his bold resolution was executed with steady and active perseverance. The woods of Mount Atlas afforded an inexhaustible nursery of timber; his new subjects were skilled in the arts of navigation and shipbuilding; he animated his daring Vandals to embrace a mode of warfare which would render every maritime country accessible to their arms; the Moors and Africans were allured by the hopes of plunder; and, after an interval of six centuries, the fleets that issued from the port of Carthage again claimed the empire of the Mediterranean.

VOYAGE OF OCTHER, A.D. 890

RICHARD HAKLUYT, *Principal Navigations, Voyages, Traffiques and Discoveries of the English Nation.* 1598–1600

OCTHER said, that the countrey wherein he dwelt was called Helgoland. Octher tolde his lord king Alfred that he dwelt furthest North of any other Norman. He sayd that he dwelt towards the North part of the land toward the West coast: and affirmed that the land, notwithstanding it stretcheth marvellous farre towards the North, yet it is all desert and not inhabited, unlesse it be very few places, here and there, where certeine Finnes dwell upon the coast, who live by hunting all the Winter, and by Fishing in Summer. He said that upon a certeine time he fell into a fantasie and desire to proove and know how farre that land stretched Northward, and whether there were any habitation of men North beyond the desert. Whereupon he tooke his voyage directly North along the coast, having upon his steereboord alwayes the desert land, and upon the leereboord the maine Ocean: and continued his course for the space of 3. dayes. In which space he was come as far towards the North, as commonly the whale hunters use to travell. Whence he proceeded in his course still towards the North so farre as he was able to saile in other 3. dayes. At the end whereof he perceived that the coast turned towards the East, or els the sea opened with a maine gulfe into the land, he knew not how farre. Well he wist and remembred, that he was faine to stay till he had a Westerne wind, and somewhat Northerly: and thence he sailed plaine East along the coast still so far as he was able in the space of 4. dayes. At the end of which time he was compelled againe to stay till he had a full Northerly winde, forsomuch as the coast bowed thence directly towards the South, or at least wise the sea opened into the land he could not tell how farre: so that he

sailed thence along the coast continually full South, so farre
as he could travaile in 5. dayes; and at the fifth dayes end he
discovered a mightie river which opened very farre into the
land. At the entry of which river he stayed his course, and
in conclusion turned backe againe, for he durst not enter
thereinto for feare of the inhabitants of the land: perceiving
that on the other side of the river the countrey was thorowly
inhabited: which was the first peopled land that he had found
since his departure from his owne dwelling: whereas continually thorowout all his voyage, he had evermore on his steereboord, a wildernesse and desert countrey, except that in some
places, he saw a few fishers, fowlers, and hunters, which were
all Fynnes: and all the way upon his leereboord was the maine
ocean.

FOURTH CRUSADE AT SEA

EDWARD GIBBON, *Decline and Fall of the Roman Empire.*
Vol. VI, chap. lx. 1788

A SIMILAR armament, for ages, had not rode the Adriatic:
it was composed of one hundred and twenty flat-bottomed
vessels or *palanders* for the horses, two hundred and forty
transports filled with men and arms, seventy store-ships laden
with provisions, and fifty stout galleys well prepared for the
encounter of an enemy. While the wind was favourable, the
sky serene, and the water smooth, every eye was fixed with
wonder and delight on the scene of military and naval pomp
which overspread the sea. The shields of the knights and
squires, at once an ornament and a defence, were arranged on
either side of the ships; the banners of the nations and families
were displayed from the stern; our modern artillery was
supplied by three hundred engines for casting stones and
darts; the fatigues of the way were cheered with the sound of
music; and the spirits of the adventurers were raised by the
mutual assurance that forty thousand Christian heroes were
equal to the conquest of the world. In the navigation from

Venice and Zara the fleet was successfully steered by the skill
and experience of the Venetian pilots: at Durazzo the confederates first landed on the territories of the Greek empire;
the isle of Corfu afforded a station and repose; they doubled,
without accident, the perilous cape of Malea, the southern
point of Peloponnesus or the Morea; made a descent in the
islands of Negropont and Andros; and cast anchor at Abydos
on the Asiatic side of the Hellespont....As they penetrated
through the Hellespont, the magnitude of their navy was
compressed in a narrow channel, and the face of the waters
was darkened with innumerable sails. They again expanded
in the basin of the Propontis, and traversed that placid sea,
till they approached the European shore at the abbey of
St Stephen, three leagues to the west of Constantinople.

THE CAPE DOUBLED

WILLIAM WINWOOD READE, *The Martyrdom of Man.*
Chap. iii. 1872

IT was a fête day in Lisbon. The flags were flying on every
tower; the fronts of the houses were clothed in gorgeous
drapery, which swelled and floated in the wind; stages were
erected on which mysteries were performed; bells were ringing, artillery boomed. Marble balconies were crowded with
ladies and cavaliers, and out of upper windows peeped forth
the faces of girls, who were kept in semi-Oriental seclusion.
Presently the sound of trumpets could be heard; and then
came in view a thousand friars, who chanted a litany, while
behind them an immense crowd chanted back in response.
At the head of this procession rode a gentleman richly dressed;
he was followed by a hundred and forty-eight men in sailors'
clothes, but bare-footed, and carrying tapers in their hands.
On they went till they reached the quay where the boats,
fastened to the shore, swayed to and fro with the movement
of the tide, and strained at the rope as if striving to depart.
The sailors knelt. A priest of venerable appearance stood

before them, and made a general confession, and absolved them in the form of the bull which Prince Henry had obtained. Then the wives and mothers embraced their loved ones whom they bewailed as men about to die. And all the people wept. And the children wept also, though they knew not why.

Thirty-two months passed, and again the water-side was crowded, and the guns fired, and the bells rang. Again *Vasco da Gama* marched in procession through the streets; and behind him walked, with feeble steps, but with triumph gleaming in their eyes, fifty-five men—the rest were gone. But in that procession were not only Portuguese, but also men with white turbans and brown faces; and sturdy blacks, who bore a chest which was shown by their straining muscles to be of enormous weight; and in his hand the Captain-General held a letter which was written with a pen of iron on a golden leaf, and which addressed the king of Portugal and Guinea in these words: " *Vasco da Gama, a gentleman of thy house, came to my country, of whose coming I was glad. In my country there is plenty of cinnamon, cloves, pepper, and precious stones. The things which I am desirous to have out of thy country are silver, gold, coral, and scarlet*".

That night all the houses in Lisbon were illuminated; the gutters ran with wine; the skies, for miles round, were reddened with the light of bonfires. The king's men brought ten pounds of spices to each sailor's wife, to give away to her gossips. The sailors themselves were surrounded by crowds, who sat silent and open-mouthed, listening to the tales of the great waters, and the marvellous lands where they had been.

They told of the wonders of the Guinea coast, and of the men near the Cape, who rode on oxen and played sweet music on the flute; and of the birds which looked like geese, and brayed like donkeys, and did not know how to fly, but put up their wings like sails, and scudded along before the wind. They told how as they sailed on towards the south, the north star sank and sank, and grew fainter and fainter, until at last it disappeared; and they entered a new world, and sailed beneath strange skies; and how, when they had doubled the Cape, they again saw sails on the horizon, and the north star again rose to view. They told of the cities on the Eastern

shore, and of their voyage across the Indian Ocean, and of
that joyful morning when, through the grey mists of early
dawn, they discerned the hills of Calicut.

And then they sank their voices, and their eyes grew grave
and sad, as they told of the horrors of the voyage; of the long,
long nights off the stormy Cape when the wind roared, and
the spray lashed through the rigging, and the waves foamed
over the bulwarks, and the stones that were their cannon-shot
crashed from side to side, and the ships like live creatures
groaned and creaked, and hour after hour the sailors were
forced to labour at the pumps till their bones ached, and
their hands were numbed by cold. They told of treacherous
pilots in the Mozambique, who plotted to run their ships
ashore; and of the Indian pirates, the gipsies of the sea, who
sent their spies on board. They told of that new and horrible
disease which, when they had been long at sea, made their
bodies turn putrid and the teeth drop from their jaws. And
as they told of these things, and named the souls who had died
at sea, there rose a cry of lamentation, and widows in new
garments fled weeping from the crowd.

That night, the Venetian ambassador sat down and wrote
to his masters that he had seen vessels enter Lisbon harbour
laden with spices and with India drugs. His next letter informed them that a strong fleet was being prepared, and that
Vasco da Gama intended to conquer India. The Venetians
saw that they were ruined. They wrote to their ally, the Sultan
of Egypt, and implored him to bestir himself. They gave him
artillery to send to the India princes. They offered to open the
Suez canal at their own expense, that their ships might arrive
in the Indian Ocean before the Portuguese. On the other
hand came the terrible Albuquerque, who told the Sultan to
beware, or he would destroy Mecca and Medina, and turn the
Nile into the Red Sea. The Indian Ocean became a Portuguese
lake. There was scarcely a town upon its shores which had not
been saluted by the Portuguese bombardiers. Not a vessel
could cross its waters without a Portuguese passport.

LEPANTO, 1571

JOHN LOTHROP MOTLEY, *Rise of the Dutch Republic*.
Part v, chap. i. 1856

THE war which the Sultan had avoided in the West came
to seek him in the East. To lift the Crucifix against the
Crescent, at the head of the powerful but quarrelsome alliance
between Venice, Spain, and Rome, Don John arrived at
Naples. He brought with him more than a hundred ships and
twenty-three thousand men, as the Spanish contingent. Three
months long the hostile fleets had been cruising in the same
waters without an encounter; three more were wasted in
barren manœuvres. Neither Mussulman nor Christian had
much inclination for the conflict, the Turk fearing the consequences of a defeat, by which gains already secured might
be forfeited; the allies being appalled at the possibility of
their own triumph. Nevertheless, the Ottomans manœuvred
themselves at last into the gulf of Lepanto, the Christians
manœuvred themselves towards its mouth as the foe was
coming forth again. The conflict thus rendered inevitable,
both Turk and Christian became equally eager for the fray,
equally confident of victory. Six hundred vessels of war met
face to face. Rarely in history had so gorgeous a scene of
martial array been witnessed. An October sun gilded the
thousand beauties of an Ionian landscape. Athens and
Corinth were behind the combatants, the mountains of
Alexander's Macedon rose in the distance: the rock of Sappho
and the heights of Actium were before their eyes. Since the
day when the world had been lost and won beneath that
famous promontory, no such combat as the one now approaching had been fought upon the waves. The chivalrous young
commander despatched energetic messages to his fellow
chieftains, and now that it was no longer possible to elude the
encounter, the martial ardour of the allies was kindled. The
Venetian High-Admiral replied with words of enthusiasm.
Colonna, lieutenant of the league, answered his chief in the
language of St Peter: "Though I die, yet will I not deny
thee".

The fleet was arranged in three divisions. The Ottomans, not drawn up in crescent form, as usual, had the same triple disposition. Barbarigo and the other Venetians commanded on the left, John Andrew Doria on the right, while Don John himself and Colonna were in the centre. Crucifix in hand, the High-Admiral rowed from ship to ship exhorting generals and soldiers to show themselves worthy of a cause which he had persuaded himself was holy. Fired by his eloquence and by the sight of the enemy, his hearers answered with eager shouts, while Don John returned to his ship, knelt upon the quarter-deck, and offered a prayer. He then ordered the trumpets to sound the assault, commanded his sailing-master to lay him alongside the Turkish Admiral, and the battle began. The Venetians, who were first attacked, destroyed ship after ship of their assailants after a close and obstinate contest, but Barbarigo fell dead ere the sunset, with an arrow through his brain. Meantime the action, immediately after the first onset, had become general. From noon till evening the battle raged, with a carnage rarely recorded in history. Don John's own ship lay yard-arm and yard-arm with the Turkish Admiral, and exposed to the fire of seven large vessels besides. It was a day when personal audacity, not skilful tactics, was demanded, and the imperial bastard showed the mettle he was made of. The Turkish Admiral's ship was destroyed, his head exposed from Don John's deck upon a pike, and the trophy became the signal for a general panic and a complete victory. By sunset the battle had been won.

Of nearly three hundred Turkish galleys, but fifty made their escape. From twenty-five to thirty thousand Turks were slain, and perhaps ten thousand Christians. The galley-slaves on both sides fought well, and the only beneficial result of the victory was the liberation of several thousand Christian captives. It is true that their liberty was purchased with the lives of a nearly equal number of Christian soldiers, and by the reduction to slavery of almost as many thousand Mussulmans, duly distributed among the Christian victors. Many causes contributed to this splendid triumph. The Turkish ships, inferior in number, were also worse manned than those

of their adversaries, and their men were worse armed. Every
bullet of the Christians told on muslin turbans and embroidered tunics, while the arrows of the Moslems fell harmless on the casques and corselets of their foes. The Turks, too,
had committed the fatal error of fighting upon a lee shore.
Having no sea-room, and being repelled in their first onset,
many galleys were driven upon the rocks, to be destroyed
with all their crews.

But whatever the cause of victory, its consequence was to
spread the name and fame of Don John of Austria throughout
the world. Alva wrote, with enthusiasm, to congratulate him,
pronouncing the victory the most brilliant one ever achieved
by Christians, and Don John the greatest general since the
death of Julius Cæsar. At the same time, with a sarcastic
fling at the erection of the Escorial, he advised Philip to improve this new success in some more practical way than by
building a house for the Lord and a sepulchre for the dead.
"If", said the Duke, "the conquests of Spain be extended in
consequence of this triumph, then, indeed, will the Cherubim
and Seraphim sing glory to God." A courier, despatched post
haste to Spain, bore the glorious news, together with the
sacred standard of the Prophet, the holy of holies, inscribed
with the name of Allah, twenty-eight thousand nine hundred
times, always kept in Mecca during peace, and never lost in
battle before. The King was at vespers in the Escorial. Entering the sacred precincts, breathless, travel-stained, excited,
the messenger found Philip impassible as marble to the
wondrous news. Not a muscle of the royal visage was moved,
not a syllable escaped the royal lips, save a brief order
to the clergy to continue the interrupted vespers. When the
service had been methodically concluded, the King made
known the intelligence and requested a Te Deum.

DRAKE ENTERS THE PACIFIC

Sir Julian Corbett, *Sir Francis Drake*. Chap. vi. 1890

DRAKE boldly entered the Straits. Then from the towering snow-cones and threatening glaciers that guarded the entry the tempests swept down upon the daring intruders. Out of the tortuous gulfs that through the bowels of the fabulous Austral continent seemed to lead beyond the confines of the world, rude squalls buffeted them this way and that, and currents, the like of which no man had seen, made as though they would dash them to pieces in the fathomless depths where no cable would reach. Fires lit by natives on the desolate shores as the strangers struggled by, added the terrors of unknown magic. But Drake's fortitude and consummate seamanship triumphed over all, and in a fortnight he brought his ill-sailing ships in triumph out upon the Pacific. Then, as though maddened to see how the adventurers had braved every effort to destroy them, the whole fury of the fiends that guarded the South Sea's slumber rushed howling upon them. Hardly had the squadron turned northward than a terrific gale struck it and hurled it back. The sky was darkened, and the bowels of the earth seemed to have burst, and for nearly two months they were driven under bare poles to and fro without rest in latitudes where no ship had ever sailed. On the maps the great Austral continent was marked, but they found in its place an enchanted void, where wind and water, and ice and darkness, seemed to make incessant war. After three weeks' strife, the *Marygold* went down with all hands; and in another week Wynter lost heart, and finding himself at the mouth of the Straits, went home in despair; while the *Golden Hind*, ignorant of the desertion, was swept once more to the south of Cape Horn. Here, on the fifty-third day of its fury, the storm ceased exhausted, and Drake found himself alone. But it was no moment to repine, for he knew he had made a discovery so brilliant as to deprive even Magellan's of its radiance. He was anchored among islands southward of anything known to geographers, and before him the Atlantic and Pacific rolled together in one great flood.

In his exultation he landed on the farthest island, and walking alone with his instruments to its end, he laid himself down, and with his arms embraced the southernmost point of the known world.

THE ARMADA WRECKED, August 1588

James Anthony Froude, *History of England from the Fall of Wolsey to the Defeat of the Spanish Armada.* Vol. xii, chap. lxxi. 1870

O F the hundred and fifty sail which had left Coruña, a hundred and twenty could still be counted when Howard left them. For five days they were in the gale which he met on his way back to the Thames, and which he described as so peculiarly violent. The unusual cold brought with it fog and mist, and amidst squalls and driving showers, and a sea growing wilder as they passed the shelter of the Scotch coast, they lost sight of each other for nearly a week. On the 9th,* the sky lifted, and Calderon found himself with the *Almirante* of Don Martinez de Recalde, the galleon of Don Alonzo, the *San Marcos* and twelve other vessels. Sick signals were flying all round, and the sea was so high that it was scarcely possible to lower a boat. The large ships were rolling heavily. Their wounded sails had been split by the gusts, and masts and yards carried away. That night it again blew hard. The fog closed in once more, and the next morning Calderon was alone in the open sea without a sail in sight, having passed between the Orkneys and the Shetlands. Recalde and da Leyva had disappeared with their consorts, having as Calderon conjectured gone north. He himself stood on west and southwest. On the 12th, he saw a number of sails on the horizon; on the 13th he found himself with Sidonia and the body of the fleet, and Sidonia signalled to him to come on board. Observations showed that they were then in 58° 30′ North latitude. Their longitude they did not know. They were probably a hundred and fifty miles west north-west of Cape

* The dates here given are in Old Style.

Wrath. Sidonia asked anxiously for Recalde and da Leyva. Calderon could but say where he had last seen them. He supposed that they had gone to the Faroe Isles or to Iceland, where there were German fishing stations which had a trade with Spain.

Again a council was held. The sickness had become frightful. Those who had escaped unwounded were falling ill from want and cold, and the wounded were dying by hundreds, the incessant storms making care and attention impossible. Calderon and the French pilot insisted that at all costs and hazards they must keep off the Irish coast. Diego Florez, distressed for the misery of the men, to whose sufferings want of water had become a fearful aggravation, imagined that along the west shore there must be a harbour somewhere; and that they would find rest and shelter among a hospitable Catholic people. The Bishop of Killaloe, a young Fitzmaurice, and a number of Irish friars were in the fleet. Diego Florez had possibly heard them speak of their country and countrymen, and there were fishing connections between Cadiz and Valencia and Galway, which he and many others must have known of, though they had not been on the coast in person. But the Irish themselves were with Alonzo da Leyva, and Sidonia happily took the opinion of the pilots. The day was fine and the sick were divided; those which could be moved were transferred wherever there was most room for them, and as Calderon passed to and fro among the galleons with his medicines and his arrowroot, he was received everywhere with the eager question, where was Alonzo da Leyva? There was scarcely a man who did not forget his own wretchedness in anxiety for the idol of them all.

The calm had been but an interlude in the storm. The same night the wild west wind came down once more, and for eleven consecutive days they went on in their misery, unable to communicate except by signals, holding to the ocean as far as their sailing powers would let them, and seeing galleon after galleon, Oquendo's among them, falling away to leeward amidst driving squalls and rain, on the vast rollers of the Atlantic. An island, which he supposed to be ten leagues from the coast, Calderon passed dangerously near. It was perhaps Achill, whose tremendous cliffs fall sheer two thousand feet into the sea, or perhaps Innisbofin or Innishark. On the 4th of September, he with Sidonia and fifty vessels, fifty-two ships only out of a hundred and fifty, leaking through every seam, and their weary crews ready to lie down and die from exhaustion, crawled past the Blaskets, and were out of danger.

And where were all the rest? Thirty, large and small, had been sunk or taken in the Channel. There remained nearly seventy to be still accounted for.

Don Martinez and da Leyva, with five and twenty of them, had steered north after passing the Orkneys. They went on to latitude 62°, meaning, as Calderon had rightly conjectured, to make for the settlement in Iceland. They had suffered so severely in the action, that they probably doubted their ability to reach Spain at all. The storms, however, which grew worse as the air became colder, obliged them to abandon their intention. One galleon was driven on the Faroe Isles; the rest turned about, and, probably misled by the Irish, made for the Shannon or Galway. As they braced to the wind, their torn rigging gave way; spar after spar, sail after sail, was carried away. Those which had suffered most dropped first to leeward. A second was lost on the Orkneys; a third fell down the coast of Scotland, and drifted on the Isle of Mull. It was one of the largest ships in the whole fleet. The commander (his name is unknown) was a grandee of the first rank, always "served in silver". He had made his way into some kind of harbour where he was safe from the elements; but the Irish Scots of the Western Isles were tempted by the reports of the wealth which he had with him. The fainting crew could not defend themselves, and the ship was fired and burnt, with almost everyone that it contained.

Their companions holding a better, but only rather better course, rolled along upon the back of Ireland, groping for the hoped-for shelter. The coming of the Spaniards had long been dreamt of by the Irish as the era of their deliverance from tyranny. It had been feared as their most serious danger by the scanty English garrison. The result of the fight in the Channel, if known at all, was known only by vague report;

and the country was thrown into a ferment of excitement, when, in the first week of September, Spanish sails were reported in numbers as seen along the western coast, off Donegal, off Sligo, in Clew Bay, at the mouth of the Shannon; in fact everywhere....

Two large galleons had rounded the point of Kerry, and had put into Dingle. They belonged to Recalde's squadron: one of them was the *Almirante* herself, with Don Martinez on board, who was dying from toil and anxiety. They wanted water; they had not a drop on board, but the dregs of the putrid puddle which they had brought with them from Spain; and they sent boats on shore to beg for a supply.... The boats were seized, the men who had landed imprisoned, and those on board the galleons, hunted already within a hair's-breadth of destruction, and with death making daily havoc among them, hoisted their ragged sails, and went again to sea.

Another galleon of a thousand tons, named *Our Lady of the Rosary*, which Calderon had watched sadly falling away before the waves, had also nearly weathered the headland of Kerry. She had all but escaped. Clear of the enormous cliffs of the Blasket Islands, she had no more to fear from the sea. Between the Blaskets and the mainland there is a passage which is safe in moderate weather, but the gale, which had slightly moderated, had risen again. The waves as they roll in from the Atlantic on the shallowing shores of Ireland boil among the rocks in bad weather with a fury unsurpassed in any part of the ocean. Strong tidal currents add to the danger, and when *Our Lady of the Rosary* entered the sound, it was a cauldron of boiling foam. There were scarcely hands to work the sails. Out of seven hundred, five hundred were dead, and most of the survivors were gentlemen, and before she was half way through, she struck among the breakers upon the island. A maddened officer ran the pilot (a Genoese) through the heart, "saying he had done it by treason". Some of the gentlemen tried to launch a boat, but no boat could live for a moment in such a sea. The pilot's son lashed himself to a plank, and was washed on shore alone of the whole company, and all the rest lay among cannon and doubloon chests amidst the rocks in Blasket Sound.

The same 10th September witnessed another and more tremendous catastrophe in Thomond. The seven ships in the mouth of the Shannon sent their cockboats with white flags into Kilrush, asking permission for the men to come on land. There were no English there, but there were local authorities who knew that the English would hold them answerable, and the request was refused. Here, as everywhere, the Spaniards' passionate cry was for water. They offered a butt of wine for every cask of water; they offered money in any quantity that the people could ask. Finally, they offered the Sheriff of Clare "a great ship, with all its ordnance and furniture", for licence to take as much water as would serve their wants. All was in vain. The Sheriff was afraid of an English gallows, and not one drop could the miserable men obtain for themselves by prayer or purchase. They were too feeble to attempt force. A galleass landed a few men, but they were driven back empty-handed; so abandoning and burning one of the galleons which was no longer seaworthy, the other six went despairingly out into the ocean again. But it was only to encounter their fate in a swifter form. They were caught in the same gale which had destroyed *Our Lady of the Rosary*. They were dashed to pieces on the rocks of Clare, and out of all their crews a hundred and fifty men struggled through the surf, to be carried as prisoners immediately to Galway....

More appalling still, like the desolation caused by some enormous flood or earthquake, was the scene between Sligo and Ballyshannon. A glance at the map will explain why there was a concentration of havoc on those few miles of coast. The coast of Mayo trends directly westward from Sligo for seventy miles, and crippled vessels, which had fallen upon a lee shore, were met by a wall of cliff, stretching across their course for a degree and a half of longitude. Their officers had possibly heard that there was shelter somewhere in the bay. Many ships were observed for days hovering between Rossan Point and Killala; but without experienced pilots they could not have found their way in the finest weather among the shoals and islands. They too were overtaken by the same great storm. The numbers that perished are unknown; there are no means to distinguish between those that foundered out in deep water and those that went to pieces on the beach....

Such was the fate of the brilliant chivalry of Spain; the choicest representatives of the most illustrious families in Europe. They had rushed into the service with an emotion pure and generous as ever sent Templar to the Sepulchre of Christ. They believed that they were the soldiers of the Almighty. Pope and bishop had commended them to the charge of the angels and the saints. The spell of the names of the apostles had been shattered by English cannon. The elements, which were deemed God's peculiar province—as if to disenchant Christendom, were disenchantment possible, of so fond an illusion—whirled them upon a shore which the waves of a hundred million years had made the most dangerous in the world; there as they crawled half drowned through the surf to fall into the jaws of the Irish wolves.

STORM OFF MAGELLAN STRAITS, 1592

RICHARD HAKLUYT, *Principal Navigations, Voyages, Traffiques and Discoveries of the English Nation*. 1598–1600

THIS night the winde began to blowe very much at West-northwest, and still increased in fury, so that wee were in great doubt what course to take: to put into the Streights wee durst not for lacke of ground tackle: to beare sayle wee doubted, the tempest was so furious, and our sayles so bad. The pinnesse come roome with us, and tolde us that shee had received many grievous Seas, and that her ropes did every houre fayle her, so as they could not tell what shift to make: wee being unable in any sort to helpe them, stood under our coarses in view of the lee-shore, still expecting our ruinous end.

The fourth of October the storme growing beyond all reason furious, the pinnesse being in the winde of us, strake suddenly ahull, so that we thought shee had received some grievous sea, or sprung a leake, or that her sayles failed her, because she came not with us: but we durst not hull in that unmercifull

storme, but sometimes tried under our maine coarse, sometime with a haddock of our sayle, for our ship was very leeward, and most laboursome in the sea. This night wee lost
the pinnesse, and never saw her againe.

The fift, our foresayle was split, and all to torne: then our
Master tooke the mizzen, and brought it to the foremast, to
make our ship worke, and with our sprit-saile we mended our
foresayle, the storme continuing without all reason in fury,
with haile, snowe, raine, and winde such and so mighty, as
that in nature it could not possibly be more, the seas such and
so lofty, with continuall breach, that many times we were
doubtfull whether our ship did sinke or swimme.

The tenth of October being by the accompt of our Captaine
and Master very neere the shore, the weather darke, the
storme furious, and most of our men having given over to
travell, we yeelded our selves to death, without further hope
of succour. Our captaine sitting in the gallery very pensive, I
came and brought him some Rosa solis to comfort him; for
he was so cold, that hee was scarce able to moove a joint. After
he had drunke, and was comforted in heart, hee began for the
ease of his conscience to make a large repetition of his fore-
passed time, and with many grievous sighs he concluded in
these words: Oh most glorious God, with whose power the
mightiest things among men are matters of no moment, I
most humbly beseech thee, that the intollerable burthen of
my sinnes may through the blood of Jesus Christ be taken
from me: and end our daies with speede, or shew us some
mercifull signe of thy love and our preservation. Having thus
ended, he desired me not to make knowen to any of the
company his intollerable griefe and anguish of minde, because
they should not thereby be dismayed. And so suddenly,
before I went from him the Sunne shined cleere; so that he
and the Master both observed the true elevation of the Pole,
whereby they knew by what course to recover the Streights.
Wherewithall our captaine and Master were so revived, &
gave such comfortable speeches to the company, that every
man rejoiced, as though we had received a present deliverance. The next day being the 11 of October, we saw Cabo
Deseado being the cape on the South shore (the North shore

is nothing but a company of dangerous rocks, Isles, & sholds). This cape being within two leages to leeward off us, our master greatly doubted, that we could double the same: whereupon the captain told him: You see there is no remedy, either we must double it, or before noon we must die: therefore loose your sails, and let us put it to Gods mercy. The master being a man of good spirit resolutely made quicke dispatch & set sails. Our sailes had not bene halfe an houre aboord, but the footrope of our foresaile brake, so that nothing held but the oylet holes. The seas continually brake over the ships poope, and flew into the sailes with such violence, that we still expected the tearing of our sayles, or oversetting of the ship, and withall to our utter discomfort, wee perceived that wee fell still more and more to leeward, so that wee could not double the cape: wee were nowe come within halfe a mile of the cape, and so neere the shore, that the counter-suffe of the sea would rebound against the shippes side, so that wee were much dismayed with the horror of our present ende. Beeing thus at the very pinch of death, the winde and Seas raging beyond measure, our Master veared some of the maine sheate; and whether it was by that occasion, or by some current, or by the wonderfull power of God, as wee verily thinke it was, the ship quickened her way, and shot past that rocke, where wee thought shee would have shored. Then betweene the cape and the poynt there was a little bay; so that wee were somewhat farther from the shoare: and when we were come so farre as the cape, wee yeelded to death: yet our good God the Father of all mercies delivered us, and wee doubled the cape about the length of our shippe, or very little more. Being shot past the cape, we presently tooke in our sayles, which onely God had preserved unto us: and when we were shot in between the high lands, the wind blowing trade, without any inch of sayle, we spooned before the sea, three men being not able to guide the helme, and in six houres wee were put five and twenty leagues within the Streights, where wee found a sea answerable to the Ocean.

THE ELIZABETHANS

RICHARD HAKLUYT's "Epistle Dedicatorie" to the first
edition of his *Principal Navigations*. 1589

To speake a word of that just commendation which our
nation doe indeed deserve: it cannot be denied, but as in all
former ages, they have bene men full of activity, stirrers
abroad, and searchers of the remote parts of the world, so in
this most famous and peerlesse governement of her most excellent Majesty, her subjects through the speciall assistance,
and blessing of God, in searching the most opposite corners
and quarters of the world, and to speake plainly, in compassing
the vaste globe of the earth more then once, have excelled
all the nations and people of the earth. For, which of the
kings of this land before her Majesty, had theyr banners ever
seene in the Caspian sea? which of them hath ever dealt with
the Emperor of Persia, as her Majesty hath done, and ob-
teined for her merchants large & loving privileges? who ever
saw before this regiment, an English Ligier in the stately
porch of the Grand Signor at Constantinople? who ever found
English Consuls & Agents at Tripolis in Syria, at Aleppo, at
Babylon, at Balsara, and which is more, who ever heard of
Englishmen at Goa before now? what English shippes did
heeretofore ever anker in the mighty river of Plate? passe
and repasse the unpassable (in former opinion) straight of
Magellan, range along the coast of Chili, Peru, and all the
backside of Nova Hispania, further then any Christian ever
passed, travers the mighty bredth of the South sea, land upon
the Luzones in despight of the enemy, enter into alliance,
amity, and traffike with the princes of the Moluccaes, & the
Isle of Java, double the famous Cape of Bona Speranza, arrive
at the Isle of Santa Helena, & last of al returne home most
richly laden with the commodities of China, as the subjects
of this now flourishing monarchy have done?

SEA POWER

FRANCIS BACON, *Essayes or Counsels Civill and Morall.*
Essay 38. 1612

To be Master of the Sea is an Abridgement of a Monarchy.
Cicero writing to Atticus, of Pompey his Preparation against
Cæsar, saith; *Consilium Pompeij planè Themistocleum est;
Putat enim, qui Mari potitur, eum Rerum potiri.* And, without
doubt, Pompey had tired out Cæsar, if upon vaine Confidence
he had not left that Way. We see the great Effects of Battailes
by Sea. The Battaile of Actium decided the Empire of the
World. The Battaile of Lepanto arrested the Greatnesse of
the Turke. There be many Examples, where Sea-Fights have
beene Finall to the warre; But this is when Princes or States
have set up their Rest upon the Battailes. But thus much is
certaine, That hee that Commands the Sea, is at great liberty,
and may take as much and as little of the Warre as he will.
Whereas those that be strongest by land are many times never-
thelesse in great Straights. Surely, at this Day, with us of
Europe, the Vantage of Strength at Sea (which is one of the
Principall Dowries of this Kindome of Great Brittaine) is
Great; Both because Most of the Kingdomes of Europe are
not meerely Inland, but girt with the Sea most part of their
Compasse; And because the Wealth of both Indies seemes in
great Part but an Accessary to the Command of the Seas.

LONDON POOL, 1724

DANIEL DEFOE, *A Tour Thro' the Whole Island of Great
Britain.* Letter 5. 1724–6

THAT Part of the River of *Thames* which is properly the
Harbour, and where the Ships usually deliver or unload their
Cargoes, is called the *Pool,* and begins at the turning of the
River out of *Lime-house* Reach, and extends to the *Custom-
house-Keys*: In this Compass I have had the Curiosity to

count the Ships as well as I could, *en passant*, and have found above Two thousand Sail of all Sorts, not reckoning Barges, Lighters or Pleasure-Boats, and Yachts; but of Vessels that really go to Sea.

It is true, the River or Pool, seem'd, at that time, to be pretty full of Ships; it is true also, that I included the Ships which lay in *Deptford* and *Black-Wall* Reaches, and in the Wet Docks, whereof, there are no less than Three; but 'tis as true, that we did not include the Men of War at the King's Yard and in the Wet Dock there at *Deptford*, which were not a very few.

In the River, as I have observed, there are from *Battle-Bridge* on the *Southwark* Side, and the *Hermitage-Bridge* on the City-Side, reckoning to *Black-Wall*, inclusive,

Three Wet Docks for laying up   ⎫
Twenty Two Dry Docks for Repairing ⎬ Merchants Ships.
Thirty Three Yards for Building   ⎭

This is inclusive of the Builders of Lighters, Hoys, &c. but exclusive of all Boat-Builders, Wherry-Builders, and above-Bridge Barge-Builders.

To enter into any Description of the great Magazines of all manner of Naval Stores, for the furnishing those Builders, would be endless, and I shall not attempt it; 'tis sufficient to add, That *England*, as I have said elsewhere, is an inexhaustible Store-house of Timber, and all the Oak Timber, and generally the Plank also, used in the building these Ships, is found in *England* only, nay, and which is more, it is not fetched from the remoter Parts of *England*, but these *Southern* Counties near us are the Places where 'tis generally found; as particularly the Counties of *Berks* and *Bucks, Surrey, Kent, Sussex, Essex* and *Suffolk*, and very little is brought farther, nor can all the Ship-Building the whole Kingdom are able to build, ever exhaust those Counties, tho' they were to build much more than they do.

COMMENT ON THE SEVEN YEARS' WAR

Sir Julian Corbett, *England in the Seven Years' War.*
Vol. ii, chap. xii. 1907

No great action took place, because the weakness of the French at sea and the exigencies of their war plan forced them to adopt a naval defensive. It was their wise policy to avoid a decision at sea, and to keep the command in dispute as long as possible, while they concentrated their offensive powers upon the army ashore. It was exactly the reverse of Pitt's system, and how nearly it came to defeating it is one of the great facts of the war.

The essence of the defensive is waiting for an opportunity to pass to the offensive, and we cannot look back upon the struggle which the French attitude so skilfully prolonged without a shudder to see how nearly they were rewarded. Had Ferdinand, the Anglophile king of Spain, died a year or two sooner than he did, Spain would certainly have joined our enemy before we had attained our object in America. As it was, the French, by preserving their fleet from a decision, prevented us for five long years from completing that easy conquest which we looked to settle in one campaign. With the Spanish fleet to help them dispute the control of the American communications, there is no saying how much longer the labour would have lasted. Again, if the Czarina Elizabeth had survived one more campaign it is impossible to see how Frederick could have maintained his position. On all the chances of war we must have been crushed; Hanover, and Holland, and the Netherlands would have been at the mercy of France, and the treaty of peace could scarcely have been on a better basis for us than the *status quo ante bellum*.

There is no clearer lesson in history how unwise and short-sighted it is to despise and ridicule a naval defensive. Of all strategical attitudes it is the most difficult to meet and the most deeply fraught with danger for the opposing belligerent if he is weak ashore and his enemy strong. The prolongation of war at sea tends to raise up fresh enemies for the dominant power in a much higher degree than it does on land, owing to the inevitable exasperation of neutrals. In the long run and by itself the defensive cannot, of course, lead to a final attainment of the command of the sea. But it can prevent its attainment by the other side, and this, taken in concert with a powerful offensive ashore, may well secure a final triumph. The real lesson of the war is not that we should treat a naval defensive with contempt, just because in this case it failed by the chance prolongation of two human lives; but that we should note the supreme necessity and difficulty of crushing it down before it has time to operate its normal effect. The primary and all-absorbing object of a superior naval power is not merely to take the offensive, but to force the enemy to expose himself to a decision as quickly as possible. One of the rare glimpses we have had into Anson's mind showed us how deeply he was impressed with this preoccupation. In his heart he never approved of Pitt's coastal operations. Great as he was as a master of naval warfare, there is no sign he ever rose to Pitt's larger conception of combined strategy. It was only because Hardwicke's broad mind grasped and approved the policy, that his silent son-in-law held his tongue and loyally gave an outward assent. We have seen that the sole use he could find in coastal expeditions was a means of forcing a decision at sea, and so far and no further he believed them justified. Much has been said of the first function of the British army being to assist the fleet in obtaining command of the sea. We may take it that in Lord Anson's opinion there was no better way in which this function could be performed than by operating over the uncommanded sea, and tempting the enemy's battleships into the open.

TRAFALGAR

Robert Southey, *Life of Nelson*. Chap. ix. 1813

A LONG swell was setting into the Bay of Cadiz. Our ships, crowding all sail, moved majestically before it, with light winds from the south-west. The sun shone on the sails of the enemy, and their well-formed line, with their numerous three-deckers, made an appearance which any other assailants would have thought formidable; but the British sailors only admired the beauty and the splendour of the spectacle; and, in full confidence of winning what they saw, remarked to each other what a fine sight yonder ships would make at Spithead!

The French Admiral, from the *Bucentaure*, beheld the new manner in which his enemy was advancing—Nelson and Collingwood each leading his line; and pointing them out to his officers, he is said to have exclaimed, that such conduct could not fail to be successful. Yet Villeneuve had made his own dispositions with the utmost skill, and the fleets under his command waited for the attack with perfect coolness. Ten minutes before twelve they opened their fire. Eight or nine of the ships immediately ahead of the *Victory*, and across her bows, fired single guns at her, to ascertain whether she was yet within their range. As soon as Nelson perceived that their shot passed over him, he desired Blackwood and Captain Prowse, of the *Sirius*, to repair to their respective frigates, and on their way to tell all the Captains of the line-of-battle ships that he depended on their exertions; and that if by the prescribed mode of attack they found it impracticable to get into action immediately, they might adopt whatever they thought best, provided it led them quickly and closely alongside an enemy....

The enemy continued to fire a gun at a time at the *Victory*, till they saw that a shot had passed through her main-topgallant sail; then they opened their broadsides, aiming chiefly at her rigging, in the hope of disabling her before she could close with them. Nelson, as usual, had hoisted several flags, lest one should be shot away. The enemy showed no colours till late in the action, when they began to feel the necessity of having them to strike. For this reason the *Santissima Trinidad*, Nelson's old acquaintance, as he used to call her, was distinguishable only by her four decks, and to the bow of this opponent he ordered the *Victory* to be steered. Meantime an incessant raking fire was kept up upon the *Victory*. The Admiral's Secretary was one of the first who fell; he was killed by a cannon-shot while conversing with Hardy. Captain Adair of the Marines, with the help of a sailor, endeavoured to remove the body from Nelson's sight, who had a great regard for Mr Scott; but he anxiously asked, "Is that poor Scott that's gone?" and being informed that it was indeed so, exclaimed, "Poor fellow!" Presently a double-headed shot struck a party of marines who were drawn up on the poop, and killed eight of them, upon which Nelson immediately desired Captain Adair to disperse his men round the ship, that they might not suffer so much from being together. A few minutes afterwards a shot struck the fore-brace bits on the quarterdeck, and passed between Nelson and Hardy, a splinter from the bit tearing off Hardy's buckle, and bruising his foot. Both stopped, and looked anxiously at each other; each supposed the other to be wounded. Nelson then smiled, and said, "This is too warm work, Hardy, to last long".

The *Victory* had not yet returned a single gun. Fifty of her men had been by this time killed or wounded, and her main-topmast, with all her studding sails and her booms, shot away. Nelson declared that in all his battles he had seen nothing which surpassed the cool courage of his crew on this occasion. At four minutes after twelve she opened her fire from both sides of her deck. It was not possible to break the enemy's line without running on board one of their ships. Hardy informed him of this, and asked him which he would prefer. Nelson replied, "Take your choice, Hardy; it does not signify much". The Master was ordered to put the helm to port, and the *Victory* ran on board the *Redoutable*, just as her tiller ropes were shot away. The French ship received her with a broadside; then instantly let down her lower-deck ports, for fear of being boarded through them, and never afterwards fired a great gun during the action. Her tops, like those of all the enemy's ships, were filled with riflemen. Nelson never placed musketry in his tops. He had a strong dislike to the practice, not merely because it endangers setting fire to the sails, but also because it is a murderous sort of warfare, by which individuals may suffer, and a commander now and then be picked off, but which never can decide the fate of a general engagement.

Captain Harvey, in the *Téméraire*, fell on board the *Redoutable* on the other side. Another enemy was in like manner on board the *Téméraire*; so that these four ships formed as compact a tier as if they had been moored together, their heads lying all the same way. The Lieutenants of the *Victory*, seeing this, depressed their guns of the middle and lower decks, and fired with a diminished charge, lest the shot should pass through, and injure the *Téméraire*. And because there was danger that the *Redoutable* might take fire from the lower-deck guns, the muzzles of which touched her side when they were run out, the fireman of each gun stood ready with a bucket of water, which, as soon as the gun was discharged, he dashed into the hole made by the shot. An incessant fire was kept up from the *Victory* from both sides, her larboard guns playing upon the *Bucentaure* and the huge *Santissima Trinidad*.

It had been part of Nelson's prayer, that the British fleet might be distinguished by humanity in the victory which he expected. Setting an example himself, he twice gave orders to cease firing upon the *Redoutable*, supposing that she had struck, because her great guns were silent; for, as she carried no flag, there was no means of instantly ascertaining the fact. From this ship, which he had thus twice spared, he received his death. A ball fired from her mizzen-top, which in the then situation of the two vessels was not more than fifteen yards from that part of the deck where he was standing, struck the epaulette on his left shoulder, about a quarter after one, just in the heat of action. He fell upon his face, on the spot which was covered with his poor Secretary's blood. Hardy, who was a few steps from him, turning round, saw three men raising him up. "They have done for me at last, Hardy", said he. "I hope not", cried Hardy. "Yes," he replied; "my backbone is shot through." Yet even now, not for a moment losing his presence of mind, he observed, as they were carrying him down the ladder, that the tiller ropes, which had been shot away, were not yet replaced, and ordered that new ones should be rove immediately; then, that he might not be seen by the crew, he took out his handkerchief, and covered his face and his stars....

The *Redoutable* struck within twenty minutes after the fatal shot had been fired from her. During that time she had been twice on fire—in her fore-chains and in her forecastle.

The French, as they had done in other battles, made use in this of fire-balls and other combustibles; implements of destruction which other nations, from a sense of honour and humanity, have laid aside; which add to the sufferings of the wounded without determining the issue of the combat: which none but the cruel would employ, and which never can be successful against the brave. Once they succeeded in setting fire, from the *Redoutable*, to some ropes and canvas on the *Victory's* booms. The cry ran through the ship, and reached the cockpit; but even this dreadful cry produced no confusion; the men displayed that perfect self-possession in danger by which English seamen are characterized; they extinguished the flames on board their own ship, and then hastened to extinguish them in the enemy, by throwing buckets of water from the gangway. When the *Redoutable* had struck, it was not practicable to board her from the *Victory*; for, though the two ships touched, the upper works of both fell in so much, that there was a great space between their gangways; and she could not be boarded from the lower or middle decks, because her ports were down. Some of our men went to Lieutenant Quilliam, and offered to swim under her bows, and get up there; but it was thought unfit to hazard brave lives in this manner.

*　　　*　　　*　　　*

The death of Nelson was felt in England as something more than a public calamity. Men started at the intelligence, and turned pale, as if they had heard of the loss of a dear friend. An object of our admiration and affection, of our pride and of our hopes, was suddenly taken from us; and it seemed as if we had never, till then, known how deeply we loved and reverenced him. What the country had lost in its great naval hero—the greatest of our own, and of all former times—was scarcely taken into the account of grief. So perfectly indeed had he performed his part, that the maritime war, after the battle of Trafalgar, was considered at an end. The fleets of the enemy were not merely defeated, but destroyed. New navies must be built, and a new race of seamen reared for them, before the possibility of their invading our shores could again be contemplated.

SEA POWER

ALFRED THAYER MAHAN, *The Influence of Sea Power upon History*, 1660–1783. Chap. xi. 1890

WHATEVER may be the determining factors in strifes between neighboring continental States, when a question arises of control over distant regions, politically weak,— whether they be crumbling empires, anarchical republics, colonies, isolated military posts, or islands below a certain size,—it must ultimately be decided by naval power, by the organized military force afloat, which represents the communications that form so prominent a feature in all strategy. The magnificent defence of Gibraltar hinged upon this; upon this depended the military results of the war in America; upon this the final fate of the West India Islands; upon this certainly the possession of India. Upon this will depend the control of the Central American Isthmus, if that question take a military coloring; and though modified by the continental position and surroundings of Turkey, the same sea power must be a weighty factor in shaping the outcome of the Eastern Question in Europe.

If this be true, military wisdom and economy, both of time and money, dictate bringing matters to an issue as soon as possible upon the broad sea, with the certainty that the power which achieves military preponderance there will win in the end.

MUDROS IN LEMNOS

JOHN MASEFIELD, *Gallipoli*. Chap. ii. 1916

IN fine weather in Mudros a haze of beauty comes upon the hills and water till their loveliness is unearthly, it is so rare. Then the bay is like a blue jewel, and the hills lose their savagery, and glow, and are gentle, and the sun comes up from Troy, and the peaks of Samothrace change colour, and all the marvellous ships in the harbour are transfigured. The land of Lemnos was beautiful with flowers at that season, in the brief Ægean spring, and to seawards always, in the bay, were the ships, more ships, perhaps, than any port of modern times has known; they seemed like half the ships of the world. In this crowd of shipping strange beautiful Greek vessels passed, under rigs of old time, with sheep and goats and fish for sale, and the tugs of the Thames and Mersey met again the ships they had towed of old, bearing a new freight, of human courage. The transports (all painted black) lay in tiers, well within the harbour, the men-of-war nearer Mudros and the entrance. Now in all that city of ships, so busy with passing picket-boats, and noisy with the labour of men, the getting of the anchors began. Ship after ship, crammed with soldiers, moved slowly out of harbour in the lovely day, and felt again the heave of the sea. No such gathering of fine ships has ever been seen upon this earth, and the beauty and the exultation of the youth upon them made them like sacred things as they moved away. All the thousands of men aboard them gathered on deck to see, till each rail was thronged. These men had come from all parts of the British world, from Africa, Australia, Canada, India, the Mother Country, New Zealand, and remote islands in the sea. They had said good-bye to home that they might offer their lives in the cause we stand for. In a few hours at most, as they well knew, perhaps a tenth of them would have looked their last on the sun, and be a part of foreign earth or dumb things that the tides push. Many of them would have disappeared for ever from the knowledge of man, blotted from the book of life none would know how—by a fall or chance shot in the darkness, in the blast of a shell, or alone, like a hurt beast, in some scrub or gully, far from comrades and the English speech and the English singing. And perhaps a third of them would be mangled, blinded or broken, lamed, made imbecile or dis-figured, with the colour and the taste of life taken from them, so that they would never more move with comrades nor exult in the sun. And those not taken thus would be under the ground, sweating in the trench, carrying sandbags up the sap, dodging death and danger, without rest or food or drink, in the blazing sun or the frost of the Gallipoli night, till death seemed relaxation and a wound a luxury. But as they moved out these things were but the end they asked, the reward they had come for, the unseen cross upon the breast. All that they felt was a gladness of exultation that their young courage was to be used. They went like kings in a pageant to the imminent death. As they passed from moorings to the man-of-war anchorage on their way to the sea, their feeling that they had done with life and were going out to something new welled up in those battalions; they cheered and cheered till the harbour rang with cheering. As each ship crammed with soldiers drew near the battleships, the men swung their caps and cheered again, and the sailors answered, and the noise of cheering swelled, and the men in the ships not yet moving joined in, and the men ashore, till all the life in the harbour was giving thanks that it could go to death rejoicing. All was beautiful in that gladness of men about to die, but the most moving thing was the greatness of their generous hearts. As they passed the French ships, the memory of old quarrels healed, and the sense of what sacred France has done and endured in this great war, and the pride of having such men as the French for comrades, rose up in their warm souls, and they cheered the French ships more, even, than their own.

They left the harbour very, very slowly; this tumult of cheering lasted a long time; no one who heard it will ever forget it, or think of it unshaken. It broke the hearts of all there with pity and pride: it went beyond the guard of the English heart. Presently all were out, and the fleet stood across for Tenedos, and the sun went down with marvellous colour, lighting island after island and the Asian peaks, and those left behind in Mudros trimmed their lamps knowing that they had been for a little brought near to the heart of things.

THE WORKS OF MAN

It is all work and forgotten work, this peopled, clothed, articulate-speaking, high-towered, wide-acred World. The hands of forgotten brave men have made it a World for us; —they,—honour to them; they, in spite of the idle and the dastard. . . . Work? The quantity of done and forgotten work that lies silent under my feet in this world, and escorts and attends me, and supports and keeps me alive, wheresoever I walk or stand, whatsoever I think or do, gives rise to reflections! Is it not enough, at any rate, to strike the thing called "Fame" into total silence for a wise man.

THOMAS CARLYLE, *Past and Present*, 1843

DIVISION OF LABOUR

Adam Smith, *Wealth of Nations.*
Book i, chap. i. 1776

O bserve the accommodation of the most common artificer
or day-labourer in a civilised and thriving country, and you
will perceive that the number of people, of whose industry a
part, though but a small part, has been employed in procuring him this accommodation, exceeds all computation.
The woollen coat, for example, which covers the day-labourer,
as coarse and rough as it may appear, is the produce of the
joint labour of a great multitude of workmen. The shepherd,
the sorter of the wool, the wool-comber or carder, the dyer,
the scribbler, the spinner, the weaver, the fuller, the dresser,
with many others, must all join their different arts in order
to complete even this homely production. How many merchants and carriers, besides, must have been employed in
transporting the materials from some of those workmen to
others who often live in a very distant part of the country?
How much commerce and navigation in particular, how many
ship-builders, sailors, sail-makers, rope-makers, must have
been employed in order to bring together the different drugs
made use of by the dyer, which often come from the remotest
corners of the world? What a variety of labour, too, is necessary
in order to produce the tools of the meanest of those workmen! To say nothing of such complicated machines as the
ship of the sailor, the mill of the fuller, or even the loom of
the weaver, let us consider only what a variety of labour is
requisite in order to form that very simple machine, the shears
with which the shepherd clips the wool. The miner, the
builder of the furnace for smelting the ore, the feller of the
timber, the burner of the charcoal to be made use of in the
smelting-house, the brickmaker, the bricklayer, the workmen
who attend the furnace, the millwright, the forger, the smith,
must all of them join their different arts in order to produce
them. Were we to examine, in the same manner, all the different

parts of his dress and household furniture, the coarse linen shirt which he wears next his skin, the shoes which cover his feet, the bed which he lies on, and all the different parts which compose it, the kitchen-grate at which he prepares his victuals, the coals which he makes use of for that purpose, dug from the bowels of the earth, and brought to him, perhaps, by a long sea and a long land-carriage, all the other utensils of his kitchen, all the furniture of his table, the knives and forks, the earthen or pewter plates upon which he serves up and divides his victuals, the different hands employed in preparing his bread and his beer, the glass window which lets in the heat and the light, and keeps out the wind and the rain, with all the knowledge and art requisite for preparing that beautiful and happy invention, without which these northern parts of the world could scarce have afforded a very comfortable habitation, together with the tools of all the different workmen employed in producing those different conveniences; if we examine, I say, all these things, and consider what a variety of labour is employed about each of them, we shall be sensible that, without the assistance and co-operation of many thousands, the very meanest person in a civilised country could not be provided, even according to, what we very falsely imagine, the easy and simple manner in which he is commonly accommodated. Compared, indeed, with the more extravagant luxury of the great, his accommodation must no doubt appear extremely simple and easy; and yet it may be true, perhaps, that the accommodation of an European prince does not always so much exceed that of an industrious and frugal peasant, as the accommodation of the latter exceeds that of many an African king, the absolute master of the lives and liberties of ten thousand naked savages.

METAL AND STONE

WALTER HORATIO PATER, *Greek Studies.* (Beginnings
of Greek Sculpture.) 1895

THE history of Greek art, then, begins, as some have fancied
general history to begin, in a golden age, but in an age, so to
speak, of real gold, the period of those twisters and ham-
merers of the precious metals—men who had already discovered the flexibility of silver and the ductility of gold, the
capacity of both for infinite delicacy of handling, and who
enjoyed, with complete freshness, a sense of beauty and fitness
in their work—a period of which that flower of gold on a silver
stalk, picked up lately in one of the graves at Mycenæ, or the
legendary golden honeycomb of Dædalus, might serve as the
symbol. The heroic age of Greek art is the age of the hero as
smith.

There are in Homer two famous descriptive passages in
which this delight in curious metal-work is very prominent;
the description in the Iliad of the Shield of Achilles, and the
description of the house of Alcinous in the Odyssey. The
shield of Achilles is part of the suit of armour which He-
phæstus makes for him at the request of Thetis; and it is
wrought of variously coloured metals, woven into a great
circular composition in relief, representing the world and the
life in it. The various activities of man are recorded in this
description in a series of idyllic incidents with such complete
freshness, liveliness, and variety, that the reader from time
to time may well forget himself, and fancy he is reading a
mere description of the incidents of actual life. We peep into
a little Greek town, and see in dainty miniature the bride
coming from her chamber with torch-bearers and dancers, the
people gazing from their doors, a quarrel between two persons
in the market place, the assembly of the elders to decide upon
it. In another quartering is the spectacle of a city besieged,
the walls defended by the old men, while the soldiers have
stolen out and are lying in ambush. There is a fight on the
river-bank; Ares and Athene, conspicuous in gold, and marked
as divine persons by a scale larger than that of their followers,

lead the host. The strange, mythical images of Kêr, Eris, and Kudoimos mingle in the crowd. A third space upon the shield depicts the incidents of peaceful labour—the ploughshare passing through the field, of enamelled black metal behind it, and golden before; the cup of mead held out to the ploughman when he reaches the end of the furrow; the reapers with their sheaves; the king standing in silent pleasure among them, intent upon his staff. There are the labourers in the vineyard in minutest detail; stakes of silver on which the vines hang; the dark trench about it, and one pathway through the midst; the whole complete and distinct, in variously coloured metal. All things and living creatures are in their places—the cattle coming to water to the sound of the herdsman's pipe, various music, the rushes by the water-side, a lion-hunt with dogs, the pastures among the hills, a dance, the fair dresses of the male and female dancers, the former adorned with swords, the latter with crowns. It is an image of ancient life, its pleasure and business. For the centre, as in some quaint chart of the heavens, are the earth and the sun, the moon and con-stellations; and to close in all, right round, like a frame to the picture, the great river Oceanus, forming the rim of the shield, in some metal of dark blue.

Still more fascinating, perhaps, because more completely realisable by the fancy as an actual thing—realisable as a delightful place to pass time in—is the description of the palace of Alcinous in the little island town of the Phæacians, to which we are introduced in all the liveliness and sparkle of the morning, as real as something seen last summer on the sea-coast; although, appropriately, Ulysses meets a goddess, like a young girl carrying a pitcher, on his way up from the sea. Below the steep walls of the town, two projecting jetties allow a narrow passage into a haven of stone for the ships, into which the passer-by may look down, as they lie moored below the roadway. In the midst is the king's house, all glittering, again, with curiously wrought metal; its brightness is "as the brightness of the sun or of the moon". The heart of Ulysses beats quickly when he sees it standing amid plantations ingeniously watered, its floor and walls of brass throughout, with continuous cornice of dark iron; the doors are of gold, the door-posts and lintels of silver, the handles, again, of gold—

> The walls were massy brass; the cornice high
> Blue metals crowned in colours of the sky;
> Rich plates of gold the folding-doors incase;
> The pillars silver on a brazen base;
> Silver the lintels deep-projecting o'er;
> And gold the ringlets that command the door.

Dogs of the same precious metals keep watch on either side, like the lions over the old gate-way of Mycenæ, or the gigantic, human-headed bulls at the entrance of an Assyrian palace. Within doors the burning lights at supper-time are supported in the hands of golden images of boys, while the guests recline on a couch running all along the wall, covered with peculiarly sumptuous women's work.

*   *   *   *

Greek art is for us, in all its stages, a fragment only; in each of them it is necessary, in a somewhat visionary manner, to fill up empty spaces, and more or less make substitution; and of the finer work of the heroic age, thus dimly discerned as an actual thing, we had at least till recently almost nothing. Two plates of bronze, a few rusty nails, and certain rows of holes in the inner surface of the walls of the "treasury" of Mycenæ, were the sole representatives of that favourite device of primitive Greek art, the lining of stone walls with burnished metal, of which the house of Alcinous in the Odyssey is the ideal picture, and the temple of Pallas *of the Brazen House* at Sparta, adorned in the interior with a coating of reliefs in metal, a later, historical example. Of the heroic or so-called Cyclopean architecture, that "treasury", a building so imposing that Pausanias thought it worthy to rank with the Pyramids, is a sufficient illustration. Treasury, or tomb, or both (the selfish dead, perhaps, being supposed still to find enjoyment in the costly armour, goblets, and mirrors laid up there), this dome-shaped building, formed of concentric rings of stones gradually diminishing to a coping-stone at the top, may stand as the representative of some similar buildings in other parts of Greece, and of many others in a similar kind of architecture elsewhere, constructed of large many-sided blocks of stone, fitted carefully together without the aid of cement, and remaining in their places by reciprocal resistance. Characteristic of it is the general tendency to use vast blocks of stone for the jambs and lintels of doors, for instance, and in the construction of gable-shaped passages; two rows of such stone being made to rest against each other at an acute angle, within the thickness of the walls.

So vast and rude, fretted by the action of nearly three thousand years, the fragments of this architecture may often seem, at first sight, like works of nature. At Argos, Tiryns, Mycenæ, the skeleton of the old architecture is more complete. At Mycenæ the gateway of the *acropolis* is still standing with its two well-known sculptured lions—immemorial and almost unique monuments of primitive Greek sculpture—supporting, herald-wise, a symbolical pillar on the vast, triangular, pedimental stone above. The heads are gone, having been fashioned possibly in metal by workmen from the East. On what may be called the *façade*, remains are still discernible of inlaid work in coloured stone, and within the gateway, on the smooth slabs of the pavement, the wheel-ruts are still visible. Connect them with those metal war-chariots in Homer, and you may see in fancy the whole grandiose character of the place, as it may really have been. Shut within the narrow enclosure of these shadowy citadels were the palaces of the kings, with all that intimacy which we may sometimes suppose to have been alien from the open-air Greek life, admitting, doubtless, below the cover of their rough walls, many of those refinements of princely life which the Middle Age found possible in such places, and of which the impression is so fascinating in Homer's description, for instance, of the house of Ulysses, or of Menelaus at Sparta. Rough and frowning without, these old *châteaux* of the Argive kings were delicate within with a decoration almost as dainty and fine as the network of weed and flower that now covers their ruins, and of the delicacy of which, as I said, that golden flower on its silver stalk, or the golden honeycomb of Dædalus, might be taken as representative. In these metal-like structures of self-supporting polygons, locked so firmly and impenetrably together, with the whole mystery of the reasonableness of the arch implicit within them, there is evidence of a complete artistic command over weight in stone, and an understanding of the "law of weight". But over weight only; the ornament still seems to be not strictly architectural, but, according to the notices of Homer, tectonic, borrowed from the sister arts, above all from the art of the metal-workers, to whom those spaces of the building are left which a later age fills with painting, or relief in stone. The skill of the Asiatic comes to adorn this rough native building; and it is a late, elaborate, somewhat voluptuous skill, we may understand, illustrated by the luxury of that Asiatic chamber of Paris, less like that of a warrior than of one going to the dance. Coupled with the vastness of the architectural works which actually remain, such descriptions as that in Homer of the chamber of Paris and the house of Alcinous furnish forth a picture of that early period—the tyrants' age, the age of the *acropoleis*, the period of great dynasties with claims to "divine right", and in many instances at least with all the culture of their time. The vast buildings make us sigh at the thought of wasted human labour, though there is a public usefulness too in some of these designs, such as the draining of the Copaic lake, to which the backs of the people are bent whether they will or not. For the princes there is much of that selfish personal luxury which is a constant trait of feudalism in all ages. For the people, scattered over the country, at their agricultural labour, or gathered in small hamlets, there is some enjoyment, perhaps, of the aspect of that splendour, of the bright warriors on the heights—a certain share of the nobler pride of the tyrants themselves in those tombs and dwellings. Some surmise, also, there seems to have been, of the "curse" of gold, with a dim, lurking suspicion of curious facilities for cruelty in the command over those skilful artificers in metal—some ingenious rack or bull "to pinch and peel"—the tradition of which, not unlike the modern Jacques Bonhomme's shudder at the old ruined French donjon or bastille, haunts, generations afterwards, the ruins of those "labyrinths" of stone, where the old tyrants had their pleasures. For it is a mistake to suppose that that wistful sense of eeriness in ruined buildings, to which most of us are susceptible, is an exclusively modern feeling. The name *Cyclopean*, attached to those desolate remains of buildings which were older than Greek history itself, attests their romantic influence over the fancy of the people who thus attributed them to a superhuman strength and skill. And the Cyclopes, like all the early mythical names of artists, have this note of reality, that they are names not of individuals but of classes, the guilds or companies of workmen in which a certain craft was imparted and transmitted. The Dactyli, the *Fingers*, are the first workers in iron; the savage Chalybes in Scythia the first smelters; actual names are given to the old, fabled Telchines—Chalkon, Argyron, Chryson—workers in brass, silver, and gold respectively. The tradition of their activity haunts the several regions where those metals were found. They make the trident of Poseidon; but then Poseidon's trident is a real fisherman's instrument, the tunny-fork. They are credited, notwithstanding, with an evil sorcery, unfriendly to men, as poor humanity remembered the makers of chains, locks, Procrustean beds; and, as becomes this dark, recondite mine and metal work, the traditions about them are gloomy and grotesque, confusing mortal workmen with demon guilds.

ST MARK'S, VENICE

JOHN RUSKIN, *The Stones of Venice.*
Vol. II, chap. IV. 1851

THROUGH the heavy door whose bronze network closes the place of his rest, let us enter the church itself. It is lost in still deeper twilight, to which the eye must be accustomed for some moments before the form of the building can be traced; and then there opens before us a vast cave, hewn out into the form of a Cross, and divided into shadowy aisles by many pillars. Round the domes of its roof the light enters only through narrow apertures like large stars; and here and there a ray or two from some far-away casement wanders into the darkness, and casts a narrow phosphoric stream upon the waves of marble that heave and fall in a thousand colours along the floor. What else there is of light is from torches, or silver lamps, burning ceaselessly in the recesses of the chapels; the roof sheeted with gold, and the polished walls covered with alabaster, give back at every curve and angle some feeble gleaming to the flames; and the glories round the heads of the sculptured saints flash out upon us as we pass them, and sink again into the gloom. Under foot and over head, a continued succession of crowded imagery, one picture passing into another, as in a dream; forms beautiful and terrible mixed together; dragons and serpents, and ravening beasts of prey, and graceful birds that in the midst of them drink from running fountains and feed from vases of crystal; the passions and the pleasures of human life symbolized together, and the mystery of its redemption; for the mazes of interwoven lines and changeful pictures lead always at last to the Cross, lifted and carved in every place and upon every stone; sometimes with the serpent of eternity wrapped round it, sometimes with doves beneath its arms, and sweet herbage growing forth from its feet; but conspicuous most of all on the great rood that crosses the church before the altar, raised in bright blazonry against the shadow of the apse.

THE EDDYSTONE

SAMUEL SMILES, *Lives of the Engineers*. Vol. II.
1861–2

BEFORE Smeaton had proceeded very far, he had come to the firm conviction that the new lighthouse must be built of Stone. Nevertheless he resolved to preserve the conical form of Rudyerd's building, but to enlarge considerably the diameter of the foundation, and thus increase the stability of the whole superstructure....

Another point which he long and carefully studied, was the best mode of bonding the blocks of stone to the rock and to each other, in such a way as that not only every individual piece, but the whole fabric, should be rendered proof against external force. Binding the blocks together by iron cramps was considered, but dismissed as insufficient, as well as impracticable. Then the process of dovetailing occurred to him —a practice then generally applied to carpentry, though scarcely as yet known in masonry. Still more suitable for his purpose was the method which he had observed adopted in fixing the kerbs along the London footpaths, by which the long pieces or stretchers were retained between the two headers or bond-pieces, whose heads being cut dovetail-wise, adapted themselves to and bound in the stretchers; and the tye being as good at the bottom as at the top, this arrangement, he conceived, was the very best that could be devised for his purpose.

From these beginnings he was readily led to think that if the blocks themselves, both inside and out, were all formed into large dovetails, they might be arranged so as mutually to lock themselves together, being first engrafted into the rock; and in the round and entire courses, along the top of the rock, they might all proceed from and be locked into one large centre stone. By thus rooting the foundations into the rock, and also binding every stone to every other stone in each course, upon which the sea could only act edgeways, he conceived that he would be enabled to erect a building of a strength sufficient to resist the strongest force of winds and waves that was likely to be brought against it. . . .

The building on the rock was fairly begun in the summer of 1757, sheers having been erected and the first stone, of two and a quarter tons weight, having been landed and securely set in its place on the morning of Sunday the 12th of June. By the evening of the following day the first course of four stones was safely laid. . . .

The careful manner in which the details of the foundation work were carried on is related by Smeaton at great length. One of his expedients is worthy of notice—the method by which he gave additional firmness to the stones dovetailed into the rock, by oak-wedges and cement inserted between each. To receive the wedges, two grooves were cut in the waist of each stone, from the top to the bottom of the course, an inch in depth and three inches in width. The carpenters dropped into each groove two of the oaken wedges, one upon its head, the other with its point downwards, so that the two wedges in each groove lay heads and points; on which the one was easily driven down upon the other. A couple of wedges were also pitched at the top of each groove; the dormant wedge, or that with the point upward, being held in the hand, while the drift wedge, or that with its point downward, was driven with a hammer. The object of this wedging was to preserve the whole mass steady together, in opposition to the violent agitation of the sea. In addition to this, a couple of holes being bored through every piece of stone, one course was further bound to another by oak trenails, driven stiffly through, and made so fast that they could more easily be torn asunder than pulled out again. "No assignable power", says Smeaton, "less than would by main stress pull these trenails into two, could lift one of these stones from their beds when so fixed, exclusive of their natural weight, as all agitation was prevented by the lateral wedges...."

The fundamental Solid was completed by the 8th of August, 1758; and, the fine weather continuing, the Solid work, which included the passage from the entry-door to the well-hole for the stairs, made great progress; until, on the 24th of September, 1758, the twenty-fourth course was finished, which completed the solid part of the pillar and formed the floor of the storeroom. The building had now been raised thirty-five feet four inches above its base, or considerably beyond the heavy stroke of the waves. Above this point were to be formed the requisite apartments for the lighthouse-keepers. The walls of these were twenty-six inches thick, constructed in circles of hewn blocks, sixteen pieces forming each circle, all joggled and cramped, so as to secure perfect solidity. The stones were further grooved at the ends, and into the grooves tightly-fitting pieces (rhombs) of Purbeck marble were fixed solid with well-tempered mortar, making the whole perfectly firm and water-tight....

At the beginning of October, the twenty-eighth and twenty-ninth courses were laid, and very strongly secured. A groove was cut round their upper surfaces, in which was placed a circular chain of great strength. Upon each chain, when placed within the grooves, melted lead was poured until the cavities were filled up. They were thus *hooped* as it were, round the building. The reason of such excessive strength at this part of the work was, that these courses received the vaulted floor which formed the ceiling of the under storeroom and the floor of the upper one....

The third year's operations had now ended, and the engineer proceeded with the designs for the iron rails of the balcony, the cast and wrought iron and copper works, as well as with the glass for the lantern, all of which were, like the rest of the work, manufactured under his own eye. The year 1759 was so stormy that it was not before the 5th of July that the workmen could land upon the rock, and recommence their building operations for the year; but from that point they proceeded with great rapidity—the whole of the stones being now in readiness to be placed—so that in thirteen days two entire rooms with their proper coverings had been erected; and by the 17th of August the last pieces of the corona were set, and the forty-six courses of masonry were finished complete.

The column was now erected to its specified height of seventy feet. The last mason's work done was the cutting out of the words "LAUS DEO" upon the last stone set over the door of the lantern. Round the upper storeroom, upon the course under the ceiling, had been cut, at an earlier period, "Except the Lord build the house, they labour in vain that build it". The iron work of the balcony and the lantern were next erected, and over all the gilt ball, the screws of which Smeaton fixed with his own hands, "that in case", he says, "any of them had not held quite tight and firm, the circumstance might not have been slipped over without my knowledge...".

The engineer's work was now so nearly ended, and his anxiety had become so great, that he could not leave it, but took up his abode in the lighthouse, putting his own hands to the finishing of the window-fittings and seeing to the minutest details in the completion of the undertaking. At length the lantern was glazed, the lightning conductor fixed, the rooms were fitted up, and the builder looked upon the work of his hands as finished and complete. The light was first exhibited on the night of the 16th of October, 1759, and the column still stands as firm as on the day on which it was erected....

The Eddystone Lighthouse has now withstood the storms of more than a century. Sometimes, when the sea rolls in with more than ordinary fury from the Atlantic, driven up the channel by the force of a south-west wind, the lighthouse is enveloped in spray and its light is momentarily obscured. But again it is seen shining clear like a star across the waters, a warning and a guide to the homeward-bound. Occasionally, when struck by a strong wave, the water shoots up the perpendicular shaft and leaps quite over the lantern. At other times, a tremendous wave hurls itself upon the lighthouse, as if to force it from its foundation. The report of the shock to one within is like that of a cannon: the windows rattle, the doors slam, and the building vibrates and trembles to its very base. But the tremor felt throughout the lighthouse in such a case, instead of being a sign of weakness, is the strongest proof of the unity and close connection of the fabric in all its parts.

*　　　*　　　*　　　*

By means of similar lights, of different arrangements and of various colours, fixed and revolving, erected upon rocks, islands, and headlands, the British Channel is now lit up along its whole extent, and is as safe to navigate in the darkest night as in the brightest sunshine. The chief danger is from fogs, which alike hide the lights by night and the land by day. Some of the homeward-bound ships entering the Channel from North American ports first make the St Agnes Light, on the Scilly Isles, revolving once in a minute, at a height of 138 feet above high water. But most Atlantic ships keep further south, in consequence of the nature of the soundings about the Scilly Isles; and hence they oftener make the Lizard Lights first, which are visible about twenty miles off. These are two in number, standing on the bold headland forming the most southerly point of the English coast, against which the sea beats with tremendous fury in south-westerly gales.

From this point the coast retires, and in the bend lie Falmouth (with a revolving light on St Anthony's Point), Fowey, the Looes, and Plymouth Sound and Harbour; the coast-line again trending southward until it juts out into the sea, in the bold craggy bluffs of Bolt Head and Start Point, on the last of which is another house with two lights,—one revolving, for the Channel, and another, fixed, to direct vessels inshore clear of the Skerries shoal. But between the Lizard and Start Point, which form the two extremities of this bend in the land of Cornwall and Devonshire, there lies the Eddystone Rock and Lighthouse, standing fourteen miles out from the shore, almost directly in front of Plymouth Sound and in the line of coasting vessels steaming or beating up Channel. From this point the Channel gradually contracts, and the way becomes lighted on both sides up to the Downs.

On the south are seen the three Casquet Lights on the Jersey side; and on the north the two fixed lights on Portland Bill. The next is St Catherine's, a brilliant fixed light on the extreme south point of the Isle of Wight. Next are the lights exhibited at different heights on the Nab, and then the single fixed light exhibited on the Owers vessel. Beachy Head, on the same line, exhibits a powerful revolving light 285 feet above high water, its interval of greatest brilliancy occurring every two minutes. Then comes Dungeness, exhibiting a fixed red light of great power, situated at the extremity of the low point of Dungeness Beach. Next are seen Folkestone, and then Dover, harbour lights; whilst on the south are the flash light, recently stationed on the Varne Bank; and, farther up Channel, on the French coast, is seen the brilliant revolving light on Cape Grisnez.

The Channel is passed with the two South Foreland Lights, one higher than the other, on the left; and the Downs are entered with the South Sandhead floating light on the right: and when the Gull and the North Sandhead floating lights have been passed on the one hand, and the North Foreland on the other, then the Tongue, the Prince's Channel, and the Girdler, are passed. The Nore Light comes next in sight; and from thence it is as easy for the navigator to pilot his ship up the Thames as for a foot-passenger to thread his way along the streets of London.

ART OF THE GREEK CHURCH

Hon. Robert Curzon, *Visits to the Monasteries of the Levant.* Introduction and chap. xix. 1849

It is for their architecture that the monasteries of the Levant are more particularly deserving of study; for, after the remains of the private houses of the Romans at Pompeii, they are the most ancient specimens extant of domestic architecture. The refectories, kitchens, and the cells of the monks exceed in point of antiquity anything of the kind in Europe. The monastery of St Katherine at Mount Sinai has hardly been altered since the sixth century, and still contains ornaments presented to it by the Emperor Justinian. The White Monastery and the monastery at Old Cairo, both in Egypt, are still more ancient. The Monastery of Kazzul Vank, near the sources of the Euphrates, is, I believe, as old as the fifth century. The greater number in all the countries where the Greek faith prevails were built before the year 1000. Most monasteries possess crosses, candlesticks, and reliquaries, many of splendid workmanship, and of the era of the foundation of the buildings which contain them, while their mosaics and fresco-paintings display the state of the arts from the most early periods....

The Greek Church, debased as it is by ignorance and superstition, has still the merit of carefully preserving and restoring all the memorials of its earlier and purer ages. If the fresco-painting of a saint is rubbed out or damaged in the lapse of time, it is scrupulously repainted, exactly as it was before, even to the colour of the robe, the aspect of the countenance, and the minutest accessories of the composition. It is this systematic respect for everything which is old and venerable which renders the interior of the ancient Eastern churches so peculiarly interesting. They are the unchanged monuments of primæval days. The Christian who suffered under the persecution of Diocletian may have knelt before the very altar which we now see, and which was then exactly the same as we now behold it, without any additions or subtractions either in its form or use.

JERRYBUILDING

George Macaulay Trevelyan, *History of England.*
Book v, chap. vii. 1926

JERRYBUILDING was perhaps the gravest evil of the
Industrial Revolution. It was much, no doubt, that the
immensely increased population was housed at all. Nor is it
clear that on the average men were, in the strictly material
sense, worse "housed" in the new urban areas than in the old
country cottages whence they or their fathers had come. But
cellar and one-room tenements for families were dreadfully
common for the lower class of labour, whether in London,
Glasgow, Manchester or the mining districts. A large proportion of the wage-earners and all the large class of commercial
"clerks" were better housed. But even their dwellings were
monotonous and sordid in appearance; town-planning and
any effort to brighten or embellish the face of the street were
alien to the ideas of the age. The enterprising employer wanted
dwellings where the new hands he wished to employ could
live. The builder looked to make money on the transaction.
No one else gave the matter a thought. Thus was the new
England built.

ART THE EXPRESSION OF SOCIETY

Lisle March Phillipps, *The Works of Man.*
Chap. vii. 1911

ART is always a somewhat mysterious subject to deal with,
but we may say this about it with some confidence, that it
never manifests itself with certainty, and least of all in the
shape of a great architectural style, until it has behind it a
combined and united effort. It has in it something of the
nature of a solution of life's problem. So far as the particular
race which creates it is concerned, it is an answer to the question how to live. And for this very reason a great creative

epoch in art never can occur where society is uncertain of itself and distracted in its aims. Art being the expression of a solution, it follows that the solution must be reached in life before it can be expressed in art. There have been very few great creative epochs in art. The Greeks, we may almost say, lived in such an epoch. But to the Greeks was given in their own way, a finite way perhaps, an extraordinarily clear perception of what, so far as they were concerned, life meant. The Italian Renaissance was another creative epoch, much less sure of itself, it is true, than the Greek, but still for the time being assured that in its novel sense of intellectual expansion lay the answer to life's problems. For the time being, Renaissance art did, more or less adequately, express the life of its age, and was therefore genuine.

But, further, all manifestations of art, even those quite minor and subordinate ones which are more than fashions, but less than genuine creative epochs, demand an effort of a certain weight and unanimity to back them. For example, such movements as the Louis Quinze and Louis Seize periods bear witness to the influence which at that time was supreme in France, the influence of an idle and luxurious upper class detached from yet dominating the life of the nation. So, too, if the English aristocratic style of art of the same time was less thorough than the French, it was because the aristocratic ideal had less completely gained a hold upon English than upon French life. If such minor manifestations as these seem trivial when compared with the great art epochs, the reason is to be found in the fact that they interpret the life, not of a people but of a class. Their importance is less to the degree in which the conviction of a single section of society is weaker than the conviction of the whole of it. In each case the power and sincerity of the movement in art is determined by the extent to which the idea inspiring it has already possessed itself of life and penetrated life. An idea that has collected a great deal of life will inspire a robust art. An idea that has collected but a little life will inspire a feeble art. But always the idea must have established itself in life, and made its hold upon life before it can manifest itself in art.

TRADE: FIRST CENTURY

EDWARD GIBBON, *Decline and Fall of the Roman Empire.*
Vol. I, chap. ii. 1776

THE most remote countries of the ancient world were ransacked to supply the pomp and delicacy of Rome. The forests of Scythia afforded some valuable furs. Amber was brought over land from the shores of the Baltic to the Danube; and the barbarians were astonished at the price which they received in exchange for so useless a commodity. There was a considerable demand for Babylonian carpets and other manufactures of the East; but the most important and unpopular branch of foreign trade was carried on with Arabia and India. Every year, about the time of the summer solstice, a fleet of an hundred and twenty vessels sailed from Myos-hormos, a port of Egypt, on the Red Sea. By the periodical assistance of the Monsoons, they traversed the ocean in about forty days. The coast of Malabar, or the island of Ceylon, was the usual term of their navigation, and it was in those markets that the merchants from the more remote countries of Asia expected their arrival. The return of the fleet of Egypt was fixed to the months of December or January; and as soon as their rich cargo had been transported on the backs of camels, from the Red Sea to the Nile, and had descended that river as far as Alexandria, it was poured, without delay, into the capital of the empire. The objects of oriental traffic were splendid and trifling: silk, a pound of which was esteemed not inferior in value to a pound of gold; precious stones, among which the pearl claimed the first rank after the diamond; and a variety of aromatics, that were consumed in religious worship and the pomp of funerals.

TRADE: EIGHTEENTH CENTURY

Joseph Addison, *The Spectator*. No. 69. 1711

Nature seems to have taken a particular care to dissemin-
ate her blessings among the different regions of the world,
with an eye to this mutual intercourse and traffick among
mankind, that the natives of the several parts of the globe
might have a kind of dependence upon one another, and be
united together by their common interest. Almost every
degree produces something peculiar to it. The food often
grows in one country, and the sauce in another. The fruits of
Portugal are corrected by the products of Barbadoes: the
infusion of a China plant sweetened with the pith of an Indian
cane. The Philippick Islands give a flavour to our European
bowls. The single dress of a woman of quality is often the
product of a hundred climates. The muff and the fan come
together from the different ends of the earth. The scarf is sent
from the torrid zone, and the tippet from beneath the pole.
The brocade Petticoat rises out of the mines of Peru, and the
diamond necklace out of the bowels of Indostan.

If we consider our own country in its natural prospect,
without any of the benefits and advantages of commerce,
what a barren uncomfortable spot of earth falls to our share!
Natural historians tell us, that no fruit grows originally among
us, besides hips, and haws, acorns and pig-nuts, with other
delicacies of the like nature; that our climate of itself, and
without the assistance of art, can make no further advances
towards a plum than to a sloe, and carries an apple to no
greater a perfection than a crab: that our melons, our peaches,
our figs, our apricots, and cherries, are strangers among us,
imported in different ages, and naturalised in our English
gardens; and that they would all degenerate and fall away
into the trash of our own country, if they were wholly neglected by the planter, and left to the mercy of our sun and
soil. Nor has traffick more enriched our vegetable world, than
it has improved the whole face of nature among us. Our ships
are laden with the harvest of every climate; our tables are
stored with spices, and oils, and wines: our rooms are filled

with pyramids of china, and adorned with the workmanship of Japan: our morning's draught comes to us from the remotest corners of the earth: we repair our bodies by the drugs of America, and repose ourselves under Indian canopies. My friend Sir Andrew calls the vineyards of France our gardens: the spice-islands our hot-beds; the Persians our silk-weavers, and the Chinese our potters. Nature indeed furnishes us with the bare necessaries of life, but traffick gives us greater variety of what is useful, and at the same time supplies us with everything that is convenient and ornamental. Nor is it the least part of this our happiness, that whilst we enjoy the remotest products of the north and south, we are free from those extremities of weather which give them birth; that our eyes are refreshed with the green fields of Britain, at the same time that our palates are feasted with fruits that rise between the tropicks.

For these reasons there are no more useful members in a commonwealth than merchants. They knit mankind together in a mutual intercourse of good offices, distribute the gifts of nature, find work for the poor, add wealth to the rich, and magnificence to the great. Our English merchant converts the tin of his own country into gold, and exchanges his wool for rubies. The Mahometans are clothed in our British manufacture, and the inhabitants of the frozen zone warmed with the fleeces of our sheep.

STOCK-JOBBING

DANIEL DEFOE, *A Tour Thro' the Whole Island of Great Britain.* Letter 5. 1724–6

HERE are the *South Sea* Company, the *East India* Company, the *Bank*, the *African* Company, etc. whose Stocks support that prodigious Paper Commerce, called *Stock-Jobbing*; a Trade, which once bewitched the Nation almost to its Ruin, and which, tho' reduced very much, and recover'd from that terrible Infatuation which once overspread the whole Body of the People, yet is still a Negotiation, which is so vast in its Extent, that almost all the Men of Substance in *England* are more or less concerned in it, and the Property of which is so very often alienated, that even the Tax upon the Transfers of Stock, tho' but Five Shillings for each Transfer, bring many Thousand Pounds a Year to the Government; and some have said, that there is not less than a Hundred Millions of Stock transferred forward or backward from one Hand to another every Year, and this is one thing which makes such a constant Daily Intercourse between the Court Part of the Town, and the City; and this is given as one of the principal Causes of the prodigious Conflux of the Nobility and Gentry from all Parts of *England* to *London*, more than ever was known in former Years, viz. That many Thousands of Families are so deeply concerned in those Stocks, and find it so absolutely necessary to be at Hand to take the Advantage of buying and selling, as the sudden Rise or Fall of the Price directs, and the Loss they often sustain by their Ignorance of Things when absent, and the Knavery of Brokers and others, whom, in their Absence, they are bound to trust, that they find themselves obliged to come up and live constantly here, or at least, most Part of the Year.

This is the Reason why, notwithstanding the Encrease of new Buildings, and the Addition of new Cities, as they may be called, every Year to the old, yet a House is no sooner built, but 'tis tenanted and inhabited, and every Part is crouded with People, and that not only in the Town, but in all the Towns and Villages round....

But let the Citizens and Inhabitants of *London* know, and it may be worth the Reflection of some of the Landlords, and Builders especially, that if Peace continues, and the publick Affairs continue in honest and upright Management, there is a Time coming, at least the Nation hopes for it, when the publick Debts being reduced and paid off, the Funds or Taxes on which they are established, may cease, and so Fifty or Sixty Millions of the Stocks, which are now the solid Bottom of the *South-Sea Company, East-India Company, Bank*, etc. will cease, and be no more; by which the Reason of this Conflux of People being removed, they will of Course, and by the

Nature of the Thing, return again to their Country Seats, to avoid the expensive living at *London* as they did come up hither to share the extravagant Gain of their former Business here....

Then, I say, will be a Time to expect the vast Concourse of People to *London*, will separate again and disperse as naturally, as they have now crouded hither: What will be the Fate then of all the fine Buildings in the Out Parts, in such a Case, let any one judge.

TRANSPORT

Sir Arthur Quiller-Couch, *Studies in Literature.* (The Commerce of Thought.) First Series. 1918

LET your imagination play on these old trade-routes, and you will not only enhance your hold on the true springs of history; you will wonderfully seize the romance of it. You will see, as this little planet revolves back out of the shadow of night to meet the day, little threads pushing out over its black spaces—dotted ships on wide seas, crawling trains of emigrant waggons, pioneers, tribes on the trek, men extinguishing their camp-fires and shouldering their baggage for another day's march or piling it into canoes by untracked river sides, families loading their camels with figs and dates for Smyrna, villagers treading wine-vats, fishermen hauling nets, olive-gatherers, packers, waggoners, long trains of African porters, desert caravans with armed outriders, dahabeeyahs pushing up the Nile, busy rice-fields, puffs of smoke where the expresses run across Siberia, Canada, or northward from Capetown, Greenland whalers, Newfoundland codfishers, trappers around Hudson's Bay....

The main puzzle with these trade-routes is that while seas and rivers and river valleys last for ever, and roads for long, and even a railroad long enough to be called a "permanent way", the traffic along them is often curiously evanescent.

Let me give you a couple of instances, one in quite recent times, the other of today, passing under our eyes.

A man invents a steam-engine. It promptly makes obsolete the stage-coaches, whose pace was the glory of England. Famous hostelries along the Great North Road put up their shutters; weeds begin to choke the canals; a whole nexus of national traffic is torn in shreds, dissipated. A few years pass, and somebody invents the motor-car—locomotion by petrol. Forthwith prosperity flows back along the old highways. County Councils start re-metalling, tar-spraying; inns revive under new custom: and your rich man is swept past a queer wayside building, without ever a thought that here stood a turnpike gate which Dick Turpin or John Nevinson had to leap.

For a second change, which I have watched for a year or two as it has passed under my own eyes at the foot of my garden at home.—As you know, the trade of Europe from the West Coast of America around the Horn is carried by large sailing-vessels (the passage being too long for steamships without coaling stations). One day America starts in earnest to cut the Panama canal. Forthwith the provident British shipowner begins to get quit of these sailing-vessels: noble three- and four-masters, almost all Clyde-built. He sells them to Italian firms. Why to Italian firms? Because these ships have considerable draught and are built of iron. Their draught unfits them for general coasting trade; they could not begin to navigate the Baltic, for instance. Now Italy has deep-water harbours. But the Genoese firms (I am told) buy these ships for the second reason that they are of iron: because while the Italian Government lays a crippling duty on ordinary iron, broken-up ship-iron may enter free. So, after a coastwise voyage or two, it pays to rip their plates out, pass them under the rollers and re-issue them for new iron; and thus for a few months these beautiful things that used to wing it home, five months without sighting land, and anchor under my garden, eke out a new brief traffic until the last of them shall be towed to the breakers' yard. Even in such unnoted ways grew, thrived, passed, died the commercial glories of Venice, Spain, Holland.

COAL

Benjamin Disraeli, Lord Beaconsfield, *Sybil*.
Book III, chap. i. 1845

THE last rays of the sun, contending with clouds of smoke that drifted across the country, partially illumined a peculiar landscape. Far as the eye could reach, and the region was level, except where a range of limestone hills formed its distant limit, a wilderness of cottages, or tenements, that were hardly entitled to a higher name, were scattered for many miles over the land; some detached, some connected in little rows, some clustering in groups, yet rarely forming continuous streets, but interspersed with blazing furnaces, heaps of burning coal, and piles of smouldering iron-stone; while forges and engine chimneys roared and puffed in all directions, and indicated the frequent presence of the mouth of the mine, and the bank of the coal-pit. Notwithstanding the whole country might be compared to a vast rabbit warren, it was nevertheless intersected with canals, crossing each other at various levels, and though the subterranean operations were prosecuted with so much avidity, that it was not uncommon to observe whole rows of houses awry, from the shifting and hollow nature of the land, still, intermingled with heaps of mineral refuse, or of metallic dross, patches of the surface might here and there be recognized, covered, as if in mockery, with grass and corn, looking very much like those gentlemen's sons that we used to read of in our youth, stolen by the chimneysweeps, and giving some intimations of their breeding beneath their grimy livery. But a tree or a shrub—such an existence was unknown in this dingy rather than dreary region.

It was the twilight hour; the hour at which in southern climes the peasant kneels before the sunset image of the blessed Hebrew maiden; when caravans halt in their long course over vast deserts, and the turbaned traveller, bending in the sand, pays his homage to the sacred stone and the sacred city; the hour, not less holy, that announces the cessation of English toil, and sends forth the miner and the collier to breathe the air of earth, and gaze on the light of heaven.

They come forth: the mine delivers its gang and the pit its bondsmen; the forge is silent and the engine is still. The plain is covered with the swarming multitude: bands of stalwart men, broad-chested and muscular, wet with toil, and black as the children of the tropics; troops of youth—alas! of both sexes—though neither their raiment nor their language indicates the difference; all are clad in male attire; and oaths that men might shudder at, issue from lips born to breathe words of sweetness. Yet these are to be—some are—the mothers of England! But can we wonder at the hideous coarseness of their language, when we remember the savage rudeness of their lives? Naked to the waist, an iron chain fastened to a belt of leather runs between their legs clad in canvas trousers, while on hands and feet an English girl, for twelve, sometimes for sixteen hours a day, hauls and hurries tubs of coal up subterranean roads, dark, precipitous and plashy; circumstances that seem to have escaped the notice of the Society for the Abolition of Negro Slavery. Those worthy gentlemen too appear to have been singularly unconscious of the sufferings of the little trappers, which was remarkable, as many of them were in their own employ.

See, too, these emerge from the bowels of the earth! Infants of four and five years of age, many of them girls, pretty and still soft and timid; entrusted with the fulfilment of most responsible duties, and the nature of which entails on them the necessity of being the earliest to enter the mine and the latest to leave it. Their labour indeed is not severe, for that would be impossible, but it is passed in darkness and in solitude. They endure that punishment which philosophical philanthropy has invented for the direst criminals, and which those criminals deem more terrible than the death for which it is substituted. Hour after hour elapses, and all that reminds the infant trappers of the world they have quitted and that which they have joined, is the passage of the coal-wagons for which they open the air-doors of the galleries, and on keeping which doors constantly closed, except at this moment of passage, the safety of the mine and the lives of the persons employed in it entirely depend.

IRON

WILLIAM COBBETT, *Rural Rides*. Northern Tour. 1830

ALL the way along from Leeds to Sheffield it is coal and iron, and iron and coal. It was dark before we reached Sheffield; so that we saw the iron furnaces in all the horrible splendour of their everlasting blaze. Nothing can be conceived more grand or more terrific than the yellow waves of fire that incessantly issue from the top of these furnaces, some of which are close by the way-side. Nature has placed the beds of iron and the beds of coal alongside of each other, and art has taught man to make one to operate upon the other, as to turn the iron-stone into liquid matter, which is drained off from the bottom of the furnace, and afterwards moulded into blocks and bars, and all sorts of things. The combustibles are put into the top of the furnace, which stands thirty, forty, or fifty feet up in the air, and the ever-blazing mouth of which is kept supplied with coal and coke and iron-stone from little iron waggons forced up by steam, and brought down again to be refilled. It is a surprising thing to behold; and it is impossible to behold it without being convinced that, whatever other nations may do with cotton and with wool, they will never equal England with regard to things made of iron and steel. This Sheffield, and the land all about it, is one bed of iron and coal. They call it black Sheffield, and black enough it is; but from this one town and its environs go nine-tenths of the knives that are used in the whole world; there being, I understand, no knives made at Birmingham; the manufacture of which place consists of the larger sort of implements, of locks of all sorts, and guns and swords, and of all the endless articles of hardware which go to the furnishing of a house. As to the land, viewed in the way of agriculture, it really does appear to be very little worth. I have not seen, except at Harewood and Ripley, a stack of wheat since I came into Yorkshire; and even there, the whole I saw; and all that I have seen since I came into Yorkshire; and all that I saw during a ride of six miles that I took into Derbyshire the day before yesterday; all put together would not make the one-half of what I have many times seen in one single rick-yard of the vales of Wilt-shire. But this is all very proper: these coal-diggers, and iron-melters, and knife-makers, compel us to send the food to them, which, indeed, we do very cheerfully, in exchange for the produce of their rocks, and the wondrous works of their hands.

SUPERIMPOSED CIVILISATIONS

GEORGE MACAULAY TREVELYAN, *British History in the Nineteenth Century*. Introduction. 1922

DURING the last hundred and fifty years, the rate of pro-gress in man's command over nature has been ten times as fast as in the period between Cæsar and Napoleon, a hundred times as fast as in the slow prehistoric ages. Tens of thousands of years divided man's first use of fire from his first applica-tion of it to iron. Even in the civilised era, when literature, science and philosophy were given us by Greece, the art of writing preceded the printing-press by tens of centuries. In those days each great invention was granted a lease of many ages in which to foster its own characteristic civilisation, before it was submerged by the next. But in our day, in-ventions, each implying a revolution in the habits of man, follow each other thick as the falling leaves. Modern history, beginning from the England of 1780, is a series of dissolving views. In each generation a new economic life half obliterates a predecessor little older than itself.

One example will suffice, that of inland transport. In the reign of George III the civilisation of the riding-horse and the pack-horse gave way to that of the coach, the waggon and the barge, because the soft road was at length superseded by the hard road, flanked by the canal. But no time was given to develop a new civilisation on that basis; Macadam had not yet taught Lord Eldon and the Duke of Wellington that they were living in a new world, before Stephenson's locomotive in its turn replaced the barge, the waggon and the coach. And then, before the society based on steam has worked out its peculiar destiny, petrol in our own day gives a new life to the old roads, and opens out the pathways of the air.

THE WEST AND THE FAR EAST

GOLDSWORTHY LOWES DICKINSON, *Appearances*.
Part II, chap. vii. 1914

WESTERN civilisation, wherever it penetrates, brings with it water-taps, sewers, and police; but it brings also an ugliness, an insincerity, a vulgarity never before known to history, unless it be under the Roman Empire. It is terrible to see in China the first wave of this western flood flinging along the coasts and rivers and railway lines its scrofulous foam of advertisements, of corrugated iron roofs, of vulgar, meaningless architectural forms. In China, as in all old civilisations I have seen, all the building of man harmonises with and adorns nature. In the West everything now built is a blot. Many men, I know, sincerely think that this destruction of beauty is a small matter, and that only decadent æsthetes would pay any attention to it in a world so much in need of sewers and hospitals. I believe this view to be profoundly mistaken. The ugliness of the West is a symptom of a disease of the Soul. It implies that the end has been lost sight of in the means. In China the opposite is the case. The end is clear, though the means be inadequate. Consider what the Chinese have done to Tai Shan, and what the West will shortly do, once the stream of Western tourists begins to flow strongly. Where the Chinese have constructed a winding stairway of stone, beautiful from all points of view, Europeans or Americans will run up a funicular railway, a staring scar that will never heal. Where the Chinese have written poems in exquisite caligraphy, *they* will cover the rocks with advertisements. Where the Chinese have built a series of temples, each so designed and placed as to be a new beauty in the landscape, *they* will run up restaurants and hotels like so many scabs on the face of nature.

I say with confidence that they *will*, because they *have* done it wherever there is any chance of a paying investment. Well, the Chinese need, I agree, our science, our organisation, our medicine. But is it affectation to think they may have to pay too high a price for it, and to suggest that in acquiring our material advantages they may lose what we have gone near to lose, that fine and sensitive culture which is one of the forms of spiritual life? The West talks of civilising China. Would that China could civilise the West!

LUCULLUS

PLUTARCH OF CHAERONEIA, *Lives of the Noble Greeks and Romans*, c. A.D. 80. Translated by Sir Thomas North. 1579

FOR my part, reading Lucullus' life: methinks that I read an ancient comedy, the beginning whereof is tedious, and the latter end joyful. For at the beginning of his life, you find notable exploits done by him in wars, and great good government also in peace: but in the end they all turned into feasts and banquets, and lacking little of masks and mummeries, dancing with torches, and all other such delights fit for young men. For I bring within the compass and reckoning of his fineness and pleasures, his sumptuous buildings, his stately walls and galleries, his hot-houses and stoves, his tables and pictures, his statues also: and the great workmanship and curiosity he had besides of all other arts by him gotten together out of all parts to his infinite charge, abusing therein the world of goods and treasure gotten and won in the wars, in time of his charge and office of general, and otherwise. Insomuch, that notwithstanding excess and superfluity hath ever since increased until this present time, yet they reckon the gardens Lucullus made, to be the most sumptuous and delicatest places that the emperors have. And therefore Tubero the Stoic philosopher, having seen these stately works which Lucullus had caused to be made near unto Naples, by the seaside (where there are mountains cut through, light as day, and hanged upon vaults) and great ditches cast by force to make the sea pass and run through his houses, to keep fish therein, and lodgings also that he built in the sea itself: he called Lucullus, Xerxes the gownman, as if he would have said, Xerxes the Roman. For even so did Xerxes in old time cause the mountain Athos to be cut in sunder, and a channel to be digged there to pass his ships through. He had also many other pleasant places within the territories of Rome near unto Tusculum, where there were great large halls set upon terraces to see round about far off in the day time. And Pompey going thither sometime to see him, reproved him greatly, telling him that he had built a marvellous fair sommer house, but not to be dwelt in the winter season. Lucullus laughing, answered him: Do you think me to have less wit and reason than storks or cranes, that I cannot shift houses according to the season? Another time there was a prætor of Rome, that making plays to shew the people pastime, sent unto Lucullus to borrow certain purple clokes to set forth his players: Lucullus made him answer, that he would cause his folks to look if he had any. And the next morning demanding of him how many he should need, the other answered, that a hundred would serve his turn. Whereupon Lucullus told him again, he would furnish him with two hundred, if his case so required. And therefore the poet Horace writing this story, addeth to a notable exclamation against superfluity, saying: That men think that a poor house, where there is no more riches than necessary, and where there is not more than appeareth in sight, and that the maister knows of. He was a vain man in his ordinary service at his board, not only in that his beds whereon he fed, were covered with rich carpets of purple, and himself served in gold and silver vessels set with precious stones, and that there was dancing, music, plays, and other suchlike pastimes of ordinary: but also for that he was continually served with all sorts of fine dainty dishes, with works of pastry, banqueting dishes, and fruit curiously wrought and prepared, which only made him to be wondred at of men of simple understanding and mean condition.

A GREAT HOUSE

Frances Parthenope Verney, *Memoirs of the Verney Family during the Civil War.* Vol. i. 1892

A great house provisioned itself, with little help from the outside world; the inhabitants brewed and baked, they churned and ground their meal, they bred up, fed and slew their beeves and sheep, and brought up their pigeons and poultry at their own doors. Their horses were shod at home, their planks were sawn, their rough iron work was forged and mended. Accordingly the mill-house, the slaughter-house, the blacksmiths', carpenters' and painters' shops, the malting and brewhouse, the woodyard full of large and small timber, the sawpit, the outhouses full of all sorts of odds and ends of stone, iron, bits of marble, carved woodwork, and logs cut for burning—the riding-house, the laundry, the dairy with a large churn turned by a horse, the stalls and styes for all manner of cattle and pigs, the apple and root chambers, show how complete was the idea of self-supply and independence of trade of any kind at Claydon as in other country houses. Of the "Dove Cotts", we read continually in the letters, as a dozen pigeons were an acceptable present to friends in London, almost preferred indeed to the venison, which Sir Ralph is very generous in distributing.

In a series of graduated little pools in the garden called "the Stews", belonging to the Old Roman Catholic days, the fish caught in the larger ponds below was kept for immediate use. A supply of wild fowl was obtained from a Decoy "celebrated in the neighbourhood", observes Browne Willis, leading by a long watercourse from a great pool about a mile away into the heart of the "Charndon and great sea woods". The difficulty of keeping cattle and sheep alive in winter on the scanty stores of hay was so great that until the middle of the 17th century they were killed and salted down early in the autumn. In the Northumberland household book of the reign of Henry VII, it appears that fresh meat was eaten only between Midsummer and Michaelmas. The frequent mention of skin diseases in the Verney letters shows how the salt diet,

almost unrelieved by vegetables for many months, told upon
the health particularly of the women and children; any little
relief from fish and game was valuable.

Matters were however improving in the days of James and
Charles I. Salt meat was now only used after Martinmas,
potatoes had been introduced by Sir Walter Raleigh, and
Sir Ralph is intent upon many sorts of salad and vegetables
which he sends from France between 1644 and 1653. That they
were not altogether new, however, is evident from the cynical
remarks of his uncle, Dr Denton. On receiving the presents
of seeds and plants from his nephew, he often declares that
he "cannot see they are much better than the sallats he has
already". Ralph on his return is very anxious for the welfare
of the vines and fig trees, the roots, seeds, flowers, and ornamental trees, which he gets over from Holland and France,
and in spite of Lord Macaulay's statement to the contrary, it
is clear that great attention was beginning to be paid to
gardens and pleasure grounds. We hear of the "Persian tulips
and ranoncules" sent him by his son John at his particular
request, apparently from Holland; the pinks, gilliflowers,
melon seeds and pear-grafts, and "the exact fine gardens" at
Claydon are mentioned in 1694 by Cecilia Fiennes. The woods
were always a great feature of the Claydon Estate, and the
arts of wood-craft and forestry amongst the constant interests of its owners. Sir Ralph desires his steward to go
and see "Cozen Smith's hedges at Akeley", which are grown
in a west-country fashion, and to give him his opinion of
them.

Within doors the activity of the family and household was
as great and as multifarious as without. The spinning of wool
and flax (so universal that an unmarried woman of any class
was called "a spinster"), the fine and coarse needlework, the
embroidery, the fine cooking, the curing, the preserving, the
distillery that went on, were incessant. The excellent linen
spun at home and woven in the cottage handlooms (well
described in "Silas Marner"), was so valuable that it was left
by will with great particularity. Margaret, Lady Verney, is
as careful to which of her daughters she will leave her "best
sheets", and to whom "the second best", and the "table

clothes ", as about the destination of her diamonds, and though her children are a loving family, there is nearly a disagreeable quarrel between Sir Ralph and his sister Pen, when she prefers money, and he allows her only 8*l.* for the sheets in question. As 10*l.* at the time is the price of a good horse, this sounds a quite sufficient sum.

The work with the needle and the wheel was a very necessary part of a lady's education, and as some of the poorer relations of the family resided in great houses as "lady helps" (the equivalents of the pages of the other sex), they were useful and welcome in carrying out these important household labours. There are letters from five or six of these ladies, connected with the Verneys, well born, well bred, and as well educated as their neighbours, who seem to have been treated with great consideration. "Sir George Strickland's daughter is my lady's gentlewoman" to Lady Sussex, and Sir Ralph's cousin, Lady Hobart, is very anxious when she becomes poor and a widow, that he should obtain the place for her daughter "Frank". Doll Leake, another cousin, is living with Lady Vere Gaudy and her daughter-in-law, Lady Mary Fielding, who are both warmly attached to her. She is busy embroidering a bed on one occasion, and writes to Sir Ralph in London to help her with the silks and crewels required for it.

Lace-making had been introduced into Bucks by Catherine of Aragon, whose dowry was derived from the revenues of Steeple Claydon. She was visiting at a house in Buckingham, still standing in Sir Ralph's days, when she received the news of the victory at Flodden Field. "St Katern's day" was held as a festival in her honour until not long ago, by the makers of pillow-lace in Buckinghamshire; and the allusion to

The spinsters and the knitters in the sun,
And the free maids who weave their thread with bones,

whom Viola quotes as her authority for a song, shows that pillow-lace was commonly made in England in Shakespeare's time.

The work of the still-room, the "preserving, conserving, candying, making syrupes, jellies, beautifying washes, pomatum essences, and other such secrets", the making of vinegar and pickles, must have been held by the family to be quite as important a part of their business.

Accordingly in the fruit season the ladies are very fully occupied. Lady Gardiner is excused by her husband from writing to Sir Ralph—"being almost melted with the double heat of the weather and her hotter employment, because the fruit is suddenly ripe and she is so busy preserving", and this though their household is very large, consisting of thirty persons. Mrs Isham sends word to Lady Verney, through Sir Ralph, "I praye tell yore mother (in London) I will doe oup hur sugar if she hath corrantes a nowe, for this last wicke of windes hath bine so bige that most of them was bloed off the treeses".

The remains of queer tin vessels of many shapes with spouts at all angles, in the ancient cupboards of the Claydon still-room, and the endless recipes amongst the papers, show how the "decoctions, infusions and essences of herbs and simples" were prepared. When a doctor wrote a prescription, he directed how the medicine was to be made. "The snail water, the hiera picra, the mithridates, orbiculi, Bezoartis", and the like, are all thus explained.

The fruit syrups, raspberry vinegar, home-made wines, currant, cowslip, and elder, were important drinks when tea, coffee and chocolate were unknown. All three were introduced about the time of the Restoration. When Sir Ralph was young, the health of his bride was drunk by Sir Nathaniel Hobart "in ale and cake, my wife and aunt will do the like ", showing it was the beverage for women as well as for men. Some twenty years later, in 1650, Sir Ralph, in exile at Blois, writes anxiously to London for "the quite new drink chocolate", for his dying wife; his uncle sends directions how to make it, because "the thing itselfe is not knowne in France". The fashion however spread quickly, for a few months after another exile sends the invalid a still better kind from Paris. The next year Sir Ralph, travelling after his wife's death with his little boy through Lyons, mentions "coffee, a berry out of Turkey, ground for a drink", as a curious novelty, and Pepys, as is well known, partakes of "the new China drink, tea", for the first time in 1660, after which the use of it became common.

PUBLIC EMPLOYMENT

JOHN EVELYN, *Public Employment and an Active Life preferred to Solitude.* 1667

LET us therefore rather celebrate public employment and an active life, which renders us so nearly allied to virtue, defines and maintains our being, supports society, preserves kingdoms in peace, protects them in war; has discovered new worlds, planted the Gospel, increases knowledge, cultivates arts, relieves the afflicted; and in sum, without which the whole universe itself had still been but a rude and indigested chaos. Or if (to vie landscapes with our Celador) you had rather see it represented in picture, behold here a sovereign sitting in his august assembly of Parliament enacting wholesome laws; next him my Lord Chancellor and the rest of the reverend judges and magistrates dispensing them for the good of the people; figure to yourself a Secretary of State making his dispatches and receiving intelligence: a statesman countermining some pernicious plot against the commonwealth; here a general bravely embattling his forces and vanquishing the enemy; there a colony planting an island, and a barbarous and solitary nation reduced to civility; cities, houses, forts, ships, building for society, shelter, defence, and commerce. In another table, the poor relieved and set to work, the naked clad, the oppressed delivered, the malefactor punished, the labourer busied, and the whole world employed for the benefit of mankind. In a word, behold him in the nearest resemblance to his Almighty Maker, always in action, and always doing good.

DEO, PATRIAE, AMICIS

GEORGE GRANVILLE, LORD LANSDOWN, *In a letter to the*
Earl of Bath. September, 1711

You are placed at the head of a body of gentry, entirely
disposed in affection to you and your family: you are born
possessed of all those amiable qualities which cannot fail of
fixing their hearts: you have no other example to follow, but
to tread in the steps of your ancestors; it is all that is hoped,
or desired from you. You are upon an uncommon foundation
in that part of the world: your ancestors, for at least five
hundred years, never made any alliance, male or female, out
of the western counties. Thus there is hardly a gentleman
either in Cornwall or Devon, but has some of your blood, or
you some of theirs. I remember, the first time I accompanied
your grand-father into the west, upon his holding his parliament of tinners, as Warden of the Stannaries, when there was
the most numerous appearance of gentry of both counties,
that had ever been remembered together; I observed there
was hardly any one but whom he called cousin, and I could
not but observe at the same time, how well they were pleased
with it. Let this be a lesson for you, when it comes to your
turn to appear amongst them.

There is another particular, in my opinion of no small consequence to the support of your interest, which I would re-
commend to your imitation; and that is to make Stowe * your
principal residence. I have heard your grand-father say, if
ever he lived to be possessed of New-Hall, he would pull it
down, that your father might have no temptation to withdraw
from the antient seat of his family.

From the Conquest to the Restoration, your ancestors constantly resided amongst their countrymen, except when the
public service called upon them to sacrifice their lives for it.
Stowe, in my grand-father's time, till the civil wars broke out,
was a kind of Academy for all the young men of family in the
country: he provided himself with the best masters of all
kinds for education; and the children of his neighbours and

* In the parish of Kilkhampton, Cornwall.

friends shared the advantage with his own. Thus he, in a manner, became the father of his country, and not only engaged the affection of the present generation, but laid a foundation of friendship for posterity, which is not worn out at this day. Upon this foundation, my Lord, you inherit friends without the trouble of making them, and have only to preserve them; an easy task for you, to whom nature has been so liberal of every quality, necessary to attract affection, and gain the heart.

I must tell you the generality of our countrymen have been always Royalists: you inherit too much loyal blood to like them the worse. There is an old saying amongst them, "that a *Godolphin* was never known to want wit; a *Trelawney*, courage; or a *Granville*, loyalty". To *fear* God *and honour* the King, were injunctions so closely tacked together, that they seem to make but one and the same command: a man may as well pretend to be a good christian, without *fearing God*; as a good subject, without *honouring the King.* DEO, PATRIAE, AMICIS, was your great grand-father Sir Bevil's motto: in three words, he has added to his example a rule, which in following, you can never err in any duty of life.

WORK OF THE HUMANISTS

CHARLES BEARD, *The Reformation of the Sixteenth Century in its relation to Modern Thought and Knowledge.* Hibbert Lectures. Lecture X. 1883

THE tide of reviving interest in classical culture, which had been slowly gathering strength for a century and a half, was far too mighty to be even temporarily arrested by any defection of the Reformers. While they were occupied in internecine quarrels and the building up of rival systems of dogmatic theology, the work of recovering the mind of antiquity went steadily on. It was a longer and a more laborious task than from our present standpoint of culture we are easily able to conceive; and the men who accomplished

it are not to be measured by the worth of their visible con-
tributions to literature. When the convent libraries of east
and west had been ransacked, and every fragment of ancient
literature consigned to the safe keeping of the printing-press,
the work was only begun. Texts had to be emended, grammars
to be slowly compiled, the materials of dictionaries collected
with almost infinite toil. The whole mass of learned tradition,
on the basis of which a scholar now begins his work, had to
be painfully brought together. When, by the labours of several
generations, the philological part of the task was accomplished
with tolerable completeness—when all educated men could
read the classical authors in the original, and Greek and Latin
were written by scholars with facility and even elegance—
there remained the work of reproducing the life of the ancients; of understanding their law, their worship, their military
systems, their amusements; of re-writing their history, and
reducing their chronology to order. And this was a toil which
lasted through the eighteenth century, if indeed it can be said
to be even yet at an end. Italy soon gave up her place in
the van of classical culture. Her scholarship became mere
phrase-mongering and Ciceronianism. Not what a man had
to say, but how he said it, was the all-important thing; while
platitude was no offence at all, solecism was a mortal sin.
I have already spoken of the lack of moral fibre in the Italian
scholars of the age of the despots: when Rome became serious
under the influence of the Counter-Reformation, humanists
were warned off debateable ground, and bidden to employ
their pens in her service, if at all. The study of Greek fell into
disfavour; and when Jesuit influence came to predominate in
schools and colleges, those admirable educators had practical
ends of their own, which they cared for more than the progress
of philology. So the literary hegemony passed to France and
to Holland. Budæus, Turnebus, Casaubon, Salmasius, are
the glories of French scholarship. If the Scaligers boasted
an Italian descent, the elder lived and wrote in France; the
younger and greater, who was Huguenot to the heart, taught
in Leiden. It would be difficult to enumerate the many profound scholars who toiled in the Universities of Holland to
complete the long task the nature of which I have endeavoured

to indicate. Their labours lie concealed in the grammars and dictionaries which to-day smooth the path of classical culture to our children; in the annotations which elucidate every difficult passage and explain every obscure allusion; in that knowledge of ancient life which is part of the intellectual air we breathe. The result was at once to restore that living connection with the mind of antiquity which Christian Europe deliberately abandoned in the sixth century, and to accumulate the materials upon which the higher and more constructive criticism of a later age has worked.

EDUCATION

(i) PLATO, *Republic*, c. 390 B.C. Book III. Translated by Benjamin Jowett. 1871

(ii) SAMUEL TAYLOR COLERIDGE, *Statesman's Manual, or the Bible the best Guide to Political Skill and Foresight.* 1816

(iii) THOMAS CARLYLE, "Signs of the Times", *Edinburgh Review.* June, 1829

(i)

THEN good language and harmony and grace and rhythm depend on simplicity,—I mean the simplicity of a truly and nobly ordered mind, not that other simplicity which is only a euphemism for folly?

Very true, he replied.

And if our youth are to do their work in life, must they not make these their perpetual aim?

They must.

And all life is full of them, as well as every creative and constructive art; the art of painting, weaving and embroidery, and building, and the manufacture of vessels, as well as the frames of animals and of plants; in all of them there is grace or the absence of grace. And absence of grace and inharmonious movement and discord are nearly allied to ill words and ill nature, as grace and harmony are the sisters and images of goodness and virtue.

That is quite true, he said.

But is our superintendence to go no further, and are the poets only, to be required by us to impress a good moral on their poems as the condition of writing poetry in our State? Or is the same control to be exercised over other artists, and are they also to be prohibited from exhibiting the opposite forms of vice and intemperance and meanness and indecency in sculpture and building and the other creative arts; and is he who does not conform to this rule of ours to be prohibited from practising his art in our State, lest the taste of our citizens be corrupted by him? We would not have our guardians grow up amid images of moral deformity, as in some noxious pasture, and there browse and feed upon many a baneful herb and flower day by day, little by little, until they silently gather a festering mass of corruption in their own soul. Let our artists rather be those who are gifted to discern the true nature of beauty and grace; then will our youth dwell in a land of health, amid fair sights and sounds; and beauty, the effluence of fair works, will meet the sense like a breeze, and insensibly draw the soul even in childhood into harmony with the beauty of reason.

There can be no nobler training than that, he replied.

Is not this, I said, the reason, Glaucon, why musical training is so powerful, because rhythm and harmony find their way into the secret places of the soul, on which they mightily fasten, bearing grace in their movements, and making the soul graceful of him who is rightly educated, or ungraceful if ill-educated; and also because he who has received this true education of the inner being will most shrewdly perceive omissions or faults in art and nature, and with a true taste, while he praises and rejoices over, and receives into his soul the good, and becomes noble and good, he will justly blame and hate the bad, now in the days of his youth, even before he is able to know the reason of the thing; and when reason comes he will recognize and salute her as a friend with whom his education has made him long familiar.

(ii)

I AM greatly deceived, if one preliminary to an efficient education of the labouring classes be not the recurrence to a more manly discipline of the intellect on the part of the learned themselves, in short, a thorough recasting of the moulds in which the minds of our gentry, the characters of our future land-owners, magistrates and senators are to receive their shape and fashion.

(iii)

LET us observe how the mechanical genius of our time has diffused itself into quite other provinces. Not the external and physical alone is now managed by machinery, but the internal and spiritual also. Here too nothing follows its spontaneous course, nothing is left to be accomplished by old, natural methods. Everything has its cunningly devised implements, its preëstablished apparatus; it is not done by hand, but by machinery. Thus we have machines for Education: Lancastrian machines; Hamiltonian machines; monitors, maps and emblems. Instruction, that mysterious communing of Wisdom with Ignorance, is no longer an indefinable tentative process, requiring a study of individual aptitudes, and a perpetual variation of means and methods, to attain the same end; but a secure, universal, straightforward business, to be conducted in the gross, by proper mechanism, with such intellect as comes to hand.

ANCIENT PHILOSOPHERS AND
MODERN KNOWLEDGE

Thomas Babington, Lord Macaulay, "Essay on
Lord Bacon", *Edinburgh Review*. 1837

Suppose that Justinian, when he closed the schools of
Athens, had called on the last few sages who still haunted the
Portico, and lingered round the ancient plane-trees, to show
their title to public veneration: suppose that he had said;
"A thousand years have elapsed since, in this famous city,
Socrates posed Protagoras and Hippias; during those thousand years a large proportion of the ablest men of every
generation has been employed in constant efforts to bring to
perfection the philosophy which you teach; that philosophy
has been munificently patronised by the powerful; its professors have been held in the highest esteem by the public; it
has drawn to itself almost all the sap and vigour of the human
intellect: and what has it effected? What profitable truth has
it taught us which we should not equally have known without
it? What has it enabled us to do which we should not have
been equally able to do without it?" Such questions, we
suspect, would have puzzled Simplicius and Isidore. Ask a
follower of Bacon what the new philosophy, as it was called
in the time of Charles II, has effected for mankind, and his
answer is ready; "It has lengthened life; it has mitigated pain;
it has extinguished diseases; it has increased the fertility of
the soil; it has given new securities to the mariner; it has
furnished new arms to the warrior; it has spanned great rivers
and estuaries with bridges of form unknown to our fathers;
it has guided the thunderbolt innocuously from heaven to
earth; it has lighted up the night with the splendour of the
day; it has extended the range of the human vision; it has
multiplied the power of the human muscles; it has accelerated
motion; it has annihilated distance; it has facilitated intercourse, correspondence, all friendly offices, all despatch of
business; it has enabled man to descend to the depths of the
sea, to soar into the air, to penetrate securely into the noxious

recesses of the earth, to traverse the land in cars which whirl along without horses, and the ocean in ships which run ten knots an hour against the wind. These are but a part of its fruits, and of its first fruits. For it is a philosophy which never rests, which has never attained, which is never perfect. Its law is progress. A point which yesterday was invisible is its goal to-day, and will be its starting-post to-morrow".

FINIS RERUM

From a judgment by L.C.J. SIR RANULPHE CREWE, *on a claim to the Oxford peerage.* 1625

I HAVE laboured to make a covenant with myself, that affection may not press upon judgment; for I suppose there is no man that hath any apprehension of gentry or nobleness, but his affection stands to the continuance of so noble a name and house, and would take hold of a twig or twine-thread to uphold it, and yet time hath his revolution; there must be a period and an end to all temporal things, *finis rerum*, an end of names and dignities, and whatsoever is terrene; and why not of De Vere? For where is Bohun? Where's Mowbray? Where's Mortimer? nay, which is more, and most of all, where is Plantagenet? They are intombed in the urns and sepulchres of mortality.

JUSTIFICATA EST SAPIENTIA

(i) FRANCIS BACON, *Advancement of Learning.* Book I, viii, 6. 1605
(ii) SIR HUMPHREY DAVY, *The Director*, No. 19. 1807

(i)

LET us conclude with the dignity and excellency of knowledge and learning in that whereunto man's nature doth most aspire, which is immortality or continuance; for to this tendeth generation, and raising of houses and families; to this tend buildings, foundations, and monuments; to this tendeth the desire of memory, fame, and celebration; and in effect the strength of all other human desires. We see then how far the monuments of wit and learning are more durable than the monuments of power or of the hands. For have not the verses of Homer continued twenty-five hundred years, or more, without the loss of a syllable or letter; during which time infinite palaces, temples, castles, cities, have been decayed and demolished? It is not possible to have the true pictures or statues of Cyrus, Alexander, Caesar, no nor of the kings or great personages of much later years; for the originals cannot last, and the copies cannot but leese of the life and truth. But the images of men's wits and knowledges remain in books, exempted from the wrong of time and capable of perpetual renovation. Neither are they fitly to be called images, because they generate still, and cast their seeds in the minds of others, provoking and causing infinite actions and opinions in succeeding ages. So that if the invention of the ship was thought so noble, which carrieth riches and commodities from place to place, and consociateth the most remote regions in participation of their fruits, how much more are letters to be magnified, which as ships pass through the vast seas of time, and make ages so distant to participate of the wisdom, illuminations, and inventions, the one of the other?

(ii)

THE pleasure derived from great philosophical discoveries is less popular and more limited in its immediate effect, than that derived from the refined arts; but it is more durable and less connected with fashion or caprice. Canvas and wood, and even stone, will decay. The work of a great artist loses all its spirit in the copy. Words are mutable and fleeting; and the genius of poetry is often dissipated in translation. The compositions may remain, but the hand of execution may be wanting. Nature cannot decay; the language of her interpreters will be the same in all times. It will be an universal tongue speaking to all countries, and in all ages, the excellence of the work, and the wisdom of the Creator.

INDEX OF AUTHORS AND TRANSLATORS

SUBJECT INDEX

For EU product safety concerns, contact us at Calle de José Abascal, 56–1°, 28003 Madrid, Spain or eugpsr@cambridge.org.

www.ingramcontent.com/pod-product-compliance
Ingram Content Group UK Ltd.
Pitfield, Milton Keynes, MK11 3LW, UK
UKHW040615240426
470322UK00010B/136